GRAHAM GR
FRIEND AND BI

Leopoldo Duran is a Catholic priest and former lecturer
in English literature at the University of Madrid. He
holds doctorates in theology, English literature and
philosophy. He is the author of several books, including
La Crisis del Sacerdote en Graham Greene ('The priesthood
in the writings of Graham Greene') and *Estudio sobre El
Poder y la Gloria* (a study of *The Power and the Glory*),
together with numerous articles on Graham Greene's
work. Now retired, he lives in Vigo, Spain.

LEOPOLDO DURAN

GRAHAM GREENE: FRIEND AND BROTHER

'The trouble is I don't believe my unbelief'
GRAHAM GREENE

Translated by Euan Cameron

Fount
An Imprint of HarperCollinsPublishers

Fount Paperbacks is an Imprint of
HarperCollins*Religious*
Part of HarperCollins*Publishers*
77–85 Fulham Palace Road, London W6 8JB

First published in Great Britain in 1994 by HarperCollins*Publishers*
This edition published in 1995 by Fount Paperbacks

1 3 5 7 9 10 8 6 4 2

A catalogue record for this book is
available from the British Library

ISBN 0 00 627946-5

Printed and bound in Great Britain by
HarperCollinsManufacturing Glasgow

For my brothers Manuel and Avelino

Contents

Acknowledgements

I WOULD LIKE to acknowledge my immense debt and gratitude to Excmo D. Antonio Briva, Bishop of Astorga. It was he who discovered my specific vocation within the ministry of the priesthood. He encouraged me, with these words, to continue my study of English literature in England: 'Let me assure you that you can rely on the moral, and if necessary the material, support of your prelate.' Had this not happened, Graham Greene and I would never have met. The consequences of that meeting, including this book, are due in no small part to my dear friend, the Bishop of Astorga, who died very recently. May he rest in peace.

My thanks are also due to Professor Roger Sharrock and Professor Esteban Pujals, who supervised my doctoral thesis on Graham Greene at King's College, University of London, and at the Universidad Complutense in Madrid, respectively.

I also owe a debt of gratitude to Dr Jaime Iglesias Cendon and his family for his great friendship; his house and his hospitality were at my disposal at all times during the years in which I wrote this book. And they continue to be. His support in all manner of things has been incalculable.

Introduction

THIS IS NOT a book of investigation, but rather a living book. For I will only write about the Graham Greene I knew and the things that we discussed between ourselves. I trust it will be a lively account. How many hours of conversation there have been over so many years! Unforgettable conversations that took place over the table of a *parador*, driving around in a car, or stretched out under the trees after one of the simple picnics we so enjoyed.

The first letter Graham Greene ever wrote to me was dated 30 June 1964. Our last, lengthy telephone conversation took place on 12 February 1991, six weeks before his death. Our final meeting was to be twenty-four hours before he departed this world. I was summoned by him a week before his death to administer the sacraments and to be by his side, but no one was able to reach me until 31 March. It was half past nine on Easter Sunday evening. On 2 April, at midday, I was with him at Vevey in Switzerland in the Hôspital de la Providence. Graham died the next day at 11.40 in the morning. We were alone.

From the time of our very first trip through Spain, Graham told me very seriously at one time or another that he wanted me to be by his side during his last moments. He added that he had given my telephone number and address to the people concerned and asked them to get in touch with me. I shall always regret not having been with him during the last week of his life; but I thank God that Graham Greene saw me at his side during his final hours. I consider myself enormously fortunate to have been in his company.

Our journeys through Spain and Portugal began in the 1970s and they usually lasted a fortnight at least. On several occasions we made different journeys in the same year. When the film of *Monsignor Quixote* was being shot, Graham made four trips to Spain, for example, and there were other occasions too. Our main journey each year always took place in the summer. These travels around Spain became very important to Graham Greene in his later years. I would even go so far as to say that they affected his entire life. In my case, they made an indelible mark.

Our conversations during these 'picnics' started from the moment we took to the road, between half past eight and nine o'clock in the morning, and continued until midnight, or sometimes until one or two o'clock in the morning. During the last two or three years we would usually retire to bed a little earlier. My own visits to Antibes usually lasted about a week, especially in the early days. We would meet at his home at around 10.00 am; then lunch followed by a short walk, then a quick siesta; and after dinner, which was normally at his flat, the familiar conversations would stretch out until about midnight. In my sixteen volumes of journals, each consisting of about 190 pages, I made a synthesis of the essential details of our discussions as scrupulously as I could.

In these pages I have also recorded the gist of our most important telephone conversations. These occurred quite frequently, especially in the weeks preceding our summer 'picnics', as we called our journeys, or before meetings that had been arranged in Madrid, Vigo or Antibes. We needed to plan our routes, decide which *paradores* we would stay at, and construct a timetable.

During the five years Graham spent battling against the mafia on the Côte d'Azur, these telephone chats tended to be more frequent. In those fateful days we would also correspond more regularly, for it was not prudent to discuss delicate matters over the telephone.

It was Graham's idea, expressed on many occasions, that I ought to take notes about our 'picnics' — a diary of our conversations and jokes — with a view to writing an amusing book. He would write a prologue.

In 1983, he persisted, in a way that was unusual for him, with this idea of keeping notebooks. It was in Caleruega as we were admiring the Dominican monastery in the silence of a July afternoon. The peace and quiet contrasted with the blaring of a television set in a neighbouring bar, in which we later stopped, very briefly, for a cup of coffee. A group of peasants were listening intently to the noise. I will not forget Graham's phrase once we were outside: 'The new illiteracy.'

I never knew whether I would ever write this book, even though Graham had suggested two or three possible titles: '(Further?) Travels with a Donkey', parodying the one used by his distant relative, Robert Louis Stevenson; or 'On the Track of Murrieta', which alluded to one of our favourite wines . . .

This will not be the humorous book that Graham proposed, with its humour based on our jokes, stories and conversations, and the 'cargo of pure unlabelled Galician wine we always carry with us' or the 'Tonico Cariño', patented for us by Señor Antonio Nogueiras of Las Regadas, and everything else. I would be incapable of writing a book of that sort. It will be the factual account of our adventures, the story of the real 'Monsignor Quixote' to set against the fictionalized version which Graham wrote.

I am writing this book because no one else knows the essential characteristics of the man as I do; the man who was prepared to open his heart to me so affectionately and so unashamedly.

Graham often alluded to this putative book in his letters: 'After all you have written on the subject, I can trust your knowledge of my work – not only drawn from reading, but also from all the conversations we have had during our travels together . . . I can fully trust you to present me as a living person and not as a mere academic subject. You even know my taste in wine and whisky!'

Graham wanted to see himself described in all the small details of day to day life. He wrote to me on another occasion: 'You have always treated my novels, in your articles and essays, in depth. We have talked and travelled together for many years now and you certainly know more about what I am trying to do than anybody else in Europe.'

And in November 1986, there was further encouragement: 'I do hope that after all these years of travelling around Spain together, ceaselessly talking, you will be able to continue writing and lecturing on my work – for no one knows better than you do its nature and its source.'

Nietzsche said that three anecdotes were enough to describe a man perfectly, and it is true that they can reveal the most intimate part of a person. In writing this book I have not taken the chronological approach of the biographer, but the anecdote has been the lamp I carry in my hand so that no one will doubt the truth of what I write. For me, Graham Greene was never the 'evasive' or 'mysterious' man 'cloaked in secrecy' that everyone spoke of. He was simply someone who loved solitude and cherished his privacy, particularly where his own inner experiences were concerned. They were his chief treasure.

Writing such a book is a delicate matter for a priest. Should certain matters be left to the silence of eternity? Are there things that are left unsaid due to over-scrupulousness on my part?

I once told Graham on the telephone that I was going to write an article about him but that I would be discreet. Without a moment's hesitation he replied: 'Forget your discretion. Write it interestingly.'

●

When Graham Greene's coffin was lowered into the grave, I recited Horatio's famous words to Hamlet:

> *Now cracks a noble heart. Good-night, sweet prince,*
> *And flights of angels sing thee to thy rest.*

Yet previously Hamlet had asked Horatio:

> *Horatio, I am dead;*
> *Thou liv'st; report me and my cause aright*
> *To the unsatisfied.*

It would be the height of rashness, and in very bad taste, to apply the Prince's entreaty to myself.

A few days before I completed this book, I was invited to the University of Vigo to give some lectures on Graham Greene. The reception I was given was quite exceptional and scarcely merited. To those delightful students on the 1992–93 course, as well as those on the 1989–90 course, and all my students of English Literature at the Universidad Complutense in Madrid, many of whom are now teachers themselves, my affectionate gratitude. From the moment I first came to know all those young people, a line from *Mio Cid* has been pounding away unceasingly in my mind:

'God, how good the vassal if he had a good lord!'

Writing on behalf of my London publishers, Giles Semper wrote to me: 'The book should ... be about your relationship, and not about Greene in isolation. You should feature as strongly as he does. The "spiritual biography" will emerge in the course of the story.'

I am being asked, therefore, for a *chiaroscuro* ('tenebrista') painting. In the painting Graham will be the light and I the shadow.

PART ONE

CHAPTER I

OUR FIRST MEETING

I T TOOK PLACE at the Ritz Hotel in London on 20 August 1973. That day, I came to know in flesh and blood the man whose name and whose books had been a source of help and encouragement to me for almost twenty years. The point of departure had been *The Power and the Glory*.

Without any doubt, this was one of the most significant moments in my life. Anyone who has ever made an idol of someone in his or her imagination will readily understand. The only difference is that in this case reality surpassed the imagined ideal.

It had happened this way. One day I answered the telephone. A voice asked: 'May I speak to Father Leopoldo Durán?'

'Oh! Professor Sharrock. How are you?'

'I am not Professor Sharrock. I am Graham Greene.'

I literally almost fell out of my chair. Professor Sharrock had been my tutor at King's College, London, and I had thought the voice to have been his. I tried to explain myself but I was totally bewildered. Graham Greene was calling to see whether it might be convenient for us to meet; whether I would care to join him for lunch or dinner. At that moment my vocabulary was reduced to two words: 'yes' and 'delighted'. I spoke like some sort of robot. It was agreed that we should meet at the Ritz, at noon, two days later. I lived through the intervening hours in a state of limbo, rather like a sleepwalker. I left for the hotel with two hours to spare, but there were roadworks between the house where I was staying and the nearest underground station, and I arrived only just in time. It was ten minutes to twelve. After giving my name, I asked for Graham Greene.

'He's waiting for you in reception.'

Seated in a kind of low armchair, with his elbow resting on the arm of the chair and his face cupped in the palm of his hand, Graham appeared to be meditating. He was dressed in a grey suit and, unusually for him, he was wearing a tie.

We greeted each other with an embrace, I am not sure why, but perhaps because neither of us knew what the appropriate form of greeting should be. For Graham was also a shy man. Along with a certain natural anxiety at meeting someone for the first time, there was the added worry of my impeccable priestly garb of a black suit and snow-white Roman collar. Graham called them 'bourgeois vestments'. I feel sure that when Greene dressed Father Herrera in rather affected attire in *Monsignor Quixote*, he was trying to recreate the impression made on him at our first meeting. Except that Father Herrera appears a very self-confident, assured priest – that's why he was a close friend of the bishop's and had been his secretary – whereas I was scared stiff.

My relationship with Graham Greene was destined to be an unusual one from that first moment until his death. Within a few minutes of our meeting each of us was fully at ease and there was a mutual understanding. I went down to the hotel bar to get a non-alcoholic drink, for they seemed to be one of the hotel's specialities. All I can remember was that it was vaguely green and tasted good.

The conversation quickly became relaxed and totally natural. I told him how nervous I had been beforehand. Speaking of his own 'shyness' Graham told me that when he had been very young, a certain well-known person had invited him to visit him. To encourage him to come, he mentioned that they would be virtually alone; there would just be two or three others, among them T.S.Eliot. Graham continued:

'T.S.Eliot was at that time the most important literary figure in England and my host did not exactly cheer me up with the news.'

'It sounds rather like what I went through today,' I said.

'Oh, that was entirely different,' Graham insisted.

We had dinner in the restaurant at the Ritz. I do not recall the first course. All I remember is the roast beef and the good French wine. And as for the apple tart we had for dinner that evening . . . we were to ask for it countless times in restaurants in Spain and Portugal.

Graham hardly ever ate anything, especially after his very serious stomach operation, and virtually the only fruit he would ever touch was apple tart and occasionally strawberries. We used to select a good wine, for a glass or two of carefully chosen wine was what made dinner for Graham. I eventually came to share his point of view, and on the few occasions that I only drank water, I slightly spoiled dinner for my friend. Wine or the 'Tonico Cariño' eventually became as much of a game for us as a pleasure. Photographs taken without a glass usually looked rather lifeless, so it became almost a ritual for us always to have a glass of wine in our hands. Graham would often tell me many interesting anecdotes in which wine was the chief means of obtaining secrets and getting what one wanted.

•

I remember our first dinner in Madrid. We dined wherever we could, for our conversation had made us very late and I did not know many good restaurants in that part of town. The first wine served was very bad, and Graham scarcely bothered to taste it. I told the waiter discreetly to bring us the best wine they had and he came back with a bottle of Campo Viejo. Graham tried it and mumbled in a loud whisper to me:

'Supposing we leave it here, in the nicest possible way, as a present to the waiter who served us?'

As time went by, my knowledge of wine improved and I acquired a reasonable expertise. Graham and I were even able to dine at my house, alone, at our leisure.

Graham said that a man who knew how to appreciate different types of wine was like a man who could distinguish one writer from another and appreciate good literature. A man who was unable to appreciate a glass of good wine gave one cause for thought; he might be unpleasant or untrustworthy.

That dinner, or rather our conversation, lasted five hours. We discussed the divine and the human aspects of the Church; the Vatican, bishops, priests, religious orders. Graham Greene's relationships with both the ecclesiastical and secular authorities meant that he was unusually well informed.

Not long before, Graham had been given an audience with Pope Pius XII. It lasted about twenty minutes and the Pope never asked him to sit down. He had just attended a Mass said by His Holiness.

'Your Holiness,' said Graham, 'during my life I have heard two Masses that impressed me more than any others.'

The Pope asked which these were, and Graham replied: 'One was the Mass Your Holiness has just celebrated.'

'And the other?' asked the Pope.

'One that I heard Padre Pío say.'

Graham added: 'The Pope frowned, kept his distance and looked displeased.'

Nevertheless, before he left, Graham Greene asked the Pope to pray for his friend, Bishop Matthews, who was seriously ill. Afterwards, he learned that his friend had received a box of chocolates which the Pope had arranged to be sent from a shop in Rome.

Later, Graham told me more about the Mass celebrated by Padre Pío whom he loved and admired. After this Mass, which made a great impression on him, he always carried a little holy picture of Padre Pío in his wallet. The Mass took place at five o'clock in the morning, for that was what the Vatican required of this saintly man. The public had been waiting at the door of the church for hours in order to be allowed to enter and set eyes on the 'saint'. Padre Pío appeared on the altar wearing mittens to hide the marks of the stigmata of the Passion. He enunciated every word of the Mass very slowly and clearly, but to Graham it seemed that it had lasted no longer than the normal half hour. Only when he left the church and looked at his watch did he realize that Padre Pío had been on the altar for between an hour and a quarter and ninety minutes. A slanderous article published in England at the time suggested that Graham had left Mass before the end because he found it too long.

A friend of Graham's wanted to take him to the sacristy before or after the Mass so that he could meet Padre Pío, but he refused because he was frightened of finding himself face to face with a saint. Later, Padre Pío asked Graham's friend: 'What became of your English friend, the one who would not dare to come and see me?'

Nobody had previously said a word to Padre Pío about this 'English friend'.

•

At dinner, Graham questioned me about my work as a priest, and asked my opinion of Opus Dei. At the time I knew very little about the inner workings of 'la Obra', and I know no more today. I have some close friends within Opus Dei who are truly fine people, but we never discuss the subject. Graham Greene did not care for it very much and was suspicious of its cloak of secrecy. His description of 'la Obra' in Monsignor Quixote is reminiscent of a silver stiletto:

It occurred to Father Quixote that such a man was almost certainly a member of Opus Dei – that club of

intellectual Catholic activists whom he could not fault
and yet whom he could not trust.

He once said something which amused me: 'If you belonged to Opus
Dei you would be a very dangerous individual.' I burst out laughing.
He was joking . . .

Graham wanted to know why I had left the Vincentians to become
a secular priest, and whether there had been any difficulties in making
the transition. Although it happened long ago, it had been a difficult
period in my life and one that had left its mark on me. Many years
later, I told him that I had no right to complain about life, but he
remembered what I had once said, and reminded me of my remarks
that evening.

There and then at the Ritz, we started planning future journeys
through Spain and elsewhere. Graham told me that he wanted us to
be constantly in touch. He gave me his addresses in Antibes, Paris
and Anacapri, and his telephone numbers.

I had heard about Graham's travels, and I was familiar with
Orwell's remark about him being 'our first Catholic fellow traveller'.
I had heard that in one year alone he might travel 67,000 miles. I
asked him whether this was true. 'I don't know', he replied with a
smile.

We talked about the danger of so many aeroplane flights. Graham
never paid any attention to danger whatsoever, and much later I came
to realize that he attached no importance to his own death either.
He told me of the time that he and Carol Reed were travelling to
the United States on business to discuss the film of *The Third Man*.
They were due to land at San Diego, California. They made a very
bad landing. The passengers were terrified, children were crying and
there was general turmoil. Carol Reed was furious with the American
crew and complained to the airhostess, who told him: 'You can count
yourself lucky. We were obliged to make a forced landing along the
coast.'

The conversation naturally moved on to the subject of the cinema,
something that Graham had been involved with in one way or another
throughout his life. He told me about his first meeting with Alexander
Korda. Korda got in touch with Graham because he had been writing
very critical reviews of his films. They became great friends, even
though Graham continued to judge Korda's films severely.

That day I took away with me a copy of *The Honorary Consul* which he inscribed for me with these words: 'For Father Durán at our first long-delayed meeting of two friends'.

The Honorary Consul is dedicated to Victoria Ocampo. Seeing her name as he inscribed the book, I was reminded of this marvellous woman and her rich life. She had been a great friend of Graham's. Graham had come to know her in New York at the end of World War II and they had become friends. She edited the famous Argentinian literary review *Sur*, ran a publishing house of the same name, and corresponded with many famous people.

She came from a distinguished family who obliged her to take part in an arranged marriage at the age of seventeen with a man whom she did not love. During her honeymoon in Rome, she fell in love with an Argentinian and so began a love affair which was to last for several years. She was very rich and she bought a house by the River Plate where she would meet her lover. He would remain locked inside the house until he was sure no one would see him come out, but one day a maid discovered the lovers and from that moment on, the husband never spoke to Victoria again. When the husband died, there was no longer time to marry the lover, for both of them were of an advanced age.

Victoria Ocampo was a marvellous person. She always dressed in trousers, she translated several of Greene's plays, and ran the influential literary magazine *Sur* as well as the publishing house of the same name. She was a friend of Ortega, Valéry, Keiserling and many other famous people, and she had letters from all of them. She wrote her intimate memoirs and gave them to Greene to read. He liked them and believed they should be published, but where are they today? Does one of her sisters have them?

Chapter II

A MODEST MAN

I HAVE OFTEN BEEN asked what the characteristic was that I found most attractive in Graham. I would have to say that it was his modesty, both in public and in private. Throughout our journeys together there were many instances of this, as well as his extraordinary simplicity, humility and delicacy. Graham must have known the value of this modesty, but he did so with wonderful humility. He often told me not to use the word 'humility', but instead, 'modesty', since the word in English had a different meaning from the Spanish.

On one occasion, we were travelling from Galicia to the Basque Country and we were in a small town in Asturias called Soto de Luina. Graham had noticed that our friend Miguel, our 'Third Man' or driver at that time, was growing tired. We decided to stop for the night at a modest inn on the main road. The proprietress of the inn did all she could to dissuade us. 'There's nothing suitable', she kept saying. She had another place which was much better but all the rooms there were taken. Judging by appearances, and in view of what the lady had said, I was of the opinion that we should continue on our way. Graham, however, wanted to see the accommodation. All that was available were some tiny rooms in the attic, without running water and basic conveniences. Restraining his humour and ignoring my look of disapproval, Graham thought only of Miguel and how tired he was. He laughed and said enthusiastically: 'Yes, they are fine! If you had seen some of the places in Tabasco, in Africa and elsewhere, that I have had to sleep in . . .'. He reminded me of the time in Mexico when his mule had refused to budge any further under the burning Palenque sun. And so there we stayed. The good lady prepared us an excellent supper. She allowed us to drink our own Las Regadas wine, for I had whispered to her that we were on a diet and that this wine had been specially prescribed for us . . .

•

Many years later, during one of my visits to Antibes, we went out shopping one morning to buy something for supper when a lady came into the shop where we were waiting to be served and, noticing two smoked trout in Graham's shopping basket, asked him where she could obtain them. Graham immediately left me in charge of the purchases and accompanied the lady to the shop where he had bought the trout.

I remember the time when he was due to come to Madrid for the first time. I went to a hardware shop and bought some kitchen utensils: a stainless steel teapot, and special dishes for butter and marmalade. In fact, they were never used, but years later, I showed him what I had bought and told him how nervous I had been. He laughed aloud. I had not known then that Graham was only too happy with a glass of good wine, a Spanish omelette and a few biscuits.

His tastes were simple and he was quite happy with the most basic essentials. I remember when he was obliged to buy a pair of decent shoes to attend the dinner that Mrs Thatcher gave when the King and Queen of Spain visited Britain. Ties irritated him enormously too; he only ever wore one when it was impossible not to wear a suit.

On another occasion in Madrid, he was astonished to see a pile of shirts in my cupboard. I excused myself, saying that shirts were far cheaper in London than in Madrid and so whenever I went there I bought a few. Later, on my return from some visit or other to London, Graham telephoned me and asked: 'Any more shirts?' Eventually, I stopped buying them so that I would not have to lie to Graham. He had only two or three suits, and half a dozen shirts were quite sufficient for him.

There was a directness in everything that Graham Greene said or did – even when he was being ironic. Many years ago when he was in the United States, where he knew he was being watched, Graham took a taxi and crossed over the border from Texas into Mexico, where he changed money to pay the driver. He did this at an official 'Exchange' but he was given money that had been withdrawn from circulation. Later, when a United States Treasury official wrote to him enquiring how he had left the country, for he had to keep his records up to date, Graham replied simply: 'By taxi.'

•

Graham's modesty as a writer was equally admirable. He was never really satisfied with any of his own work and only happy with a few of his novels. It was with difficulty that one persuaded him that some of his books might become literary classics. When I told him that the reason why everybody praised him was because there was something special about his work, he replied with complete conviction: 'Virtually everyone who has ever spoken about me has understood very little or nothing. Look, writing is a disease like any other.'

'Do most people in Antibes know who you are?' I once asked him.

'No,' he replied, 'at best the odd person may have read one of my books.'

Naturally, I discussed with Graham the most important points on my two doctoral theses on his work. I told him that much of his work needed to be analysed and could not simply be read. But he thought there was no point in such analysis; at least not in most of his work. When I asked what his reaction would be to a book entitled 'The Thought of Graham Greene', he told me with sincerity and total conviction that such a title was too imposing for his work; it would be better to call it the 'Fantasies' or 'Phantasmagoria' of Graham Greene.

When Graham came to Madrid in July 1980, on an official visit at the invitation of the Mayor, Enrique Tierno Galván, a journalist at the airport asked whether he considered himself to be a great novelist. He replied: 'Dickens, for example, was a great novelist. I write novels, some of which are a little better than others.' He was appalled that the price second-hand bookdealers were asking for one of the two novels he had refused to allow to be reprinted was as much as £1,000, while a first edition of Dickens or Trollope – writers he greatly admired – might only fetch £200 or £300.

On the occasion of Graham's eightieth birthday, his brother Hugh tried to persuade him to accept an invitation to go to the National Film Theatre in London to answer questions from the audience. Eventually, he accepted, but he was with me in Spain until just before the event and I shall never forget how much he regretted his acceptance. 'This is nonsense, nonsense', he repeated continually. He had agreed some time beforehand, but as the day approached, the idea became intolerable. The original plan was that the event should be televised and that he would bring the evening to a close. He refused on both counts. The evening would start with his replying to questions and it would end with a showing of the film *Doctor Fischer of Geneva*. (Graham paid a fine tribute that evening to the actor James Mason, describing how he had been made to shoot the film at night on snow-covered mountains in Switzerland, when he was elderly and unwell.)

Sometimes his modesty was scarcely believable. I remember once telling him that the Sunday edition of the Spanish newspaper *Ya* carried a photograph of Alec Guinness and himself in colour on the front page, and that by eleven o'clock that morning it was impossible to find a copy in Madrid. With absolute conviction, Graham replied: 'I don't think my picture, or Alec's, on the cover has anything to do with it. It must be your article.'

On another occasion we had arrived together at Osera one evening, and at supper they told us that on a number of occasions people had asked about Graham Greene. He appeared surprised to hear this. Ingenuously, the 'Third Man' told him that it was hardly surprising that people should ask after him there, since he was a very well known and famous person, and it was common knowledge that he visited that particular monastery. With a rather sullen air, Graham denied it flatly: 'I am not important, nor am I famous.'

Graham was very bashful when speaking about such matters. I was given many examples of this. During one of my last visits to Antibes, he read me the introduction to *A World of My Own*, the book he had written about his dreams. He used an epigraph from Heraclitus which I liked very much and asked him to read to me again. He blushed slightly – even after all those years of friendship! – and replied: 'Once is enough'. On another occasion, he inscribed a copy of *The Lawless Roads* to Estebán Pujals, a well-known professor at Madrid University, with a long and handsome dedication. 'Do you think this has any merit?' he asked me. Graham believed that his friend Shusaku Endo's novel *Silence* was a better book than *The Power and the Glory*.

Just as Graham was always careful that friendship and trust should not impose any burdens, he always did his best to be helpful to others. We were once in a restaurant in Lisbon when a journalist came up and asked whether she could have a very short interview with him. Graham refused politely: 'I am here for a few days to have a rest.' The girl apologized and did not persist. Next day, he was a little anxious and felt guilty about not agreeing to the interview. He thought he might have seemed a little irascible, but I assured him that he had done all he should and that if he did not behave in this way, then in future people would not leave him alone. But he asked me: 'Would you be entirely happy if that girl had approached you as Father Durán, the professor from Madrid University, asking to speak to you and you had refused?'

Somewhat taken aback, I replied: 'If she had come to me as a teacher, I should have felt entirely justified in not speaking to her because it is neither the time nor the place. Had she approached me as a priest, it would be another matter.'

•

Graham Greene was a courteous and affectionate man, but an extremely sensitive one. One could frequently see from his eyes that he was overcome with emotion, either from a sense of tenderness or on account of the suffering of others. For Graham, literature – the aesthetic beauty of literary art – was his life and, according to him, encompassed both human sorrow and joy.

He once told me a story about the son of the owner of the hotel where I used to stay on my visits to Antibes. Apparently, the household economy was in dire shape and, when Graham had gone to reserve my room, everything appeared to have virtually ground to a halt. He asked the owner whether the hotel was open, whereupon the lady started to cry. She told him how her son had become involved with some unscrupulous people and how the police had come to search their home. The boy was now serving an eighteen-month prison sentence. The woman had thought she had lost Graham's custom because of her son's behaviour, but Graham assured her that he had known nothing about what had happened. When he went home he took out a copy of the French edition of *Monsignor Quixote*, inscribed it to her and presented it to her. The woman told him that this gesture had totally changed her outlook on life.

He could be deeply affected by the suffering of others. Another example of this concerned his flat in Paris, where he kept his best books and favourite paintings, and which he never normally lent to anyone. Although he had a house on Anacapri, it was constantly being used by friends, and Graham never liked to say anything even when he felt the need to go and work there in solitude. Living above him in Paris, however, in a one-room garret flat, was his former literary agent Marie Biche, an old and ailing woman. She had worked under the famous Resistance heroine Denise Clairoin, Graham's first French agent, who died in a German concentration camp. Graham told her that she could live in his flat whenever he was not in Paris.

When he did go to Anacapri, there was not even a telephone to bother him and many of his best known plots and characters were created on the island. When he had first gone to live there, he had come to know the humble proprietor of the local bar. The man spoke no English and Graham did not speak Italian at that time, but he soon discovered that the man had very special qualities, and whenever he visited Anacapri he always spent some time with him. After the man died, Graham spent far less time there, just the occasional few days when he felt a need for the monastic but creative silence of the place to set his characters on their fictional paths. The absence of the bar owner was too painful for him.

I think I could recall enough experiences to write a short book about Graham Greene's extreme sensitivity, for I spent many years observing scenes such as these. Once, in Verin, a student from Santiago recognized Graham in a café. She and her boy friend were very tactful and eventually she came up to me and whispered in my ear, asking whether the gentleman with me was Graham Greene. I smiled and sipped my camomile tea, and said that I scarcely ever knew the people I was travelling with, but Graham must have heard his name spoken, for he later went out of his way to shake hands with the girl as we were leaving.

I want to give one final example of this extraordinary respect for other people. We were staying in the Carthusian monastery of Miraflores, an immense and wonderful oasis of silence which impressed Graham profoundly. The sun was setting, and he lingered for some time in the garden with its red roses whose petals are used by the nuns to make their famous scented rosaries. I whispered to Graham that I wanted to take a photograph of him and the monk who was escorting us around the monastery against the background of the rose bushes, but he mumbled back: 'It may show a lack of respect to this monk.'

CHAPTER III

A GREAT FRIENDSHIP

W HERE FRIENDSHIP WAS concerned, Graham Greene was
capable of making the most heroic sacrifices. During the six
unending years spent battling against the mafia on the Côte d'Azur,
a battle that he undertook out of friendship and affection, I mentioned
a certain passage in one of his books that I very much admired. He
replied: 'If it would prevent those who I love from suffering so much
(he was referring to Martine, the daughter of his close friend Yvonne
Cloetta, and her family) I would give every one of the words that I
have written. Without any doubt whatsoever.' I was astonished for a
moment, but of course I understood. It was then that I realized how
well I already knew him.

The President of Nicaragua, Daniel Ortega, had to go to London
to see Mrs Thatcher and ask for aid and support for his country. On
the face of it, Mrs Thatcher was not exactly an Ursuline nun and she
was likely to side with the Americans over Nicaragua. Daniel Ortega
asked Graham whether he would kindly come and help him in
London. Steadfast in his friendship, Graham agreed. People spoke
about the public embrace he gave Ortega. Graham only knew the
path that he had chosen was the one he sincerely believed to be the
right one. He had been to Nicaragua on several occasions and supported the Sandinistas. He knew what the situation had been like
under Somoza, and considered that Ortega was trying to cope as best
he could. He did not reckon Ortega to be a communist, nor any of
the priests who were then members of the government, in spite of
the fact that they had been excommunicated. Was Graham right
about this? It is open to debate. But he certainly thought that he was,
and he believed the Sandinistas were improving the country in a
number of ways, particularly its culture and social services.

At the time Ortega had telephoned, Greene had just fallen down
in his flat in Antibes. He felt a slight pain, but friendship – for
Nicaragua more than for Ortega – was an analgesic and it overcame

all other considerations. Only after Ortega had left London did Graham go to see his doctor. He had broken two ribs. Graham joked when he told me about this. 'Because of being incapacitated,' he said, 'I even heard my name mentioned on the television news in connection with Ortega that afternoon.'

Evelyn Waugh and Graham Greene were true friends. Graham often spoke to me about him. On more than one occasion, we both listened to the amusing talk Graham had given about Waugh and his work on the BBC.

Evelyn Waugh, who was only one year older than Graham, although Graham outlived him by twenty-five years, never tired of talking about his dear friend, both in Britain and in America, always presenting him as the greatest English Catholic writer. However, something put it into Evelyn Waugh's head that the character of Querry in *A Burnt-Out Case* was actually a portrait of his dear friend Graham, the author of the book. He had written to him: 'You are exasperated by the reputation which has come to you unsought of a "Catholic" writer.'

God only knows how much these two friends suffered on account of Waugh's unfortunate notion. They exchanged a series of letters, but there was no way of making the author of *Brideshead Revisited* see reason.

Waugh's allusion to a 'Lost Leader' particularly upset Graham. In his Introduction to *A Burnt-Out Case* he relates exactly what happened. A great deal of pain is contained in Graham Greene's simple words: 'for had I not always regarded him as *my* leader?'

Eventually, Graham bought a postcard on Brighton pier and sent it to Waugh, making light of what had happened. For Graham that friendship was a part of his very soul. Evelyn and Graham were devoted friends until death. How often Graham talked to me about one of Evelyn's daughters, and about his son Auberon, whose review of *Monsignor Quixote* almost seemed to suggest that Graham and I had been to a brothel!

Enrique Tierno Galván, the mayor of Madrid, made a big impression on Greene during his official visit in July 1980. They each came to have a high regard for one another and, as a result, a character in *Monsignor Quixote* came to be based on the Mayor. However, Don Enrique died not long afterwards. A rumour came to Graham's attention that Galván's widow was not being treated with the respect she deserved, in particular by those people from the Town Council who owed everything to Don Enrique. I discussed this with Graham and he asked me to try to find out whether there was any truth in the story. I did so, and was assured that it was not the case. Graham would have been quite prepared to return his 'honorary citizen of Madrid' medal, conferred at the time Don Enrique was mayor, to the Town Council.

•

Ten years after I had first met him, our friendship was still something of a secret as far as I was concerned, but Graham Greene talked about it several times in interviews with the press whenever the subject of our travels in Spain, Portugal and elsewhere arose. I once thanked him for mentioning my name in several English newspapers, and he replied humorously: 'Oh, you are becoming very famous indeed.'

At the time *The Human Factor* was published in 1978, his sister Elisabeth, Graham and I went to Berkhamsted; we wanted to see some of the places associated with the novel and I was keen to get to know the town in which Graham had been born. I wanted to see the school where his father had been headmaster and where he had been so unhappy. Above all, I longed to see that green baize door which formed a frontier, and which later took on a symbolic significance for him. The frontier could not be crossed!

We spent a wonderful day in Berkhamsted. We walked down the High Street and I was shown 'The Swan', the pub from which Castle sent his last message. We also saw the fine church, the first school that Graham had attended and the Public School where his father had been headmaster, with its famous green door. We drove to the celebrated castle and up to the Common after lunch. The Common was important in Graham's life because it was the place he escaped to and where he could hide. Graham told me all about this at length as we walked along: 'This was the path I took to go to the Common. It was over there', and he indicated with his hand.

'How old were you?'

'About fifteen.'

'But did you intend to come back; was it a joke?'

'Oh no. I meant to run away forever.'

As we walked back to the car, Graham told me:

'This is where Castle hid, and where he sees the other car approaching through the night. . . .'

Both Elisabeth and Graham spoke about their memories of Berkhamsted. They were quite moved, although the emotion was contained. Elisabeth had lived here until she was twelve years old; Graham, until he had left Oxford.

As we drove along, we spoke of many things in a light-hearted way and Graham began to pull my leg: 'Well, well; apparently you are ashamed of your friends. I have spoken about our friendship a number of times, but you never do so in your articles. You must be ashamed of your friends.'

I felt myself blushing and simply told him to stop this tomfoolery.

But from that time on, I did occasionally mention our friendship in the various articles I wrote about Graham's books and began to speak about our travels, for it was a relationship that had long since reached its maturity.

•

From June 1964 onwards, we had occasionally written letters to each other (indeed I have a copy of *A Sort of Life* that was inscribed to me in 1971) but our friendship had really begun after our first meeting, in the early seventies.

The beginning of our friendship was like the source of a river. From the moment we first met, his letters were immediately very affectionate. That first day, Graham asked me whether I had 'a communion set', with which to say Mass on our travels. I did not have one; I always said Mass at a church whenever I travelled on my own. Graham went to great lengths to obtain a magnificent 'communion set' for me, though, as always, it was Elisabeth who actually acquired it.

One day, my guardian angel dictated a letter to me in which I spoke to Graham of some autographs written by him, according to his will. I would send him a good quality bound album to write on and I would call it my 'Picasso'. Graham's quick answer was: 'Of course, send me your "Picasso".' And seven years later, at the *parador* at Oropesa, he handed me over something which I call 'my greatest treasure'.

It was about these years when I also made another very delicate request to Graham: it was my desire to possess a complete collection of all his work. He replied with a very affectionate letter in which he wrote, amongst other things: 'But I can't deny you anything.'

•

Graham was always extravagant with favours to his friends.

For three or four years, I had been seriously troubled by some nodules in the throat and it had become difficult for me to give lectures at the University. I was living in Madrid in the 1980s and although I went to see a number of specialists, they were unable to diagnose what was wrong. At that time, I had not yet met my friend, Dr Antonio Martinez Vidal, and I had been going to speech therapy classes for two years simply in order to try to keep going.

The speech therapist had prescribed exercises which had to be done twice a day at least. For three years, whenever Graham and I were travelling together in the summer, I would sit in the back of the car and at the required moment, I would begin my exercises: a, e, i . . . Normally, I would let the others know when I was about to start, but at other times they would suddenly hear my high-pitched voice pronouncing the letter 'a'. Alarmed by the sudden noise, or else in order to tease me, Graham would hunch up his shoulders.

Once, in the garage of the *parador* in Tordesillas, I was taken for a drunkard who had lost his way. Graham and the 'Third Man' had stayed behind in our rooms preparing the glasses and the ice for our whiskies while I went to the car to get a bottle of J & B. I had not done my exercises and this bit of countryside, a little way away from the *parador*, seemed the ideal place to make my remedial gargling noises. With the bottle in my hand, I wandered to and fro near the garage making these strange sounds. As I was walking back towards the garage, I noticed a car parked just in front of the entrance and inside were a lady and a young girl who were having a wonderful time watching the behaviour of this good-natured drunk. I went up to them and, in order to avoid any misconceptions, I explained the problem with my throat.

I had not realized that Graham had been very concerned and had imagined that I might possibly have cancer of the throat. His brother Raymond had been operated on for this disease totally successfully. So it was that one Monday morning, during one of our telephone chats, Graham told me with the utmost tact that he thought it might be wise to go to London to see a well-known specialist. He never mentioned the word cancer, but gradually he succeeded in convincing me, and I flew to London that very afternoon. Everything had been organized perfectly by Elisabeth: I met the kindly Dr King Lewis, the Greenes' family doctor, and the celebrated specialist, Mr H.J. Shaw, who was to operate on me on 7 July. However, he and his speech-therapist, Mrs Christopherson, endured a long battle with my throat with infinite patience for four long months. The thought of the bill terrified me, but the fee proposed by these wonderful people was extremely reasonable. Just one Our Father was all that was requested! It was out of respect for Graham, naturally; and perhaps also because I was a Catholic priest – in Protestant England too!

I spent a total of five months in London because of the operation to my throat, and later, back in Spain, there were two further operations, and I had a serious car accident as well. Graham Greene really had met 'my Father Durán' at the worst time. Elisabeth and Graham had been very worried indeed. When it was all over, Graham confessed to me: 'I was terrified.'

Further proof of his munificence came when I was obliged to retire from my University post because of a law that obliges one to retire at a certain age and, depending on the number of years spent teaching, to live on a percentage of one's final salary. I have spent the greater part of my life doing research in both Spanish and foreign universities so as to be able, now and again, to pass on some useful ideas to my students. It has always seemed shameful to me that someone who has only graduated in June should be able to start teaching the following September. Whatever my merits, when I arrived at Complutense I already had three doctorates: one in Theology (from Angelicum, Rome), in English Literature (King's College, London), and in English Philology (Complutense, Madrid). However, I had only taught at the university for thirteen years. The other thirty years which I had spent teaching or doing research did not qualify me legally. The State is all-powerful and to oppose it is useless.

The last payment I received as a fully active professor was about £1,000 on 30 September 1986 and my first meagre monthly pension as a retired professor, drawn on 1 March 1988, was the equivalent of £150. Need I say more?

This matter of my retirement was of great concern to Graham Greene. It even occurred to him to write to the highest authorities in Spain. I convinced him that it would be a waste of time. Only our dear friend, Enrique Tierno Galván, would have been prepared to listen and to see whether anything could be done, but he was already in another world where Truth had taken the place of politics. Graham was quite prepared to write to whoever I told him to. He was game for anything: 'Make me a rough copy listing the points to be dealt with. I'll look after the rest.'

He wrote a number of letters to me on the subject. Here is one:

My dear Leopoldo,

I was very distressed, and I'm sure all your students are, to hear of the miserable pension on which you are retiring. In your twelve years you have done more original and valuable work than most academics do in a quarter of a century.

Perhaps I am a little prejudiced for, during most of that period, I have gained so much not only from our friendship, but from all the critical articles you have devoted to my work. If Spain is one of the countries where my books have the widest circulation I think it is largely due to you. You have shown great critical understanding of works which might well have displeased you as a priest. A quality you share with Pope Paul VI who told me in a private audience: 'Your books are sure to offend some Catholics, and you shall pay no attention to that.' Well, I don't pay attention and you have never been offended.

I do hope that after all these years of travelling around Spain together, ceaselessly talking, you will be able to continue writing and lecturing on my work – perhaps to a larger audience than a university provides – for no one knows better than you do its nature and its source.

Perhaps when I next visit you your Astorga friends will join us in killing a couple of bottles of my favourite Murrieta wine!

With all my love,
Graham

P.S. I have received an essay by Father Huerta on the relation between Don Quixote and the works of Unamuno, Carlos Fuentes, and myself. The part devoted to me consists mainly of quotations from you!

CHAPTER IV

MUTUAL CONFIDENCES

I F GRAHAM GREENE were writing this chapter, it is possible that he might start by recounting a dream he once had in which the Prince of Wales told him in confidence: 'I tell you this in all secrecy. I am homosexual. I don't like women.' I would like to share just a few of the confidences that we shared over the course of the years.

The intimacy that grew up between us made me reflect seriously upon my priesthood, though it is quite possible that our discussions, such as they were, might never have taken place had I not been a priest. My being a priest was the magic key that opened our private worlds to each other. We never used that overworn phrase – and one that is so often broken! – 'this is secret'. We took trust for granted.

Graham often recounted his dreams to me. In dreams his creative imagination seems to have had a tendency to veer in the direction of Buckingham Palace. One night he was surprised to find himself in the very same bedroom as the Queen. Love was beckoning, but suddenly the Duke of Edinburgh burst into the room and placed himself between Graham and the Queen. And so nothing happened. Such things happen in dreams when the will has no power over the instinct. In fact, the writer had great affection and respect for Her Majesty!

One should not imagine that Graham Greene's dreams always had this slightly erotic edge to them. It was not always like that. I remember once when we were in Oropesa that after our siesta, Graham and the 'Third Man' were drinking whisky before dinner. We shared a bottle and a half of good wine between the three of us. Graham told us that he dreamed every night, and that night he had dreamt about a very beautiful girl. But he was simply contemplating her; her lovely face, her fine hands.

When two people tell each other their dreams, truthfully, night after night, a considerable amount of trust is bound to develop. I go quite frequently to the Cistercian monastery at Osera. One night I dreamt that I was at Osera and I had just walked into the sacristy to remove my vestments after Mass. What should be my surprise when Graham Greene also came in, holding a chalice in both hands, his eyes lowered and looking pensive. He had just said Mass and was also coming to remove his vestments. This dream made an enormous impression on me. What extraordinary mystery of human psychology had put such a dream into my brain? In my first free moment the next morning, I wrote to Graham and told him about it. He replied: 'When I converted to Catholicism, I knew I was taking on responsibilities that would not always be easy to fulfil. But they were not quite as grave as those your dream appears to suppose.'

•

On one occasion, on the eve of his departure for Antibes after our summer jaunt, we were alone in my house when Graham told me that he was worried that our friendship might damage my university career, or affect my competitive examinations, and that I might meet opposition in the future. I quote his words almost exactly: 'As you know, my work has been much discussed from a Catholic viewpoint. It may be the case that here in Catholic Spain, it might not reflect well on you that you should study my work so closely. I say this because I was told by X that the person who came out top in the public examinations had published nothing apart from some reviews and one or two short articles. How could that be?'

This conversation took place in Madrid on 26 July 1978. Graham was referring to the competitive open examinations in my country. I had been one of those to have failed in recent public competitions. I told him, briefly, that his friendship and my studies on his work were of the greatest value to me and would continue to be, at least where certain sectors of Spanish society are concerned, whether he was a communist or an atheist. I told him more about the examination boards in Spain; of how I had no idea about the 'human factor' in many of the competitive examinations and postings in my country; about the serious publications which were conspicuous by their absence . . .

Graham was genuinely surprised. It was incomprehensible to him that someone who had not published anything of any real importance could be appointed to a university teaching post.

•

Some years later, as we were walking past a beautiful garden, flanked with hundred-year-old eucalyptus trees, Graham told me about something that had just occurred. He had been asked in Moscow whether he would accept the Order of Lenin for his literary achievement but he had decided against doing so for fear that people would think he had been a communist for many years. He asked me my view, but I had nothing to add.

As long as I knew Graham, he spent his life refusing honours and invitations. Along with this Order of Lenin, I recall the two Spanish universities which wanted to confer an *honoris causa* doctorate on him, which he wisely refused. Some years ago, I was contacted by the organizer of some summer courses and asked whether Graham Greene would kindly come and give a lecture. When I told them that there was not the slightest possibility, they resorted to human vanity: 'Would it not at least be possible to pay us a visit if you were to accompany him?' No comment.

There was worse than this. I was once telephoned by the professor of North American literature at a Spanish university. He wanted some information about the fee Graham Greene would charge for a series of conferences. The subject under discussion was something to do with the political situation – or was it something literary? – in the Dominican Republic or Haiti. What could I say to a professor who had not the slightest idea of the sort of man Graham Greene was? When I told him about it, he laughed but looked rather sad.

Our walk through that garden in the shade of the ancient eucalyptus trees was an interesting one. Graham told me that I should put away my Roman collar and not always dress in black. 'It would be more suitable for the university life. You would look more approachable to some people. You would seem more human, though no less divine.'

•

We would often laugh about some of the intimate stories that were told during our conversations. As a young man, Graham had been very good looking, and male and female beauty delight the devil, who is only too happy to provide charming temptations to lure the unwary.

For Graham, the eyes really were the mirror of the soul. Within them, you could see the truth reflected and what a person was really like. He confessed that visiting prostitutes as a young man had been bad for him. A girl with an attractive, lively expression never disappointed him subsequently. Sometimes he felt attracted by a beautiful body, but if the eyes were dead, he always realized, after the event, what a waste of time and of money it had been.

In this context, a very curious thing once happened to him. He was introduced to an extremely sweet and intelligent streetwalker, who said: 'Why should you pay to sleep with me? If we made love in front of the television cameras, you would earn a great deal of money?'

'These things are completely private', replied Graham.

He had been very struck by the girl, but when he went to call on her on another occasion, she had disappeared for good.

The night he had been with the girl, Graham had had an interesting dream. He found himself in a place full of small pieces of gold. He hurried to pick up as many as he could. However, he realized later that it was forbidden to take gold out of that country. What could he do to cross the frontier?

On occasion, I have thought that wherever he went Graham was haunted by the notion of the frontier. More than once, I laughed when I recalled, a trifle ironically, the title (which he liked) of the lecture I failed to give: 'You can't cross the frontier.'

Pretty girls remained etched in his memory. He was particularly drawn to a Vietnamese girl, married to a North American diplomat, whom we had met at a reception given in the gardens of the Retiro in Madrid. It happened when he came to the city on an official visit. Perhaps she reminded him of Phuong in *The Quiet American*. He often spoke to me of her. Graham used his eyes as a camera. Later, everything would be developed in the laboratory of his mind. There was no need for the photographic apparatus. That was why mine irritated him so!

In relating these little events, I don't want to sound like the late Anthony Burgess. Graham mentioned his fellow Catholic novelist to me on several occasions. Apparently, Burgess once wrote an article which revealed that Graham was living with a woman at his home in Antibes and he informed his readers that when the woman's husband arrived, there had been a tremendous fracas outside in the street.

Graham laughed: 'As you can see, I live on the fourth floor. The poor man cannot have found it easy to hear what was going on at street level.'

He went on: 'I wrote a letter to Anthony Burgess in which I said that either he had invented a lie, or else he was out of his mind. I advised him to go and see a doctor quickly.'

He continued: 'I don't understand the man. He once wrote a highly favourable article about the political aspects of my work. Only recently, he praised Maria Couto's book on the political content of my work. He even dedicated one of his books to me. And now he comes out with this . . .'

And I replied: 'I, too, think there is something strange at times about Anthony Burgess. He accuses you of Jansenism, whereas I don't believe anyone could be less Jansenistic than you. Jansenists assure us that "only the elect shall be saved, for Christ died for them alone", yet you joke and pull my leg sometimes by saying that there may not even be a hell. You would even save your enemy Franco, for you want everyone, without exception, to go to heaven.'

'Exactly,' replied Graham, 'exactly.'

●

Shortly afterwards, we spoke at length about Bishop Christopher Butler, the distinguished theologian, scholar and writer. We both agreed that he was one of the best intellectual minds in the Catholic church and that his thinking left its mark on the Second Vatican Council. His career had been similar to that of Cardinal Newman's: he had been at Oxford, he became a convert to Catholicism, then a priest and later a bishop. It may be that he was not made a cardinal because of his age. Or did he refuse it himself because he did not want to look after a London diocese? As it happened, they elected another Benedictine, Basil Hume, to be cardinal. When *The Heart of the Matter* was published, Butler wrote a defence of Greene and his work. Many years later, the Bishop would write an Introduction to my own book *La Crisis del Sacerdote en la Obra de Graham Greene* ('The Priesthood in the Writings of Graham Greene'). This learned bishop invited me to dinner and asked me to tell Graham how much he would like to meet him too. Graham arranged it as soon as he could. They dined at the Atheneum Club in London: a dinner of two geniuses. They discussed the thorniest of problems: birth control and the Church's view on the subject, among other things.

'We agreed about everything. He is a delightful man', concluded Graham. Later, Bishop Butler wrote to me to say that he would love to have another talk with Graham. I passed this on to Graham, who said that he would like that too, but so hectic is modern life that in fact they never did manage to meet again.

Cardinal Heenan also invited Graham to lunch at his residence in Westminster. The conversation was enjoyable and was mostly concerned with Malcolm Muggeridge. The Cardinal was very keen on him and wrote to Rome about his possible conversion to Catholicism. Greene knew Muggeridge well; it was he who had recruited him to the Secret Service. Graham thought he rather tended to flirt with religion. Why, for example, when he was talking about the Trappists, did he have to appear on the television screen all the time? Graham once wrote him a rather sarcastic postcard. Malcolm Muggeridge did, of course, become a Catholic.

On one occasion, it was midnight and Graham had just finished reading to me the second chapter of *Monsignor Quixote* in manuscript, and we had been chatting into the small hours. I told him about my early life: about my family's humble origins; about the wonderful human qualities of my parents who could only read with difficulty. I told him that I had been born in Penedo de Avión, a village in the province of Orense, a place Graham would later visit several times, and about the three watersheds in a life spent searching for a place where I could have the freedom to dedicate myself to books: as a priest with the Vincentians; as a parish priest in Astorga; and as a professor at the Complutense University in Madrid.

Graham asked me to tell him about my life with the Vincentians and I gave him a resumé from the time of my entry to the novitiate up until my transfer to the diocese of Astorga. He was much impressed by the details of my life as a novice, and asked about the amount of money the Vincentians gave to those of us who were already priests for our personal expenses. Could one, for example, buy a book that one wanted? Things were improving – up from twenty pesetas a month to one hundred, but only on condition that the four Masses that we were free to say for our own intentions each month were said for the Superior's intention!

I told him how the Superior of our Province went to visit the Vincentian houses in the United States. On his return, as a present for the professors of the seminary at San Pablo (Cuenca), he brought us each a little packet of ten razor blades. 'It is fantastic, unbelievable', commented Graham. But I told him that these things could not be understood outside their 'medieval' context, and that thanks to these eccentricities, the persevering side of my character was forged. I also told him – to remove any stain from my own name! – that I had some great friends who continued to be Vincentians.

I remember that it was already quite late, but we were in no hurry and we were resting on the two beds in his room in Sintra. Graham told me about a hoax letter he had received. An American lady had written to him saying that she was immensely rich and that she wanted to leave her entire fortune to him. Greene showed the letter to a number of people who considered it to be authentic and sincere. He wrote back to the woman saying that he had no need of the money and advising her to distribute it to charity. She had insisted on leaving it all to Graham, so in a second letter he wrote that, if she liked, she could give a third of it to Daniel Ortega, the Nicaraguan president, so that he could buy arms to defend his country.

On the face of it, the letter was a hoax. Graham fully expected to see it published in the press at any moment. Reagan had been informed about it. It reassured him, at least, to know that he had not asked anything for himself.

Graham made me laugh a good deal when he told me a story about a woman who was a professor at an American university. She came to see him at Antibes and invited him to America with the idea of marking his eightieth birthday. Everything, including the journey, would be paid for. There would be the occasional photograph. The woman insisted on putting her hand on his shoulder . . . She left, but not long afterwards he received a letter from her in which she offered to become his secretary, cook, and anything else. Graham need not pay her anything. His mere presence would be enough.

•

Everyone knows that Graham Greene belonged to the Secret Service. *The Human Factor* is dedicated to his sister, Elisabeth Dennys, 'who cannot deny some responsibility ' for it. The main character in the novel is a double agent. Graham told me about those 'parties' in London to which he used to be invited without having any idea about their true significance. He did wonder how it was possible that there were so many good things to drink when, at that period of the war, everything was rationed. They were checking him out. He had 'a very good head'.

To judge by the anecdotes he related, this Secret Service world must have been even more extraordinary than the world of Agatha Christie. When Graham Greene was working for MI6 in Sierra Leone, he was sent a secretary. This girl became involved in an affair with a Frenchman. Graham was warned by his senior officer that he should be aware of the danger of this situation, to which Graham responded: 'I'm quite well aware of the matter. She is acting under my advice.'

Walking through London one day, he pointed out the building – the door, the room, the window – where he and Kim Philby had worked. We often spoke about Philby. They were friends and continued to be so even after Philby's defection. He had been Greene's boss.

Graham and Philby went on writing letters to each other – although there were only one or two a year – until the day Graham felt obliged to stop the correspondence. A former officer in MI6, 'C', had died and a journalist had subsequently published some of the things that 'C' had told him, including information about the correspondence between Graham and Philby.

'It's the last thing I would have expected of "C"', Graham told me. But he exonerated him: 'He was a dying man', Graham said.

'It's always the same,' I concluded, 'some journalists simply have no scruples.'

Graham agreed. He had suffered badly from such treatment himself. In every profession there are examples of people who lack honour. It must have been a great disappointment for Philby. What he looked forward to, more than anything else, was a letter from Graham and, above all, his very occasional visits.

In one of his letters, on the subject of the invasion of Afghanistan, Philby wrote to Graham: 'What may surprise you is that no one approves of it here, at least as far as I know.' He also told him that the KGB was not in favour of the invasion, but they involved the army so as to discredit it. Graham did not think that Philby's letter was sincere, but a year later he had changed his mind. When *The Human Factor* was published, Kim Philby wrote a letter to Graham in which he said it was clear that Dr Percival is based on someone in the British Secret Service.

When Graham Greene was invited to the World Congress of Intellectuals in Moscow, Forum on Peace and Human Rights, he went to see Philby. Philby said, 'I don't want you to ask any questions, Graham.'

'Of course', Greene replied, and they spoke in a relaxed way about matters that did not compromise anyone.

Philby's wife told Graham it had been one of the happiest conversations of his life.

On 15 May 1988, Graham rang me to say that Philby had died. He was greatly affected by it. The obituary notice in *The Times* particularly upset him. Some uncouth person had written that he hoped 'his agony had been a long one'. Graham wanted to know who could have been so cruel when everything else written about Philby had been quite moderate. However, one of his reasons for going to Russia had gone and Graham was no longer eager to visit Moscow. This was why he refused the invitation to go to the gathering of Christians in that city. Kim Philby had once been a friend, although not everyone approved of this friendship. One incensed lunatic had even gone so far as to write: 'Graham Greene's books should be thrown on a bonfire.'

When the whole subject of Philby was called into question, Macmillan defended him in the House of Commons; but it is not true, Graham thought, that Macmillan resigned, just because the truth had been discovered and a mistake had been made. In the face of all the rumours about a Russian double agent, a high-ranking official went to see him. There was a meeting, and the following day Philby left aboard a Russian ship and was taken to Moscow, where he was well received. It would have been quite likely, Graham thought, that Philby would have become head of the British Secret Service.

I asked Graham how Philby was regarded in Russia now. Graham replied: 'People said that Andropov wanted to convince the members of the Politburo that the Russian Secret Service should be organized on British lines, and that Philby should be put in charge. I don't know whether there is any truth in that.'

Latterly, Graham had an unusual dream about Philby which intrigued him and which he planned to analyse in the light of his correspondence with him, but unfortunately I never heard any more details about it.

•

Whenever I went to Antibes, Graham usually had something extraordinary to tell me. I always had the feeling that there were two household gods waiting for me there: Tragedy and Comedy. On this occasion, although his number was ex-directory, Graham had received an anonymous telephone call a few days previously. A gruff voice asked whether he would receive three members of the Red Brigade at his home. Graham replied with a firm 'no'. The gruff voice continued: 'Why?'

'Because I would have to leave France the following day', answered Graham.

Greene informed the Ministry of Justice about this call. At the Ministry they were familiar with the criminal milieu in Nice and knew that it was a hide-out for members of the Italian Red Brigades, just as France was also a refuge for Basque terrorists at that time.

As we were leaving the block of flats in Antibes, the concierge told us that the call had come from Spain. The man identified himself as 'Alvarez' and said he was a member of the Spanish government. He had then rung the concierge a second time and asked for Graham Greene's telephone number. Señor Alvarez assured her he had written, or received a letter from Mr Greene.

We were in no further doubt. Graham telephoned Elisabeth and she confirmed that she had received a long telegram signed by someone whose name was illegible. The proposal was that a film should be made based on *Ways of Escape* and others of his books. It would be called 'From Guernica to Berlin'. They would be delighted if Graham would accept their invitation to come to Bilbao, together with his friend 'the Jesuit, Father Leopoldo Durán', to discuss plans and start work on the film.

Obviously, we thought, this had something to do with Herribatasuna, or one of the political wings of ETA, the Basque separatist movement. We didn't think it had anything to do with the autonomous Basque government. Of course, it would never even have occurred to Greene to accept anything like this.

At supper that night Graham told me all about a trip he had just made to Communist Poland. He spoke, in particular, about his meetings with Boleslaw Piasecki and his celebrated Peace movement. This good man tried to frame Graham, but the trick rebounded on him.

At a conference he attended, there were a number of writers and political figures who tried to introduce him to a girl at a reception. He did not find her particularly attractive, but he began to be suspicious and wonder why the girl should have been 'offered' to him. Instead, he started talking to another young woman, and it was clear that they both felt attracted to one another. In all probability, they would have ended up sleeping together. Very suddenly, however, this girl was removed from the reception. They realized that she and Graham had become too familiar with each other much too quickly.

Piasecki was alone with Graham after the gathering. 'We started drinking "heavily"', Graham told me. Eventually, they decided to leave. Graham was rather unsteady on his feet as they walked towards the car, but his companion was in an even worse state. Piasecki was driving. A few minutes later, they collided with something. It might have been fatal. This was when Graham said to me: 'Thank God I have a good head.'

CHAPTER V

TWO CONVERSATIONS

O UR TALKS TOGETHER ranged over a wide variety of subjects. Greene's conversation was always stimulating and entertaining, and he had a wonderful gift for detailed observation. Two particular evenings stick in my mind for the quality of the conversations, and may help to give an idea of what it was like to be in his company. The first was in Maria Newall's house at Sintra in Portugal, the second at the Ritz, during one of Graham's periodic visits to London.

•

On 19 July 1977, we had arrived at the Quinta de Piedade, on the outskirts of Sintra. Maria Newall, an Englishwoman who had been an old friend of Graham's ever since the Mau Mau rebellion in Kenya, was waiting for us in the way a mother might wait for her children. Dinner was on the dot, for whatever this exceptional woman did, she was always punctual. The table was lit with candles and, just by Maria's hand, stood a silver bell. The conversation at dinner and afterwards was immensely entertaining. Maria Newall was a Catholic in the fullest sense. She had been very well instructed and she loved to take part in and listen to high-level religious discussions. Among other things, I remember Graham told her about how Sean O'Faolain had returned to the faith. He had previously been a practising Catholic but had abandoned the spiritual life. One day, as he arrived at St Peter's in Rome, he threw himself into the arms of a bishop or monsignor, and from that moment he had become an exemplary Catholic.

At about midnight, we retired to the comfort of our rooms, which were the cosiest I have ever seen in my life. Maria had had a small outhouse built with two apartments, separated by a staircase, for guests. It was situated in the middle of an immense garden, and at night the scent of a thousand plants and flowers transformed the room into a paradise. Every morning we were awoken by the sounds of a thousand different types of birds inviting us to start each new day in the happiest of moods. A week there made us feel like new men.

The conversation that took place the next day was unforgettable. At ten o'clock there was Mass, at which everyone assisted. For this woman, to hear Mass in her own home was something too good to be true. Maria was tranquillity itself; the only thing that could upset her equilibrium was the unthinkable prospect that there might one day be an American pope at St Peter's in Rome. 'Of course it's impossible', she assured herself, and she smiled. You cannot prevent people having such illogical notions!

We had breakfast and then spent the whole day in that enormous and wonderful garden. Laying aside all modesty for the moment, I was reminded of Plato and the garden of the Academy, and his conversations with his disciples on the subject of the 'Banquet'.

We discussed the youth of today and why they behave as they do. Perhaps it was because so many have everything handed to them on a silver plate? But Greene objected, saying that he had not suffered a great deal either at that age. At Oxford in the twenties, one was surrounded by everything one could possibly wish, and it was all paid for by one's parents; yet, in spite of all his pranks, he still dreamt of doing something with his life. We suggested that he had been searching for a path in life and reminded him of the struggles he had had in order to publish his first books.

Graham loved young people, but he would become seriously annoyed about the way young men behaved in relation to girls. He thought they were often selfish and cruel, and did not bother if they made a girl pregnant. When he was young, he always carried some 'French letters' with him should the need arise. We were appalled at the apparent number of pregnant adolescent girls. Each of those crippled lives became a scar on our society.

We moved on to the genius of Newman. We all agreed that he may perhaps have been the greatest figure of the nineteenth century. The works of his that we rated most highly were *Apologia Pro Vita Sua* and *The Idea of a University*. Graham had read both these books more than once at his leisure. We discussed the three 'Discourses' on theology and other sciences: 'Theology: A Branch of Knowledge', 'The Bearing of Theology on Other Branches of Knowledge' and 'The Bearing of Other Branches of Knowledge on Theology'.

We were in agreement on the almost total ignorance of

theology among professors of humanities at universities. Out of this stemmed the endless superficiality that one found everywhere. How could someone honed and shaped in the philosophy of life teach people if he or she had never sampled theology, the queen of sciences?

We recalled Newman's far-reaching lectures on literature. After *Brighton Rock* was published and people began to refer to Graham Greene as a Catholic novelist, he defended himself with Newman's ideas: 'I am a novelist who also happens to be a Catholic. There is no such thing as Catholic literature; there is literature, and, occasionally, it is concerned with religious themes, whether Catholic or otherwise.' Greene said he planned to read *The Dream of Gerontius* again.

Graham asked me whether I remembered Newman's advice about seminaries: 'All seminarists should read literature. Why? So as to avoid the 'shocks' of later life.'

We were very close to Lisbon, and someone mentioned the name of Otero de Cabalho, a minor Portuguese military figure of the period, who was well known for his lack of bravery. Graham decided to amuse us. After all, this talk of Newman had become far too serious. Graham had once planned to interview Otero de Cabalho. The interview had been arranged by a friend who was on the far right, through a man whose wife was Otero's mistress. The interview never took place, not that this mattered to Graham in the least.

Graham must have decided to provide us with a little light relief. He told us about the first time he had fallen in love, with his sister Elisabeth's governess. Like Carlotta, the heroine of Goethe's *Werther*, she was already engaged to be married and was several years older than Graham. They used to dance with the lights turned low and they would meet to kiss in private. One day Graham's mother surprised them in the act of kissing and things rather changed, though it was not true that the governess had been given her notice by his mother.

Falling in love was hardly the best way for Graham to start life at Oxford. For three months he lived in a continually drunken state. He drank beer. He began drinking from the moment he woke up each morning and continued to do so for three months until, with one exception, he was cured for ever from drinking too much. One day he came across a group of his friends in Oxford who had been drinking too much beer in Graham's rooms. Not to be outdone, he drank half a bottle of gin and got completely drunk. After that he came to loathe neat gin, and never drank it again without adding tonic water. During the three months he spent drinking at Oxford, the time eventually came when he had to attend a tutorial. Two friends managed to carry him there and helped him to sit down on the chair. The tutor was extremely understanding. He made the interview as short as possible and Graham returned to his rooms at Balliol.

This early love affair with his sister's governess was to blame for these problems, but at least he was fortunate not to go to his grave, playing Russian roulette, because of it. He was luckier than the wretched Werther.

After this, Graham told us about the one time that he had got drunk, with Evelyn Waugh when he had fallen asleep in the bath. There had been a girl waiting for him in the house, but Graham had completely forgotten about her.

An Italian diplomat joined us for lunch. I believe one of his close relatives was a high-ranking monsignor at the Vatican – a good source of information. As far as he was concerned, Europe was rotten; its spiritual reserves lay in Spain and Poland. (This conversation took place in the seventies.) The subject moved to communism; his opinions of Carrillo and Alvaro Cunhal; Mario Suares and his set-backs in parliament – he laughed at this. The Socialist government did not particularly seem to bother him. Taking me to one side, the Italian diplomat told me how important he thought it was to talk to Graham Greene, because his books were read all over the world.

In the afternoon, after a short siesta, we returned to the shade of our tree in the garden. Now rested, we resumed that morning's rather speculative conversation. We became slightly heated when we touched on the arguments for the proof of God. For Graham, these proved nothing or very little. In my case, they may not be conclusive individually, but taken together they were convincing. And I added, half-jokingly, that all arguments were unnecessary. All that was needed to convince me of the existence of God was a little common-sense and the ability to really look at the things that surrounded us, be it a flower or a star. I appealed to the argument of order, the sidereal order of the beauty lavished on the world. There, in that garden, we were surrounded with flowers on all sides; inside the house there were magnificent vases of hortensia and red roses. Graham replied that, as usual, he liked to play the devil's advocate, and that many things in creation were actually ugly. He saw no contradiction in this. Then we moved on to his short story 'A Visit to Morin', which I had raised; it is a story that deals with just such a philosophical-theological theme. It is also one of the best short stories he wrote.

The conversation turned to the subject of birth control once again. It was not one we had much to agree upon . . .

Among other less serious subjects, Greene related the following anecdote: after the Second World War, he and his wife went to spend a few days on the Isle of Wight. On Sunday they went to Mass. An organist was playing and a woman dressed in the worst of taste was singing horribly. When she sang her most piercing notes, the priest cringed and hunched his back and shoulders as if he were remembering bombs falling during the war. A boy of about sixteen was serving at Mass and the priest whispered a message in his ear. The server approached the organist and the singer. She was furious, and said in a loud voice that could be heard by all those nearby: 'Tell the old bugger to sing it himself'. And she left.

The priest, with the utmost calm, turned to the faithful and said simply: 'In future this Mass will be a low Mass.'

At dinner that evening we discussed pop music in church. Our opinion was that, very occasionally, this music could be beautiful. Greene cited a Mass he had heard in Paris. I mentioned the wonderful folk music and songs at the Masses I had celebrated in 1972 at the church in Milagrosa in Mexico. When they told me about the 'pop' chorus in the sacristy, I had gone up to the altar feeling quite annoyed, but those Masses will always remain something unforgettable for me; I was overwhelmed by their extraordinary spiritual beauty. I could sense the Catholic soul of the youth of Mexico pulsating within the music, and my own body pulsated too.

A greater part of our conversation at dinner turned on the complete lack of tact of many confessors and the very serious blunders which can take place in the confessional. Personally, I know many cases where an angry or rude priest has managed to put people off going to confession for life.

They very much liked my way of assisting those who said they had not been to confession for a long time. People sometimes entered the confessional in such a nervous or frightened state that they could hardly speak. It was not a problem. I would ask: 'How long is it since you have been to confession?'

'A long time, Father.'

'More than a hundred years?'

'Not as long as that, Father.'

'Fifty?'

'No.'

'In that case, it is not a long time', I would say persuasively, laughing a little. The penitent would feel relieved; wings grew on him; he was cured. How easy it is to be a marvellous confessor!

I also recounted a story about the time I told a priest that he should not sit down and hear confession if he was aware that he was in a bad mood.

It was by now late and we went up to bed, but Graham and I were now alone in our rooms, out there in the garden. A drop of the 'Tonico Carino' helped the conversation continue for another hour.

It was very late when we left each other. Around two o'clock in the morning, Graham came into my room. My door was open and there was only a short distance between our two doors.

'I am sorry,' said Graham. 'I saw your light on and I thought I heard someone crying.'

'Don't worry, Graham. I was saying my rosary. I sometimes say it aloud so that I won't fall asleep. And to think I've kept you awake. Thank you for telling me. Please go to sleep now.'

•

On 16 August 1978, Graham and I were in London. I arrived at the Ritz at 1.30 p.m. Graham came down immediately. We embraced warmly as usual, and went to have lunch at Stone's restaurant. He was carrying three books by Brian Moore which he inscribed to me later at lunch.

I can only give an outline of that two- or three-hour conversation for it would be inappropriate to say any more. We were discussing how well the media had dealt with the death of Pope Paul VI. He told me that a certain 'character' had called the Pope 'a silly old fool' on the BBC and had been sacked from his job. Graham's voice sounded quite angry. Apart from the fact that he greatly admired Paul VI, Graham could not bear to hear ill spoken of the Church, or of the hierarchy, by people who were not Catholics. It was a very different matter if the criticism came from within the Church. And yet, in this instance, the person who uttered the unfortunate remark was a Catholic whose divorce had not been recognized by Rome! It appeared that Paul VI had personally looked into the case.

He told me about his private audience with Paul VI. Graham felt it had been rather more intimate than the one he had had with Pius XII. The Pope had invited him to sit down and had been more straightforward. He told him that he had read *Stamboul Train* and that he was reading *The Power and the Glory*.

'Your Holiness is reading a book that has been banned by the Church', Graham told him.

'Who banned it?'

'Cardinal Pizzardo.'

'Cardinal Pizzardo', said the Pope, shaking his head from side to side.

Paul VI's attitude was more liberal than that of Cardinal Pizzardo. He told Graham that he ought not to worry for there would always be some Catholics who would be offended by his books; advice that Graham, naturally, had no difficulty in following. When Paul VI died, various newspapers wanted to send him to Rome for the funeral of the Pope and to cover the Conclave. But he refused: 'I don't know anyone there . . . and it's not a subject I specialize in.'

Earlier, in the fifties, when Cardinal Griffin had told Graham about Cardinal Pizzardo's demand that emendations should be made to the novel, Bishop Matthews, a great friend of Graham's, helped him compose a letter to the Holy Office. In it he said that it was ten years since *The Power and the Glory* had been published and that any changes would have to be carried out by the publishers. In order to help Cardinal Pizzardo and the Holy Office, he had included a list of publishing houses – some of them on the other side of the Iron Curtain – which the Holy Office could approach to have these changes made.

Graham talked to me at length about his brothers Hugh and Raymond. He always got on better with Hugh; Raymond was rather more snobbish – his wife especially – and Graham was totally opposed to class distinction of any kind. There had been a rather serious argument to do with this subject, concerning a marriage in the family. There were a number of things to do with his family and private friendships that were mentioned in conversation that day, but in this book I intend to avoid mentioning anything that Graham ever told me during the course of our friendship that concerned family or private matters. It is a question of basic common sense and, in my case, being bound by the secrecy of my vocation.

We talked about Tom Stoppard, the English playwright who was to write the screen play for the film based on *The Human Factor*.

Graham had been with him the day before and, apart from thinking him a good dramatist, he liked him more each time they met. We spoke about the problems of bringing an orchestra to the place where the film was being shot. Shortly after this conversation, incidentally, I was in Antibes when Graham had a very unpleasant telephone conversation with Otto Preminger, the director and producer of *The Human Factor*. Graham told him that the film was bound to be a disaster. He tried to get him to change his mind about the cast and various aspects of the film, but unfortunately Preminger was absolutely sure of what he was doing. Finally, Graham told him the film would be as big a failure as the one based on *The Comedians*. Preminger replied with a most unfortunate remark and Graham slammed down the telephone.

He told me about his recent journey to Panama and Central America. Graham said that the attempt on Eden Pastora's life was a total mystery. Pastora had refused to join the Sandinistas, a good number of whom had belonged to Somoza's National Guard. Eden Pastora was of the view that the battle against the Nicaraguan government should be political, not military. Perhaps Pastora's pride had been hurt by the fact that he had not been given a top job once Somoza had been defeated. After the attempt on his life, Pastora disappeared. Graham only met him once.

Years later, Graham told me about a curious interview connected with this attack, 'an interview which I gave to a Swedish journalist in a rushed moment'. This journalist had been present when Eden Pastora was attacked in Costa Rica. He had been shot and wounded himself, but he had powerful memories of what had happened. It had been a marvellous sensation: he felt himself flying, at unimaginable speeds, through spaces undreamt of and past ever brighter lights, filled with a feeling of unearthly happiness. Graham thought that he was describing the sensation of dying.

We recalled our travels through Spain and Portugal the previous July, a year when we had not had much luck anywhere we went. The memory of Segovia was particularly upsetting. Our friends there had shown us round with the best will in the world; but Graham and I had felt very tired walking from the Meson de Candido to the Alcazar under a burning sun – especially after lunch! If we had gone by car, we could have been there in a flash, and could have walked up the mountain to the top of Navacerrada where the water is so cool!

We did not have pleasant memories, that year, of Salamanca either

– neither the crowds in the Plaza Mayor, nor the Gran Hotel or the Restaurante Valencia which we had always loved. Perhaps it was because we had gone there on a Sunday.

On the other hand, Graham had been delighted to meet the Vincentian Fathers at Villafranca del Bierzo. He had loved the fraternal bond and that easy, familiar atmosphere; and, above all, the indelible memory of the meal we had eaten with our friend the winegrower, Antonio de las Regadas, under the biblical fig tree at his vineyard. Graham needed the peace that one breathed under that tree as well as the friendly presence of the patriarchal figure of Señor Antonio.

•

Shortly after this conversation, Graham was operated on in London for cancer of the stomach; but all went well and he improved from day to day. When I telephoned him in Antibes on 24 March, Graham told me: 'On the day after my operation, when I was in intensive care, I dreamt I was in Antibes. I got out of bed, but I saw that there were tubes all over me. The nurse came running in and she saved my life.'

Graham delighted in small details. While he was recuperating in hospital, he discovered that the girl whose job it was to clean his room at the clinic was from Galicia. She and Graham became immediate friends. Graham told her about how he and I travelled around Galicia at least once a year, and promised that we would go to visit her town that summer. The girl was called María Dolores Ramos and she came from Puente de Mera, Landoy, La Coruña. Graham seemed delighted to tell me all these details.

The nurse who looked after Graham was very kind. One day she said to him:

'My father reads many books of yours.'

'In French?' Graham asked her.

'No, in English.'

'Well, where do you come from?'

'From a very small country which you don't know, of course. I come from Belize.'

'But I am a very close friend of your Prime Minister! I was with him two years ago.'

This prime minister was called George Price. On Graham's last trip to Panama, his friend General Torrijos had asked if he would

travel to the former colony of British Honduras because he wanted
him to meet his friend the Prime Minister. Graham subsequently
wrote me a letter about him that was a thousand times more affectionate and admiring than it would have been if he were writing about
the President of the United States. This is what he wrote:

> The Prime Minister, George Peres, is an extraordinary
> character. He had wanted to be a priest, but after two
> years in the seminary, his father died and he had to leave
> to look after his ten brothers and sisters. Now he goes to
> Mass and Communion every day at 5 a.m., lives alone and
> goes to bed between 8 and 9; knew my books better than
> I do and loved talking about Teilhard and Thomas Mann
> ... Love in haste,
> Graham.

CHAPTER VI

LITERATURE AND THE
NOBEL PRIZE

WITHOUT PARTICULARLY INTENDING to, we often spoke about literature. It was almost always my fault since I would ask Graham questions on the subject whenever one occurred to me. Then, or whenever it was relevant, he discussed literature as if it were an everyday matter, but he did so with great vitality and with enormous knowledge.

I asked him what he thought about literature as it applied to the university, and he replied more or less like this: 'The university is harmful to literature. Literature cannot be taught at universities, it is something that is experienced and felt . . . Poetry is not like philosophy or theology; it is human joy and agony. It is rhythm. Although anyone who knows theology can find things in Gerard Manley Hopkins, for example, that others might not find.'

We carried on talking. I believe that the unconscious plays an important part in poetic creativity; perhaps in literary creativity in general. Although it was my intention to ask questions, I mentioned in passing the well-known idea that more unbelievable things happen in real life than they do in the most imaginative fiction.

'The novel is concerned with real life, and extraordinary events are rare in life', said Graham.

During our conversation, someone used the terms 'realism' and 'naturalism'.

'What is the difference between those two words?' asked Graham. 'I see none.'

Later, he added: 'I would not use the word "criticism", but rather "appreciation" or "condemnation".' Critics, he thought, very often behaved like 'flies'.

One day, at the *parador* at Benavente, our faithful friend, the 'Third Man', who drove the car, used the word 'culture'. Graham, who had become a little impatient with the subject we were discussing, retorted sharply: 'I detest culture. Neither Shakespeare, nor Cervantes nor Racine were cultivated men. Culture is the prerogative of pedantic professors.'

Graham improvised this phrase in one of those flashes of brilliance. It remained embedded in my mind like a bullet. Unamuno had written something similar: 'A pedant is a fool who has been damaged by culture.'

I was also reminded of his pithy retort to Mary Renault, the English novelist who lived in South Africa, who had once insulted Graham in a letter: 'I have not read any of your work,' he said. 'If I do read any of it some day, I will do so with more care than you have read mine.'

•

On 23 February 1984, Graham Greene was the principal guest at a lunch to celebrate 'The Ten Best Novels of Our Time'. It was a promotion organized by the Book Marketing Council in London in which a number of well-known authors were asked to nominate their favourite books. Graham had a bad cough and a cold, but, according to Elisabeth, he apparently made a very good and amusing speech.

'The Ten Best Novels of Our Time' is a contradiction in terms because the 'best' can only mean one. In any case, as soon as Graham read out his list of titles, various publishers ran to the telephone in order to try to acquire the rights in the books he mentioned. It was enough for Graham to write a few lines in a preface praising a book, or to recite a poem, for the work to be given a new life. This happened with *The Green Child* by Herbert Read and the work of the poet, Arthur Hugh Clough.

The names of countless authors cropped up in our conversations over the course of the years. I feel it may be useful to list some of them and to give a brief summary of Graham's opinion of their work.

Shakespeare. Graham was not very fond of *Hamlet*. The contradictions which appear in the play between what the Ghost says and what Hamlet says, may be intended to confuse the audience or reader, or may be due to Shakespeare's limited knowledge of theology. The former is the more likely. Graham preferred *Othello*, *Anthony and Cleopatra*, and *Troilus and Cressida*. In his youth, he loved *Macbeth*, but he had learned the text by heart and believed that this had spoiled his enjoyment of the play. He did not care for *The Tempest*. In Graham's view, it was not true to say that very little was known about Shakespeare. Much more was known about him than about many of his contemporaries, Marlowe among them.

Graham preferred **Webster**'s best plays – *The White Devil* and *The Duchess of Malfi* – to those of Shakepeare. He didn't much like **Marlowe**'s *Faustus*.

We often spoke about **D.H.Lawrence**. Graham did not consider him a great novelist, nor much of a lesser one. *Women in Love* was perhaps his best novel. But he did consider him one of the great English masters of the short story. He also thought highly of him as a poet and considered some of his poems to have great spiritual depths. The rather false sexual content of his novels, which Graham attributed to his highly-sexed German wife, Frieda, ruined his work. Frieda had apparently once offered herself to A.S. Frere, the former Managing Director of Heinemann, who was Graham's first publisher, as well as the publisher of Lawrence's work.

I told Graham that one of my pupils wanted to write a thesis on his fictional work. He replied: 'He should take as his subject the destruction of the myth of Lawrence.'

Graham told me that he did not much like **Hemingway**, apart from his short stories and *The Old Man and the Sea*, although he did not particularly care for that novel. He felt that *For Whom the Bell Tolls* lacked verisimilitude. The girl should not have been beautiful, but rather, ugly and ordinary, and she should have fallen in love with a Spanish patriot, rather than an American.

Why did Hemingway commit suicide? Greene's opinion was that he could see that his reputation as a writer could go no further . . . He could no longer produce ideas. His creativity had run dry and that was intolerable. There was no substitute, not even love. Shortly before he died, Graham told me that if he were not able to go on working, it would be better to die.

He had a high opinion of *Waiting for Godot*, but he felt that in his other plays **Beckett** seemed to be extolling his own lack of hope. This playwright did not interest him and at the time we spoke he had just read a highly critical article about him.

For Graham Greene, **Donne** was perhaps as profound as **Hopkins**. Hopkins had written some excellent poems, but also some worthless ones. He showed me a sonnet of Donne's that reminded him of Hopkins and he recommended his poem 'The Crosse' to me:

> *Since Christ embrac'd the Crosse it selfe, dare I*
> *His image, th'image of his Crosse deny?*

He also had a high regard for **Arthur Hugh Clough**, particularly his poem 'Easter Day', and he often quoted to me:

> *We are most hopeless who had once most hope*
> *We are most wretched that had most believed.*
> *Christ is not risen.*

Graham had very much enjoyed **David Lodge**'s novel *How Far Can You Go?*, which dealt humorously with birth control, but he did not understand a word of a book of criticism that Lodge had brought out.

T.S. Eliot was frequently the subject of our discussions. Graham told me about Eliot's friendship for John Hayward, who had helped T.S. Eliot a great deal with his powerful criticism. They had flats on the same floor of the same building and Hayward, who was paralysed and died young, had a bell with which he used to summon Eliot if he felt unwell during the night. When Eliot married a second time, he left the flat without saying a word to Hayward, 'probably so as not to upset him, but he actually succeeded in hurting him much more'. The dedication of *The Waste Land* to Ezra Pound, 'although seemingly gracious may actually have been a little derogatory. Nevertheless, it is clear that *The Waste Land* would not have been what it is without the critical help of Ezra Pound', he said, although Graham felt that Eliot should not have allowed one of the passages to be suppressed. Graham did not understand the Cantos of **Ezra Pound**, but he had a high regard for the early poems. He did think very highly of Eliot as a poet, naturally, but he did not rate him as highly as **Yeats** and **Hardy**.

Trollope is one of the English novelists Greene most admired. In his view, he was possibly a better novelist than **Dickens**. He very much liked his short *Autobiography* although he sometimes found it a bit sentimental. He preferred the political novels, *The Way We Live Now* and *The Eustace Diamonds* to his 'Barchester' novels.

With regard to **Joyce** he preferred his collection of short stories, *Dubliners*, and *A Portrait of the Artist as a Young Man*. He thought *Ulysses* contained many good things but also much obscurity. As for *Finnegan's Wake*, he told me to listen to it on a record, read by the author. When he mentioned *Dubliners* he also recommended the short stories of **J.F. Powers** most highly.

Graham had just reread **Miguel de Unamuno's** *Life of Don Quixote and Sancho*. We discussed Unamuno's theory that Cervantes derived his inspiration from St Ignatius Loyola when he had created the character of the knight, Quixote himself. 'What had Cervantes intended when he wrote his marvellous book?' asked Graham. 'Is it not a book filled with the philosophy of life?'

As I have said, Greene was a great admirer of **Thomas Hardy's** poetry. He did not consider him a great novelist, although he liked *The Trumpet Major* and *The Mayor of Casterbridge*.

He very much liked the religious poet **George Herbert** whose work he sometimes took on his trips.

Graham loved the simplicity of **Pablo Neruda's** work too. They had met when Neruda was Chilean ambassador to Paris and they immediately adopted the less formal 'tu' style of addressing each other. I mentioned his rather coarse poems written against Franco, Mola and other generals in the Spanish Civil War, but Graham blamed the passions of the moment and the conflicting ideological parties, and felt it was understandable in the circumstances.

We spoke about **Maurice Baring** on several occasions. Graham did not care much for his novels, but he very much liked his essays and travel books – *What I Saw in Russia*, for example. He recounted the story Baring told of a Russian military chaplain. This chaplain liked alcohol and one Sunday got completely drunk. His battalion wanted to hear Mass and there was no other priest. They waited as long as they could for the priest to show some sign that he had recovered his senses, then they ducked his head and shoulders in a tub of icy water until it looked as if he was more or less ready to be able to say Mass. Having heard Mass, and relieved that they had now fulfilled their duty to God, they discharged him with the following words: 'Go to hell now, son of a bitch.' How cleverly those soldiers distinguished between the man and his ministry!

Graham Greene was very keen on **Harold Pinter** and very much wanted the dramatist to write a screen play for one of his films. It was something they had both discussed before.

We spoke of the last American Nobel prize winner, **Saul Bellow**. Apparently, there is a dominating mother figure in many of his books. Graham only liked his novel *Herzog* and he did not care much for the American literary scene in general. Writers such as **Fowler, Henry**

Watson, etc., he considered to be difficult to read because of the 'philosophical' language they used.

He told me a lot about **Norman Douglas**. His best book, according to Graham, was *South Wind*, his book about Capri. He was an extremely lovable man. There is an essay about him in *Collected Essays*.

On several occasions we discussed **Borges**, who was a good friend to Graham. He admired him as a writer, but even more for his wonderful character. Graham told me an excellent anecdote about him which is included in his book *Reflections*.

> He was a man of great courage. At one time, during the
> second period of Peron, when he was living with his
> old mother, there was a mysterious phone call. A male
> voice said: 'We're coming to kill you and your mother.'
> Borges' mother replied, 'I'm ninety years old, so you'd
> better come quickly. And as for my son, it will be easy
> for you, since he is blind.' This, I think, gives a picture
> of what the family was like.

He loved **Chesterton**'s prose and much of his poetry, and he admired his personality and his wit.

He respected **Milton** but did not have a high regard for his poetry. He did not rate **Thackeray** very highly, not even *Vanity Fair*, but he enjoyed *Pelham* by **Bulwer Lytton** enormously. Of **George Meredith**, he only liked the poem 'Modern Love'.

Graham Greene was not an admirer of **Jane Austen**. She was too artificial for him, both in style and in her characters.

He disliked all **Kipling**'s prose work intensely, but he liked his poetry and five or six of his short stories. He thought *Ashenden* was **Somerset Maugham**'s best book, and he enjoyed **Angus Wilson**'s short stories, though not his novels.

At one time and another, he recommended the American writer **Flannery O'Connor** to me, especially her collection of letters, *The Habit of Being*.

The dramatists **Congreve** and **Sheridan** were too 'Attic', too 'affected'. He liked **Wycherley**, particularly *The Country Wife*. He said: 'The language of the theatre is the language of life. Wycherley uses the language the people spoke'. He preferred **Dryden** to **Congreve** and **Sheridan**.

The one novel of **William Golding**'s that he admired was *The

Lord of the Flies, which he considered very good. He found the books that followed boring and gave up reading them. The same happened with **Anthony Powell**; he only liked the early work.

Keats, according to Graham, did not deserve the reputation that fame attributed to him. He admired the shorter poems, but his longer ones, such as 'Endymion' were unreadable.

During a conversation in the *parador* of Oropesa, Graham told me that England had recently lost two great poets: **Robert Graves** and **Philip Larkin**.

●

From my volumes of notebooks, I see that at the beginning of our friendship, I asked Graham which were the best novels and writers of the current era that I should read. This is a brief synthesis of what he told me:

> Ford Madox Ford: *The Good Soldier*
> George Eliot: *Middlemarch*; *The Mill on the Floss*
> Conrad: *Under Western Eyes*; *Victory*; *The Nigger of the Narcissus*; *Heart of Darkness*
> Brian Moore: One of the living novelists who Graham Greene most admired. Among his favourite books were *The Great Victorian Collection* and *Catholics*
> Muriel Spark: *Memento Mori*
> Beryl Bainbridge: *The Bottle Factory Outing*; *Winter Garden*. He had a high regard for this writer
> R.K. Narayan: *The Bachelor of Arts*; *The English Teacher*; *The Tiger of Malgudi*
> Flann O'Brien: *The Dalkey Archive*
> William Trevor: *Collected Stories*; *Fools of Fortune*
> Malcolm Lowry: *Under the Volcano*

I asked him which he considered his own best short stories. In my copy of *Collected Stories* he marked several. These are some of them: 'Doctor Crombie', 'Two Gentle People', 'Under the Garden', 'A Visit to Morin', 'Dream of a Strange Land', 'The Destructors', 'The Hint of an Explanation', 'The Basement Room'.

Graham Greene would spend long periods rereading books that

he judged to be first-rate, in order to avoid reading the new books which took up so much of his time.

•

The question of Graham Greene and why he was not awarded the Nobel Prize is one of those subjects that was worn thin by the world's press each time he failed to obtain the prize. At the time *Monsignor Quixote* was published, an article entitled 'Graham Greene at his best' on the front page of the *Washington Post Book World* said this: 'They should award him the Nobel Prize for Literature. It is time.' (12 September 1982) In the same paper, Jonathan Yardley in a fiery article, 'Nobel and the Politics of the Left' (25 October 1982) protested angrily:

> Let us contemplate the astonishing fact that the members
> of the Swedish Academy, in their collective ignorance and
> bias, have once again refused to give the award to the
> writer who deserves it above all others now living, Graham
> Greene.

Two years previously, when the prize went to the then virtually unknown Polish poet, Czeslaw Milosz, the Irish journalist Peter Lennon had been to Stockholm to ask Dr Arthur Lundkvist why his committee had once again failed to give the Nobel Prize to Graham Greene. The academician's shameful reasons appeared in the *Sunday Times Weekly Review* of 23 November 1980, and newspapers the world over echoed the continuing scandal that a man who had received two of the highest honours in his own country, the Order of Merit and Companion of Honour, as well as being made a Chevalier de la Légion d'Honneur in France, should still not have been awarded the Nobel Prize.

Needless to say, Graham Greene and I discussed the question of the Nobel prize, particularly in the early years of our friendship. Later, it was scarcely ever mentioned.

Graham Greene rose above all this type of vanity, and I can safely say that the Nobel Prize only mattered to him because of the money the award brought with it. With the £100,000 he could have done something positive. Graham would never have gone to Sweden to receive the Prize; he told me this the first time we discussed it. If they awarded the prize to him, the person who would accept the honour in his place had been in his mind from the first moment his name was mentioned as a likely candidate. She was an artist friend of his.

What was behind this? When Graham's play, *The Living Room*, had its premiere in Stockholm, the academician Dr Lundqvist had written: 'Here is yet another Catholic saying the same old things.' It was in 1953, thirty-eight years before Graham Greene's death. But I suspect Dr Lundqvist had a much more personal reason for his attitude towards Graham and his work. Frustrated passion can lead one to inconceivable folly.

Not many years ago, Dr Lundkvist confessed that Graham Greene's work was too good even for the Nobel Prize than most winners, and it caused a scandal in Sweden. The Academy called him to account, for they had forbidden any of their members to show their preferences for particular candidates.

One day, when we were talking about the Nobel Prize, Graham pulled some torn up cuttings out of his waste paper basket. It was a long interview with a Swedish journalist who had come to visit him at the time *The Human Factor* was published. Later, Graham found out that this journalist was a close friend of his enemy at the Swedish Academy. When the journalist introduced the subject of the Nobel Prize he said that it 'would certainly be awarded to him' and these were the words used in a bold headline when the article appeared. No wonder Graham had thrown it in the waste paper basket.

For many years Graham Greene was convinced they would never give him the prize, but it was not a matter that caused him to lose any sleep. Not long afterwards, another journalist raised the matter of the Nobel yet again. Graham, who was tired but in a humorous mood, stood up, looked the man in the face, and told him:

'But I am assured of a far greater prize which no one can take from me.'

'What prize is that?' asked the astonished journalist.

'Death', replied Graham.

Perhaps the joke was a prophecy. For at the time of his death, he was acclaimed by the media in every country in the world. *Time*, in its obituary (15 April 1991), considered that 'Graham Greene had invaded and shaped the public imagination more than any other serious writer this century'. Another authoritative voice, that of Camilo José Cela, himself a winner of the Nobel Prize for Literature, put forward the wonderful notion that in future the Nobel Prize should be called the Graham Greene prize.

CHAPTER VII

POLITICS AND POLITICIANS

GRAHAM GREENE HAD a vocation for politics. To parody the remark of the philosopher, nothing that took place in the world was foreign to him. Hearing the eight o'clock news in France as well as reading two or three British newspapers, was a necessary ritual for him.

Graham's interest in politics was primarily theoretical and arose from an anxiety to be in touch; he was not concerned with being active in politics. His literary vocation and his essential integrity kept him apart from personal intervention in the world of *res publica*.

The first time he became actively concerned with a political situation was in his support for Fidel Castro's men in the Sierra Maestra in 1956–59, when he made sure they received clothes. This was how his sporadic relationship with Fidel Castro, which we shall describe later, came about.

It was on 25 May 1979 that he first spoke to me about some British hostages in El Salvador who were employees of Lloyds Bank, and the steps he took to free them. Later, he would make jokes, comparing the behaviour of the bank with the people from J & B Whisky. The former merely expressed their grateful thanks for what he had done; the latter, apart from offering their thanks, sent him two boxes of his favourite whisky, because this was what Castle drank in *The Human Factor*.

The guerrillas in El Salvador were grateful to Graham Greene for his modest economic support which was given through Omar Torrijos' right-hand man, Chuchu. Graham trusted him and respected his integrity. The assassination of Archbishop Romero on the altar while he was saying Mass in 1980, reminded Graham of the murder of Thomas à Becket in Canterbury Cathedral. The government of El Salvador was responsible for this, as it was, not long afterwards, for the murder of the Jesuit priests and their colleagues at the University of Central America (UCA) run by the Society of Jesus.

Graham visited Panama for the first time in 1976. His deep friendship for Omar Torrijos was born at that moment, and from then on,
he would visit Panama every year, even accompanying the
Panamanian delegation to the signing of the Canal Treaty by Carter
and Torrijos in September 1977, when he was supplied with a
Panamanian passport. The letter he wrote to me on 4 October 1977
was a resumé of the historic ceremony.

Omar Torrijos was, in fact, the ideologue of Central America.
Graham would fly to Panama to visit him and from there he would
travel to neighbouring countries as well, principally Nicaragua. He
also went to see Fidel Castro two or three times, usually bringing
some piece of good advice from Torrijos. All these journeys, or almost
all of them, were taken on the advice of this good friend. The General
had given economic aid to the Nicaraguan guerrillas before they came
to power, as well as to those in El Salvador.

Panama therefore became a sort of headquarters for Graham, who
used the influence of his name, his articles, his economic support and
his meetings with the guerrilla fighters to help topple the Central
American dictators. He met a number of the guerrilla leaders there,
as well as Eden Pastora, Ernesto Cardenal, and many others. It was
a group of such leaders who were waiting for us on a boiling hot July
afternoon at the entrance to the Mindanao hotel in Madrid. When
we got up to our rooms, Graham explained it all to me. I was a little
surprised that these men who fought and died in the mountains of
America, doing without all the comforts of life, should stay at five
star hotels.

Graham's annual journey to Central America was an injection of
encouragement for these fighters. It meant a great deal to them to
have him there beside them, even for a few brief days. He wrote at
least one article, usually on the subject of American policy, as a result
of his trip. Graham was never an enemy of the United States –
he had friends among the senators and members of the House of
Representatives – but he could not accept American foreign policy.

•

Graham Greene's definition of a politician was awesome. 'A politician', he told me, 'is someone who is totally amoral and corrupt
through and through, with the very occasional exception.' Politics
for Greene were a necessary evil. Somebody has to take charge of
'the community known as the State; the political association' which

'aspires to the greater good of all' as Aristotle put it. The *Estagirita* speaks of the metaphysical concept of the politics of ideals. Unfortunately, politics as we know them, do not in fact aspire to the universal good of every citizen. They do so only in theory, or in the vain words of the politician who lies to the citizen in order to gain his or her vote. Having obtained this, in the name of true politics which aspire to the 'common good', the politician debases himself. He creates his personal politics, something which is no longer really politics, but egoism, since he has forgotten all about the 'common good'. From this moment on, the politician thinks only of his own well-being. In his glory, and with his money, he will no longer serve, but be served. This is the worldly 'politician' defined by Graham Greene. The only kind we know, 'with the very occasional exception'. In few areas of human understanding is there such a flagrant gulf between the real and the ideal as in the prevailing politics of everyday life.

The notion of the 'common good' is omnipresent in Greene's politics. I believe that the following anecdote, which he related himself, perfectly defines his own ideology towards *res publica*. At the time of the Spanish Civil War, Graham Greene decided to come to Spain and do something for the cause of truth. For which side should he fight? Franco was a Catholic, but Graham hated him as he hated all totalitarian systems. Neither did he care for the Communists and Socialists because they committed murder and all sorts of vandalism, particularly against the Church. He decided on a third path: to fight on the side of the Basques under the command of Aguirre. On the one hand, they were Catholics, like Greene; on the other hand, they had nothing to do with totalitarianism. In London he was supplied with some impressive credentials, covered with seals and stamps. They were an introduction to a certain person who would meet him in Marseille.

The place where he was to meet this person was worse than humble, it was miserable. Graham walked up a dimly lit staircase and there in an untidy, rambling garret room was a man shaving. Graham handed him his papers, which the man read having broken the seals. He told Graham, quite sharply: 'There is no way in which I would go back and fly over Bilbao. The other day they sent me out against Franco's planes and it's a miracle I'm still alive. No I'm not going back there.'

So ended Graham Greene's intentions of being of some use in the Spanish Civil War. When he had finished relating this anecdote, I said with a smile: 'We would have to call this story "A Mistake on the Road".' His views did not alter at all from the time he published his novel *It's a Battlefield* in 1934. Possibly no other intellectual of his generation was so loyal to his first political principles.

This is what we agreed: 'Democracy was preferable to dictatorship in normal circumstances. Democracy, that is, that respects human and personal rights. Democracy carried with it more disorders – bank robberies and things like that – but dictatorships did not respect human rights.'

Sometimes I asked Graham: 'But supposing democracy brings with it continual disorder, frequent crime etc., while right-wing dictatorships, for the most part, avoid such things?'

Graham insisted that a person's human rights were better maintained under a democracy, but he could not convince me, nor could I persuade him otherwise. So much for the advantages of one system over another – they are much better in theory than they are in practice. Human rights are trampled on daily in the name of human rights.

For me, Graham Greene always resembled some sort of political prophet. *The Quiet American* (1955) predicted the disastrous American intervention in Vietnam following the departure of the French, many years beforehand. *Our Man in Havana* (1958) mentions Soviet missiles in Cuba several years before Kruschev brought them there. *The Honorary Consul* (1973) concerns the kidnapping of a wretched British honorary consul; within a few months Greene's imagination became a reality. And *The Human Factor* (1978) contrives a Western treaty whereby the South African gold and diamond mines are prevented from falling into Moscow's hands. The treaty is called 'Uncle Remus'. Greene's novel was published in March. But the extraordinary thing is that in July of that year Zdenek Cervenka and Barbara Rogers published a book entitled *The Nuclear Axis, The Secret Collaboration between the West and South Africa* which contained documents proving the existence of such a treaty. The only difference was in the name.

Graham Greene had a clinical eye for the motives of any politician who had risen to power. On his return from his first visit to Panama, he told me: 'I don't trust the chief of the National Guard whom Torrijos has appointed. I told Chuchu that in my view, he is not to be trusted.' Time would prove him correct.

•

Graham could be prescient too; after his trip to Russia, a few months after Gorbachev had come to power, Greene was totally convinced that the saviour of Russia had arrived. He always believed that the shift in Communism in Russia would come from the army, or, more likely still, the KGB; for the brightest graduates, the best educated and those who had seen the world and knew foreign languages, belonged to that organization.

On my visit to Antibes, at Christmas 1982, we spoke of Andropov, the new Soviet leader. He came from the KGB; a cultured man and better educated than previous General Secretaries of the party. Graham was annoyed with the absurd US policies of Reagan. It was ridiculous not to listen to Andropov's proposals, or at least find out whether they were sincere in any way. He grew irritated: 'America is a disaster in its political, ethical and the economic policies', he said. 'In politics she is infantile, in ethics, totally materialistic, and in economic matters, totally selfish.'

At Nice airport, he returned to the subject of Andropov. If only he were clever enough to liberate Christianity! All the occupied nations were Christian: Poland was entirely Catholic; Russia herself was deeply religious. The American bishops were the first to mount a campaign against Reagan and the use of atomic weapons. God knows what might not happen in Russia! His words sounded prophetic.

Three years later, at the time of Chernenko, a Russian journalist invited Graham to lunch Chez Félix, the restaurant in Antibes where he always ate. He told him that his wife had cried when Andropov died. It was clear that the journalist belonged to the KGB.

Gorbachev's star was apparently in the ascendant, and the journalist discussed the possibility of his taking over if Andropov died. Another candidate was Romanov, but both Graham and the correspondent preferred the former, although he wished Gorbachev were a little stronger. Graham asked him whether the name of Romanov, with its czarist connotations, would not be an obstacle to a candidate for the leadership, but it was apparently quite a common name in Russia.

During the course of their conversation, the correspondent asked Graham where he should send the money for the interview. Graham was astonished to discover that in Russia it was the custom for the person interviewed to be paid.

It was an interesting exercise for Graham. The journalist told him that he would like to introduce him to the Russian Consul in a certain French city, and Graham agreed. The Consul came to call on Graham and they discussed a possible visit by Graham to Georgia. 'We shall do everything we can to make your stay enjoyable', the Consul assured him.

Graham believed the Consul was speaking candidly when he told him that he missed his own country, that he was homesick and that he hoped to go back to live there for at least two years.

'Where would you like to be sent afterwards?' asked Graham.

'To Latin America', he answered.

Graham had no doubts that the Soviet communist system was essentially dehumanizing. It was a system that managed to unbalance the mind. He knew all about the psychological brainwashing that went on. The proof of it lay with his friend Iva. She was the wife of a minister who had been banished to Siberia and who had died in prison there. She nevertheless defended the Communist regime and even the judge who had convicted her husband.

Graham knew that espionage in Russia was almost universal, and he thought it unlikely that one could ever know the person to whom one was speaking or what their motives were. He mentioned a Russian poet who used to visit him in Antibes who spoke about the Communist system and much else besides, but who seemed to be free to enter and leave his country as he wished. Greene did not trust him and only half let him know this. The poet took a photograph of Graham before he left. 'Perhaps it was to justify the purpose of his trip', commented Graham.

It upset him when the West regarded Gorbachev with such suspicion, 'for it's now', said Graham, 'that he needs a helping hand, just when his enemies and the difficulties he faces inside Russia risk upsetting the man's providential mission; providential not just for Russia but for the whole world.'

On 31 July 1985, on a road in the Sierra, close to Madrid, Graham said to me: 'The Americans are upset because Gorbachev is going to meet Mitterrand before he sees Reagan.' He added: 'Marchais, the French Communist Party leader, is in Moscow. Perhaps Gorbachev has told him that he should support Mitterrand in the elections. Marchais resigned from Mitterrand's govenment and now the Communists have very few seats in France.'

On 10 November 1986, Graham returned from Russia full of enthusiasm and in a very good mood. He telephoned me at an unusual time – half past one in the afternoon. Today Graham is not his usual self. His manner is normally so moderate, especially in the way he expresses his emotions.

'I had a private meeting with a member of the Politburo', he told me. 'I liked him. I told him that they should send an ambassador to the Vatican to put Cardinal Ratzinger in his place . . . .'

'You've told me that many times before. It would be a very wise diplomatic step on the part of Moscow to continue making such changes', I said.

'However, I don't know whether the Pope will allow it', added Graham.

'I believe he will. The Pope has said several times that he is ready to go to Russia, and to Peking. He wants to reach a dialogue with the whole world. It's the mission of the Church.'

During a telephone conversation on 19 December 1986, Graham told me that he believed things were starting to change in Russia. Gorbachev gave the impression of being more human, he thought. He had a pleasant expression, it appeared, and he smiled a great deal.

29 February 1987. Graham returned from Moscow after the much publicized meeting of intellectuals from all over the world. There he gave his well-known three- or four-minute speech in the presence of Gorbachev and the Russian authorities. This is how it ended:

> And I even have a dream, Mr General Secretary, that
> perhaps one day, before I die, I shall know that there is
> an ambassador of the Soviet Union giving good advice
> at the Vatican. I am sorry – this is all I have to say. Thank
> you for listening to me patiently.

As he left the podium, Gorbachev stretched out his hand to Graham, continued to hold it for a moment, and said among other things: 'I've known about you for a long time.'

Graham thought it odd that Gorbachev had heard of his name. I told him: 'He's a cultivated man, of course he has heard of you, and he may have read some of your books.'

Then Graham said: 'I'm now fully convinced that this man is sincere, and that he wants nuclear disarmament and wants peace. But he has a lot of opposition in high places.'

A little later, during the same conversation, he added: 'Change is taking place in Russia. My books are now published there without being censored or cut at all. So as to be quite certain, I asked someone to read me the passage in *The Power and the Glory* when the child greets the new priest. It tallied exactly with the original.'

'That means a great deal', I added.

'Let us hope that those who oppose him don't manage to stop it.'

16 June 1988. We had a long telephone conversation. Graham had made several visits to Russia, each of a week or two. Towards the end of the previous month he had thought of going to Moscow again. Today he tells me that he has postponed this trip, but that instead he would attend a seminar on his work that would be held there. They told him that he could ask anyone else to accompany him to this seminar, and so Graham had given them my name. (The seminar never actually took place.)

'Gorbachev is doing wonderful work, both for Russia and the world,' Graham said, 'it's a real revolution.' But he was worried that his enemies within the Soviet Union, and within the party, would wreck the changes he had made.

Graham Greene understood what Gorbachev was trying to do from the very beginning. He went to Russia to try to help his great enterprise in any way he could, for he knew the man and the difficulties he was having long before the West accepted him. On numerous occasions, he asked me to remember Gorbachev in my daily Mass.

●

Omar Torrijos, the President of Panama, and Graham Greene were great friends. It was in 1976 that General Torrijos first invited him to Panama, and Graham went immediately. Torrijos welcomed him in pyjamas and slippers, and thereafter their meetings would take place in the country house of one of the General's friends. When the General saw that Graham was not a cold intellectual, but, on the contrary, an enormously warm-hearted man, he became devoted to him.

They had much in common. Both were big-hearted; both had a propensity for rather mysterious dreams – which they would later interpret themselves; both had a tendency to boredom or psychological depression, Omar even more than Graham.

Apart from these psychological details, General Torrijos was obsessed with death. He would frequently dream about it. Once, he dreamt that a war with America had begun. He found himself bare-footed in a wood and felt very humiliated when he was captured.

Another night, he dreamt of his dead father. He was there, standing at the far side of the road. From his side, Torrijos asked him what death was like, but just as his father was about to cross the road to answer him, Torrijos woke up.

The fear that he would be assassinated was always with him. In the evenings he would feel terribly depressed. By dawn, he was euphoric again.

Torrijos was the leader of a small country – a military leader, since he granted political control, at least in name, to the president – and yet his prestige was considerable throughout Central America. He was a friend of Castro's, he helped the Sandinistas, and he was also a friend of Tito's. But Torrijos did not want a Communist system, either in Cuba or in Latin America. He was not a Communist, but a slightly left-wing socialist.

The one political idea that guided his life was the independence of the Canal. If the Treaty were not signed, or not approved by the Senate, he believed he would have to go to war. But he did not think that Panama was alone. He was supported by many neighbouring countries and, for this reason, a confrontation with America was not so absurd. They could perhaps resist for three or four days, and later resort to guerrilla warfare in the forests and mountains.

But the Treaty was finally signed between Carter and Torrijos. In his memoirs, Carter recounts how Torrijos had come to see him on the eve of the signing ceremony, and, when they were both alone, Torrijos wept. Was it from emotion?

Graham described the signing ceremony for me vividly in a long letter. There he was with his Panamanian passport seeing 'villains' such as Pinochet and Stroessner, and 'types' like Kissinger, Ford, Carter, Rockefeller etc. 'They all seemed peculiarly insignificant. The General spoke far more sensibly than Carter who was deplorably bad.' Later, when we met, he told me how Torrijos only shook hands with certain presidents, while he embraced others. The wily Pinochet wanted to be seen to be embracing Torrijos and as he approached him he put his hand on his shoulder so that in photographs it would look as if they were hugging each other. Stroessner avoided meeting Graham at the signing. A woman friend of Graham's introduced him to one of Stroessner's ministers who walked away, enraged, saying: 'Yes, you went to Paraguay once.'

Graham told me that Torrijos did not care for the Treaty but that it was the only possible one at that moment. The General believed that the Canal would belong to Panama before the year 2000.

The novelist Gabriel García Márquez also attended the signing ceremony. He wore an open collar and was the only person not to be dressed in a suit.

Graham thought that General Torrijos' problems would begin as soon as the American Senate approved the Treaty. Students and communists needed something on which to focus their attention. But the greatest danger for Torrijos lay with the speculators. The Canal Zone which would be handed over to Panama was an obvious place in which to construct elegant and sumptuous buildings, and businessmen were sure to want to build them. Torrijos wanted the Zone to be a place where poor people could relax and take the air. Differences such as this might well lead to his downfall. Torrijos' downfall, when it came, however, was to emanate from a very different source, and long before anyone thought it would happen.

Just like Graham Greene, Omar Torrijos had a taste for playing with danger. He preferred pilots who were reckless, and when his plane took off suddenly he gave the impression of being happy. Later, in the middle of a storm, he would appear to be totally lost in his thoughts.

I was once told how, when he was welcoming a foreign president, he drove his own car through the Canal Zone, followed by his National Guards in another vehicle, and ignored every single traffic light. He wanted to show the visiting president that the Canal Zone belonged to Panama and not to the United States. The Americans did not dare protest.

Omar once telephoned Graham and Chuchu urgently. 'Something very important happened today', he said suddenly.

What had happened? Torrijos' wife was the daughter of a very well-known American Jew. The day she married Torrijos, her father swore that he would never speak to her again. Now, Torrijos supported Israel in the famous Six-Day War and, later on, General Dayan, the Israeli commander, enquired of Torrijos whether there was anything he could do to thank him for his support. Torrijos asked him to talk to his father-in-law and to beg him not to reject his daughter. Dayan did so, but the American Jew refused. Much later, seeing that his hopes had been dashed, Dayan asked whether there was anything else he could do. Torrijos thanked him warmly, but said no, there was nothing.

Torrijos' wife – to whom he was unfaithful – loved her father very much. Well, it so happened that that very same day Torrijos' father-in-law telephoned his daughter. Torrijos made it quite clear that for him this was the happiest day of his life. It was the day of his Silver Wedding.

Torrijos' wife was now very fat and had lost her looks, but he still loved her. Nevertheless, he had young girls everywhere. With his carefully trimmed moustache, he was very dashing, and women were passionately attracted to him. Once, Graham, Torrijos and his mistress were discussing matters of love and sex, each giving their own opinions. The girl sided with Graham. 'But you mustn't joke about such things', Torrijos told Graham. 'Don't try to spoil my private life.'

On 5 August 1981, Graham Greene was due to leave for Panama where he planned to spend twelve days with his friend Omar. However, terrible news reached him the day before his departure: Torrijos had been killed in an aircraft accident. His head was found far from his body. If Graham had been there, he might well have been killed too. What had happened? Today, there seems little doubt that it was sabotage. General Torrijos was a hindrance and it was necessary to get rid of him. Who killed him? Was it someone from a neighbouring country? Were there people who had grudges against him inside Panama? The United States? Graham wrote *Getting to Know the General* as an act of homage to his friend. In his postscript to that book he mentions the CIA and the fact that there are only two likely hypotheses: an error by the pilot or a bomb. Later, the 'insurance company' sent to examine the plane was refused permission to visit the place of the wreckage by the Panamanian army. They said there was nothing to be seen. To begin with, Graham suspected that the commander of Torrijos' army, Colonel Flores, was in collusion with the American general in the Canal Zone. Yet Flores disappeared a few months later and was replaced by Paredes. One thing seems quite certain: Torrijos died as a result of sabotage.

The story goes that someone (the CIA?) complained that it was never known what the General's movements were. That was dangerous; it would be better to put a recording device in the plane. 'The General will tell his friends about his future journeys, and we can protect him.' A device was provided and when one of his bodyguards innocently tried to switch it on, it exploded. Among those killed was a young woman dentist, a friend of Torrijos' daughter who was herself training to be a dentist.

Omar Torrijos was a generous man. When the president whom he had removed in a *coup d'état* returned to Panama and announced that Torrijos' regime would collapse, he took no reprisals. Someone went so far as to walk past Torrijos' house letting out a stream of insults, but Torrijos always pretended he did not understand. He also sent an aeroplane to rescue refugees from Salvador fleeing another dictatorship and provided a means for them to live in Panama.

During the ghastly five-year battle with the mafia on the Côte d'Azur, Torrijos told Graham: 'I never leave my friends alone when they are in danger.' He wanted to solve the whole problem at a stroke, but Graham would not allow him to become involved.

Omar Torrijos was an outstanding figure in Latin American politics. The young president who succeeded him idolized the General and had dreams, and occasionally hallucinations, about him. He told him that once, at night, he had heard something unusual. His wife heard it too but could not see anything. Then he saw Torrijos sitting with his legs crossed. The vision disappeared immediately. On another occasion, the President dreamed that a revolution had begun and he was unable to cope with the situation. Torrijos reassured him, saying: 'You can get along without me now, I am going for a short rest.'

•

Chuchu, or Professor José Martinez, was inseparable in Graham Greene's mind from Omar Torrijos. On his first visit to Panama in 1976, General Torrijos ordered Chuchu to be at Graham's disposal whenever he was required: his bodyguard, his guide and his companion. It was his duty to make sure that Graham's trip was enjoyable. It would have been impossible to find anyone more suitable to look after him than this 'extraordinary' Chuchu. Graham and Chuchu came to know each other very well and also became lifelong friends, although Graham knew only too well that Chuchu, for all his great intellectual gifts and his capacity for friendship, was a bit of a madcap.

Chuchu was an exceptionally intelligent man. He had studied at the Sorbonne and Berlin University, and he had degrees in Philosophy and Literature from the Complutense University in Madrid. It was there that he had apparently known Professors Ortega and Morente. He spoke several languages perfectly. Graham and he travelled all over Panama together. On their journeys, Greene quoted

Hardy in English while Chuchu quoted Rilke in German, but he was equally at ease in Spanish, English, German or French.

At the time of Omar Torrijos' *coup d'état*, Chuchu was teaching philosophy at the university, but Torrijos must have known this 'rather special' man well and decided that he should teach mathematics instead of philosophy. It was a subject in which he would cause less confusion in the minds of the students.

Chuchu was ready for anything. He held the rank of sergeant in the army, but he did not want promotion. Torrijos made him his confidant and his go-between in carrying secret letters between heads of state and on his most confidential and delicate missions. Chuchu was prepared to give his all for his beloved General.

It is not easy to define Chuchu's ideology for he did not have a clear-cut one. His views on the politics of the Canal were identical to those of Omar Torrijos except that he was less calm and reasoned. Chuchu was fanatically anti-American. He used to have an American sub-machine gun which worked to perfection, but he had exchanged it for a Soviet one which kept breaking down all the time. He proudly took it with him on the first occasion he met Graham, and looked quite prepared to conquer the Canal Zone in a trice. When he went to test it, however, and saw that it jammed every time it fired, he was very disheartened. His patience was so exhausted that he threw it to the ground. And whenever he passed by the Canal, he would aim his revolver threateningly in the direction of the American zone, though he admitted – it was one of his favourite sayings – that 'a revolver is no defence'.

Where women were concerned, Chuchu was quite a case. He was married, but in these matters his liberty went unscathed and wherever he went, he always left someone behind and had no scruples about chastity. He certainly had an extraordinarily successful way with him and he reported the details of many of his conquests to Graham. 'Do you know why women like me?' he once asked him. 'It's not because I am much to look at, but because I am so gentle with them afterwards.'

Graham was so won over by this man that he decided to make him the principal character in the novel he was thinking of writing about the Canal Zone, which was to have been called 'On the Way Back'. Each time they were together – and Graham and Chuchu were constantly travelling around Panama – and whenever Graham asked him something, Chuchu's reply was invariably: 'I shall tell you on the way back.' When Graham later wrote a biography of Torrijos rather than a novel it was because Chuchu's real personality was so strong that it kept interfering with the fictional character based upon him that Graham wanted to create.

Chuchu was convinced that he would never die. He did not believe much in God, but it was clear to him that the devil existed. He reasoned thus: 'Try to open a door and you almost always find you open it in the wrong direction. Do you see? It's the devil tricking you.' The argument did not seem particularly metaphysical but for Chuchu it was unanswerable.

I remember Graham telephoning me during the spring of 1984. Chuchu was with him in Antibes. He was there to help him to revise his book about Torrijos, *Getting to Know the General*, which he had just completed. Chuchu had, after all, spent many years with the General and there was no one better to consult.

Graham announced: 'Chuchu is coming to Madrid and I want you to get to know each other. Will you make a fuss of him and give him some good wine? Here's Chuchu to speak to you.'

'How are you, Father?' came a strange voice.

'Fine. It's marvellous to hear you!' I replied.

Chuchu spoke to me for a long time. He told me about his studies in Madrid and elsewhere and promised faithfully to call on me. But he never came . . . Graham was sure that Chuchu would never come to see me. Perhaps he was frightened that a priest would force him to make a good confession and live a holy life.

On his return from England, Graham telephoned me and enquired whether Chuchu had been to see me. I replied that he hadn't and that I had waited in vain for him all weekend. 'He must have been frightened of me', I said in a rather off-hand way.

Graham said: 'You sound annoyed.'

'Good God, I'm not annoyed. When I see Chuchu I'll tell him he's a rogue.'

I sometimes think that by having him trail around Panama and Nicaragua on various occasions after Torrijos' death, Chuchu caused harm to Graham's health. Chuchu's excuse was that he wanted him to help protect Noriega who was being attacked on all sides, but who was determined to defend Panama's right to the Canal, and Graham was unable to refuse anything connected with this subject. But who knows . . . It is possible that Don Quixote might not have died when he did if he had made one more journey.

On 26 July 1985, we were having our picnic near Castillo de Javier in a beautiful park by the banks of a small river. Graham chose the moment to speak quietly again about Chuchu, whom I thought to be an intelligent but wretchedly materialistic fellow.

Chuchu's two key interests were girls and weapons. I have already said something about these two 'hobbies', but today Graham enlarged a little on the subject of guns. Chuchu had a magnificent Belgian revolver, he told me, but once again had exchanged it for a Russian model. This revolver, just like the sub-machine gun mentioned previously, often failed. On this occasion, Chuchu was accompanied by a captain who owned a superb North American sub-machine gun – one that never failed – and he and the captain were firing at a target. Chuchu insisted that Graham take aim as well, but Graham refused.

'I'm hopeless at that sort of thing', Graham said. 'It's not worth wasting a bullet which might be useful later on in the guerrilla war against the Americans!'

But Chuchu, who had not hit the target once, went on pressing him. Finally, Graham fired one shot and, by some enormous fluke, hit the very middle of the target.

Chuchu said nothing and maintained his serious expression, but he was clearly rather in awe of Graham's skill.

One day Chuchu went to meet his wife and one of his sons, who were returning from abroad. Chuchu was divorced from his wife and relations between the two of them were very strained. She was a woman of very strong character. Chuchu, fearing that he might not be able to control his emotions properly, went to meet her wearing dark glasses. Graham was worried that it was going to be rather a difficult night for Chuchu.

Next morning, however, Chuchu appeared, still wearing his dark glasses. 'Did you have a good night?' Graham asked him.

Chuchu plucked up his courage and replied: 'It was an indescribable, heavenly, marvellous night.'

Politically, Chuchu was a Communist, but there was no way in which he would want to live in a Communist country. He believed that Torrijos' regime would move gradually in the direction of Communism. But he was wrong.

Chuchu would frequently telephone Graham at two o'clock in the morning in an attempt to persuade him to go to Panama, Nicaragua or to Havana yet again. The excuse was always the same: it was for the sake of Noriega and the Canal. But once Graham arrived, the travelling never ceased and he would return home exhausted. Yet Graham loved Chuchu. In *Getting to Know the General* he emerges as something of a hero, second only to the General.

One day Graham told me that Chuchu and I were the two most extraordinary characters he had come across in his life. His enigmatic words have always bothered me. What can I possibly have in common with José Martínez? Am I also some kind of Don Juan? Graham got on well with both of us, but for rather different reasons, I think.

●

We had long and frequent conversations on the subject of Fidel Castro – about his 'Latin' style of dictatorship, so different from the Soviet mode, for example. Graham told me that from the beginning he had always felt drawn to him, though he had never liked his brother Raul. When, not long ago, the regime executed a group of soldiers, I asked him his view on the matter.

'I don't know', he replied. 'I like Fidel, but I have never cared for Raul.'

I have already said that Graham had sent aid in the form of clothes to Castro's men in the Sierra Maestra. Naturally, we also spoke about the relationship of the Church to the Cuban state. It is quite clear that the Church did not approve or agree with the changes that had been brought about, but the situation was rather different to that in the countries of Eastern Europe. Graham related a story about the consecration of a Cuban bishop by the Papal Nuncio. After the ceremony, Castro went along to the reception and, as a joke, the new bishop placed his skullcap on Castro's head. Castro was not amused. 'He went too far', Graham commented.

He also told me that Castro is apparently very partial to Italian cheese and whenever the Nuncio goes to Rome he brings packets of cheese back for him.

It would be as wrong to say that the Church in Cuba is free as it would to say that there is the sort of persecution there that once existed in Soviet Russia, or still does in China.

We spoke of the Nuncio's intervention with Castro on behalf of the three priests who accompanied the twelve guerrilla fighters who were opposed to Castro on the Sierra. The dialogue between the two was rather amusing. The Nuncio said: 'A priest has to be where there is war and people dying.' To which Castro replied: 'Yes, but three priests seem to me too many chaplains for twelve guerrilla fighters.' Castro pardoned them, but sent them into exile.

Although America had appeared to be the victor at the time of the Cuban missile crisis, when the Russians were obliged to remove their weapons from Cuban soil, to fulfil her part of the bargain, she was obliged to promise not to attack Fidel Castro's Communist regime.

Graham visited Castro several times. On one of these visits Castro asked him what diet he followed to keep so thin and agile. Greene replied: 'I eat everything.' Castro had become thin and agile himself, and he was careful to do exercises to keep fit.

On another occasion Graham Greene and Gabriel García Márquez both met Castro together and the Colombian wrote an article in which he claimed that Graham had got drunk. García Márquez said that he and Graham Greene had drunk two bottles of whisky each. I can vouch for the fact that Graham would not be capable of drinking this amount. When I asked Graham, he answered: 'García Márquez had no idea what happened. He himself was already drunk when he arrived from another party at the Spanish Embassy.'

In January 1983, Graham had visited Panama, Nicaragua and Cuba. In Havana, he had said to Castro: 'I am not a messenger, I am the message.' And he reminded him that his friend Torrijos did not want Panama to be Communist. Graham and Fidel Castro had spoken for some time on this occasion. Castro had asked Graham whether the story about his playing Russian roulette was true. Graham replied that he had played it on four occasions, although he had once fired twice. 'But you should be dead already!' said Castro, slightly alarmed.

Graham told me again that he felt drawn towards Castro, even after all these years. I asked him why and he answered that he had no idea. It might be that he was attracted by the adventurous aspects of Fidel's character, and he recalled those twelve men of the Sierra Maestra, the only survivors from the group that had embarked from Mexico in 1958. He admitted that Castro had done some unfortunate things in his country but the situation in Cuba at the time of Batista had been terrible. Havana had been the 'Americans' brothel'. When a country fought for its democracy, or fought to rid itself of American influence, then Graham supported that country and, if he could, he would try to visit it. No one could deny that from a cultural point of view Castro had done a great deal of good and he had also tried to recover some of Cuba's lost dignity. Graham thought that if the Americans had not closed the door the Cubans might not have thrown themselves into Soviet arms. 'The amount of money that Cuba is costing Russia is enormous,' he said to me in 1985.

And Graham told me another interesting thing. He reminded me of Castro's speech condemning the Soviet invasion of Czechoslovakia. In that speech Castro stated publicly that every socialist state should be in charge of its own destiny and that no country should interfere in the fate of any other, yet in a matter of one week, Fidel Castro publicly supported that invasion. What was this due to? The Italian ambassador to Cuba told Graham, in Capri, that if Cuba had not sided with Russia at that time, Castro would have been deposed by President Dorticos and other members of the far left party. Graham asked the Ambassador whether Dorticos and others in power were not merely decorative figures, and he replied: 'Not at all. They have very genuine power.'

I asked Graham about the relationship between Torrijos and Castro. They were very cordial in spite of their different political views. Torrijos apparently advised Castro to proceed cautiously.

I am sorry I never saw the book written by Castro 'in collaboration with a Brazilian Franciscan'. Graham, without realizing that it might interest me, gave it to Chuchu. When Graham mentioned the book to me my first reaction was not very kind: I smiled and said: 'A funny theologian and a poor friar.'

Over his desk in Antibes, Graham kept a very attractive painting of flowers that Castro gave him. It was a picture he liked very much.

•

We spoke so often about politics and politicians that one would need a long book just to deal with them alone. Here, however, are a few random notes on certain well-known politicians.

We talked about Salvador Allende on 17 July 1979, as we journeyed from Merida to Oropesa. According to Graham, Allende was not a communist; rather, he was a Marxist, or perhaps better, an advanced socialist, although some ministers in his government were communists.

Graham went to see him and spent several days in Chile. Allende put an aeroplane at Graham's disposal for him to visit one of the remotest parts of the country. When Graham and a companion arrived, they were unable to spend the night at the hotel and had to make do with mattresses on the floor. The manager of the hotel apologized, but they were on strike because Allende had closed down the ministry of tourism.

It was the lorry drivers' strike that destroyed Allende, but, according to Graham, these drivers were not workers, as American propaganda led one to believe, but owned their trucks. One of the various things the Americans did in their efforts to topple Allende was to try to destroy the Chilean copper industry by putting their own enormous copper reserves on the market.

Salvador Allende died like a hero, with a helmet on his head and a machine-gun in his hands. A country doctor, he was more of an idealist than Che Guevara and, for a politician, he always replied to questions directly and with unusual frankness.

When Graham Greene went to see him, many of the press thought that the visitor 'had not been the real Graham Greene', but 'the Other Man'. 'The Other Man' was someone, or perhaps several people, who had followed in Graham's footsteps and would appear here and there, sometimes passing as his double. He would then disappear, sometimes for years at a time. Once, when Graham was with me on one of our trips through Spain and Portugal, his sister Elisabeth received a letter from Madrid written by an American lady. She told Elisabeth that she had been delighted to meet her brother Graham. She had also been very impressed by the elegant way he played tennis. Since Graham was in Spain, Elisabeth initially believed the letter was genuine, but when she read that he played tennis elegantly she realized that it must be 'The Other Man' who had surfaced once again. The lady had given Elisabeth her address in the United States and had invited her to her house. She would be very pleased to welcome the sister of Graham Greene for she had spent some wonderful moments with him.

Graham had to make fun of those Chilean journalists in Santiago who had said that 'the President has been deceived by an imposter'. He later wrote in *Ways of Escape*: 'I found myself shaken by a metaphysical doubt. Had I been the imposter all the time? Was I the Other? Was I Skinner? Was it even possible that I might be Meredith de Varg?'

For many years Graham dreamt of meeting the man who led the struggle against the French in Indo-China. It seemed very difficult, for Graham was employed as the correspondent of a French newspaper, but one day he did find himself drinking tea with President

Ho Chi Minh in Hanoi. The French, like the Americans later on, had lost the war.

When Graham arrived at the entrance to Ho Chi Minh's office, the man who was supposed to introduce him to the President appeared not to understand a word of English or French. Graham tried to make himself understood in both languages, but it was in vain. Apparently not having understood a word Graham said to him, the man went into Ho Chi Minh's office. He returned, and indicated to Graham that he should now enter. And so Graham went in, was offered tea, and chatted for a reasonable time with the head of state. When it was over, Graham came out and it was as if a miracle had happened. The aide de camp now spoke to Graham in perfect French; the fact that he had taken tea with the President had transformed everything.

In the course of the interview, Ho Chi Minh promised Graham he would send him a film about the war. Graham never believed it would actually reach him, but it was sent to him some time later in Peking.

Graham Greene had lived in Antibes for many years when I knew him, and it was with French politicians that he was most closely involved. We sometimes discussed French politics and I remember talking about the reasons why the French generals had supported de Gaulle when he had promised them initially that Algeria would always be French. Graham had known General Salan, the man who had replaced General de Lattre in Indochina, personally and he had corresponded with him.

However, most of our conversations concerned the 'professionals' – those hangers-on who were striving for the presidency. Giscard d'Estaing was the one Graham cared for least. Giscard had exaggerated the importance of the Bordeaux wine scandal in order to discredit the mayor of the city, who was also a candidate for the presidency. The date when the facts about the scandal were released was fixed by Giscard who was then Minister of Finance. There was also the scandal of the Bokassa diamonds which still needs to be satisfactorily explained.

At his press conferences, Giscard always looked unnatural and too academic, unlike his predecessor Pompidou. He also drove very badly and once had a serious accident, colliding with a lorry. Giscard was not seriously injured, but Graham said that if he drove as badly as this, he could hardly be expected to 'steer' a country very successfully.

Graham grew to respect Mitterand. He once said to me: 'I don't care for either Mitterand or Giscard d'Estaing, but I like Marchais. He's a better actor than Mitterand.' Later, he came to know Mitterand personally and to appreciate him. According to him, Mitterand understood international politics, but knew nothing about the economy. Mitterand once invited him to his public appearance as President, but Graham was unable to go. Watching it afterwards on television, he cheered up: 'My God, I'm glad I didn't go.'

Between Giscard and Chirac, he much preferred the latter.

He did not much care for Kissinger and he recalled the Nobel Peace Prize, which was awarded jointly to Kissinger and a Vietnamese who refused the prize because the war was still going on. Kissinger, however, kept his prize of some $30,000.

Graham Greene believed that Churchill was very distrustful of the British generals during the war. When any of them grew too big for their boots, they were replaced. Apparently, he protested vehemently to one general because on one particular retreat not a single soldier had died. The general replied: 'I didn't know that the loss of men had anything to do with good military tactics.'

In Graham's view, Mrs Thatcher was a decent person. Not so Mr Heath, who virtually refused to speak to her the moment she became Prime Minister. However, Mrs Thatcher was too authoritarian for most people, Graham thought, although the leader of the Opposition, Neil Kinnock, was as weak as his predecessor, Michael Foot.

We spoke about Camilo Torres and Che Guevara. Graham thought that Torres was much the greater hero. The former died with a gun in his hands, defending his social ideas, whereas all that Guevara left behind were photographs of himself.

I told Graham the true story of Camilo Torres' life. He was an ordinary priest, a bit of a dreamer and someone who was perhaps not very sensible. He was chaplain at the University of Bogota. Probably because of some mistakes that Father Torres had made, there was much bad feeling towards him among his fellow priests, and so eventually the Cardinal removed him from his post.

Father Torres could not cope with such an ordeal. Those who had been opposed to him took advantage of his disgruntlement and it came into his head that he should be the 'redeemer' of his people in some other way. Convinced of the wisdom of his new mission, he confided his plans to a friend of mine. Very wisely, this person told him that he should give up these dreams. 'There is only one redeemer', my friend counselled, but he would not listen. The party was already beginning to see the use they could make of him, and convinced him that his place was in the jungle with the guerrilla fighters. The Communists knew just where he was going and they then informed the police. Father Torres could not be useful to them anywhere. The only way he could serve the Party was through his 'martyrdom'. It was easy for both them and the police to do just what they wanted: in the case of the police they were eliminating an outlaw; as for the Communists, they could claim a 'saint' who had given his life for his cause. And perhaps God took his own revenge on both organizations.

Graham Greene immortalized Father Camilo Torres in the character of Father Rivas in *The Honorary Consul* and there are many biographical details of the guerrilla priest incorporated into his portrait of Rivas.

A SENSE OF HUMOUR

Anyone who has read *Our Man in Havana* and *Monsignor Quixote* must suspect Graham Greene of being an accomplished practical joker. The story about Señor Márquez in *Monsignor Quixote* – was Graham thinking of the novelist García Márquez when he wrote it? – who was able to secure his marital rights in good conscience with the simple device of a small bell and an eavesdropping butler, is among the wittiest things he has written. So, too, is the idea of converting vacuum cleaners to clean the dust from Soviet atomic missiles an outstanding feat of the imagination.

Graham Greene was a natural joker. On our journeys through the countryside, humour and delicate irony were never far from his lips. To travel with him, in the way that we travelled, meant that apart from those times when some passing anxiety clouded his mind or sleep had failed to cast 'its rosy fingers' over the writer's eyes that night, we were almost always laughing. Graham Greene could find something amusing in any situation and he could make one laugh out loud. I remember that when the idea of *Monsignor Quixote* came to him, he said: 'So it's agreed: I'm Sancho, you're the Monsignor.'

Graham would often laugh at himself. One day I received a letter in a large brown envelope. I opened it and found a copy of *Magazine Littéraire* (November 1978). There was a splendid drawing – a head and shoulders portrait of Graham Greene – on the cover. His intense emerald green eyes had a serious expression. But Graham had covered the entire picture with humorous remarks. Across the forehead he had written: 'So many worries. Poor old chap!' Just in front of the chin, in a bubble, he had scribbled: 'A happy Christmas, Leopoldo, but isn't it time for another glass of Galician wine?' An arrow pointed upwards to the date at the top of the page, followed by another barb aimed at me: 'Oh dear, it's only November 14 – I thought it was December 14. Perhaps I'd better not have another glass.'

On my table there is a good photograph of the two of us at the summit of the Santa Tecla mountain. In the photograph it is clear that Graham has something that looks like a spectacle case in his shirt pocket and in the photograph one can see two small bumps on the left side of his chest. I had not noticed them, but when he saw them enlarged he immediately said: 'Those bumps look like two nipples. Actually, I have two sets of nipples. A doctor once told me that if they had been discovered at the time of the Inquisition, I would have been severely punished for they are associated with witchcraft.'

Graham was a very light sleeper. The nights when he slept badly were more frequent than those mornings he awoke refreshed by good sleep. He would take half a sleeping pill, with the other half placed alongside a glass of water on the bedside table in case he did not manage to sleep the first time.

Although they did not occur very often, the truth is that some very strange things either happened to Graham, or took place in his room, at night. One morning I arrived at his flat in Antibes and he told me how his musical-box had suddenly begun to start playing at one o'clock in the morning.This lasted for five minutes until the clock-work spring had run out.

'It's a poltergeist', I told him.

And he smiled: 'It could be.'

In Madrid, Graham always stayed at the Mindanao after the Hotel Don Quijote had become a military barracks. I once arrived at his hotel in the morning and he told me with complete conviction: 'Some very strange things happen to me in hotels. The washbasin in my bathroom here makes a very strange noise. When the water drains away through the plughole, it sounds exactly as if someone were saying the words "Kyrie eleison; Christe eleison".'

I could not help bursting out laughing. He laughed too, but he assured me: 'It's quite true.'

•

Graham was constantly playing jokes on me. The slightest thing would spark his sense of humour; he loved making other people laugh, as well as himself. Our haphazard journeys were certainly among the happiest and most relaxed moments during the last third of Graham Greene's life. I have no doubt that he never felt quite so natural and as much at ease as he did on our picnics. And the reason he played jokes and teased me so much (as well as the 'Third Man' ocasionally, too) was because he felt free; comedy brought him completely out of himself.

One very hot July day one year, we stopped at Talavera de la Reina, near Madrid, to have a cold drink at the bar just next to the main park. I had been feeling terribly thirsty inside the car and when I got out I drank five or six small bottles of tonic water. I would have drunk many more but I felt rather ashamed of myself. I don't remember whether I had ever drunk Schweppes tonic water before – I suppose I must have – but I am quite sure I had no idea that it contained quinine.

Graham and the 'Third Man' looked at me a little strangely and smiled at this unusual way of quenching my thirst. It was such a scorching day in Extremadura that once we reached Trujillo, I drank a further two or three bottles, and, I must say, that water tasted glorious to me. On arriving back at my room in Maria Newall's house, there on the bedside table were two small bottles of Schweppes tonic water. Only then did I catch the drift of their humour.

But this was only the beginning of the real joke. A week or two later, Graham returned to Antibes and began to look forward to next summer's picnics. Months later, I received a letter from Antibes. Inside the envelope was a cutting from the *Daily Telegraph* with the headline

'TONIC, NOT GIN CAUSES PILOT'S DOUBLE VISION.'

Attached to it was a small piece of paper on which, in Graham's hand, was written:

'Beware, dear Leopoldo, beware. You are in DANGER.
An anonymous friend.'

And there was nothing else in the letter.

Graham loved sending these little notes with messages. One afternoon, we were having a drink and something to eat at a very pretty hotel near Sintra. Suddenly, we were interrupted by a close friend of mine, an air hostess with Iberia, who was spending a few days there. She and I moved away to another table to chat. The minutes can sometimes pass by rather more quickly than one realizes, and when the woman and I realized the time, my friends had gone. On the table Graham had left a note written on a paper napkin saying: 'I hope you have a nice time. It's not far to walk.'

What! Quinta de Piedade was three or four kilometres away and it was late by now. However, there they were, the car slightly hidden but not too far away, waiting for me.

I provided an inexhaustible excuse for Graham to tell jokes and stories about his friend the 'Generalissimo'; this delighted him. Greene disliked Franco, though I have always admired him. I think he was a discerning man and brought recovery to Spain. One afternoon we were having a brief conversation on a subject that was a constant topic with us: Graham's faith. After chatting half-seriously for a while, Graham, who was not feeling on top form that day, eventually admitted: 'Well, I keep a toe in the door' (of the Church).

We had also been talking about Franco, and so in order to pull his leg slightly over his false doubts and to surprise him a little, it occurred to me to say something that was far from being the case: 'If I were Pope, I would canonize Franco immediately.'

Graham replied in a flash: 'Then I would close the door.'

When we met next morning, I could see that Graham had slept well and that he was on top form. Before we had gone to bed, we had touched on the subject of hell. He recounted the following: 'I had a peculiar dream. I don't know whether it was some sort of revelation. Franco fell into a very long sleep ... He was digging his tomb and crowds had gathered around. This was his purgatory. God took pity on him. And well ... he was sent to heaven.'

I gave him a questioning look, as if to say: do you mean to tell me that God's mercy is so infinite that there may be no place in hell even for Franco? Graham laughed. We agreed about most things, if not always about Franco, and one or two other minor matters.

Although our picnics were usually merry affairs, Graham would sometimes make a serious comment when one least expected it. They were often remarks made against himself. A case in point occurred when we were staying with Maria Newall at Quinta de Piedade. We had set off one afternoon to have a drink at Setais, and on our way home, Graham made some joke about the fact that I had asked for a glass of milk at the hotel instead of the two sherries that I drank later. He related how when he was in Poland, at the time of Stalin, they advised him to carry with him a small flask of oil and to take a spoonful at odd moments, because people would try to make him drunk.

'I only took it once, for I soon realized that I could cope with their drinks easily', he said.

Once we were back at Maria Newall's home, Graham helped her inside. She was leaning on her sticks with some difficulty. He warned her good-humouredly: 'Be careful, because I have had three Martinis and this is a case of the blind leading the blind.'

Later, we were chatting in Graham's room for a few moments before going to bed, and it was then that Graham remarked: 'Until I was about sixty, I was extremely selfish. I let a lot of people down.'

I tried to cheer him up by making him see the enormous amount of good he had done through his work, but it was always difficult to convince Graham that he had done anything worthwhile in his life.

Here is another anecdote which was told me during the summer of 1978. As a present the previous Christmas, Graham had sent me a little book, printed in a limited edition, entitled *A Wedding Among the Owls*. It was an early chapter from *The Human Factor* which had just been published. It seems that a woman friend of Graham's had a most unusual hobby, which was to collect porcelain owls. This good woman had filled her home with owls in such a way that one only had to move to risk knocking one of the creatures and smashing it to pieces.

Graham had decided to poke a little fun at his friend's curious hobby and so he devoted a chapter of his novel to her. In the novel, it is Colonel Daintry's wife who becomes a collector of these owls. Her daughter is to be married and the reception is to take place at her home. The inevitable happens: somebody – no less than 'C' – knocks a grey owl with a piece of cake and it breaks into pieces. The collector is at her wit's end: that owl was irreplaceable. Just like poor Davis, poisoned by Percival.

'I wanted to tease her,' Graham told me.

There was another occasion when we had dined and spent the night at the big *parador* at Siguenza and, after visiting the cathedral and the tomb of Don Alvaro de Luna and his page, we set off in the direction of Madrid. We stopped for our picnic between Guadalajara and Alcala de Henares and this time we made a bad mistake. A mechanical digger was making an infernal noise and creating dust. We were obliged to pick up our tablecloth – two or three pieces of newspaper – and move away, but there was very little shade and no water at all. Graham wrote on a paper napkin, in capital letters: BAR SANCHO and stuck it on the windscreen of the car.

While we were there, some devil prompted us to play a rather disrespectful hoax on our Holy Mother the Church. I call it a semi-heretical sin! Graham Greene's diabolical idea was that we should try to arrange for *Monsignor Quixote* to be condemned by some bishop or other. This would provide us with a joke which we could laugh about for a good long while afterwards and it would also increase the sales of the book. Graham decided that an anonymous layman, a student of the priestly life, would write the letter. This man would not disclose his name because he thought it rather bold to offer advice on these matters to a prelate of the Church. The recipient of the complaint was to be the Bishop of Orense, Monsignor Angel Temiño, who was something of a standard-bearer for the Spanish ecclesiastical hierarchy in these matters. He was, after all, the person responsible for a theory about the causality of grace in the sacraments. The letter would be sent to His Grace through the offices of a personal friend, a priest who had some influence with his lordship.

What were to be the reasons to condemn the book? This Father Quixote must either be a total innocent or a complete fool. Which-ever he was, it was dangerous for the Church. He is promoted to the rank of monsignor because an ambassador from the Vatican – who is certainly not well disposed to Father Quixote's bishop – disregards all the usual conventions in such matters, just because the priest has shown himself in a good light by filling his glass with wine more times than he should have done and, through a stroke of luck, had repaired his luxurious Mercedes. It is as if he wanted to harm the church hierarchy. When His Grace the Bishop calls on the priest, the words which the author of the book puts into the mouth of Father Quixote make the bishop look ridiculous – and far less intelligent than the wretched priest. To cap it all, he is then made to look oppressive because he suspends the priest *a divinis*. From the Vatican to the Roman curia – which is compared to the Soviet politburo! – the Church is portrayed disgracefully.

What else would one expect from Graham Greene? Cardinal Pizzardo had condemned his novel, *The Power and the Glory*, and Cardinal Griffin had 'by implication' condemned *The End of the Affair*.

In the end, we thought better of it and decided it would be rather a disrespectful joke, so we never actually sent the letter.

Graham Greene was a born practical joker. He once even suggested to me that perhaps he should don the Roman collar a priest wears so that when I arrived at the Customs at Nice airport he could take care of my briefcase in which I always hid a few bottles.

•

Despite his sense of humour, it was always evident that Graham Greene had a very nervous disposition. He often told me that he was not 'a steady person' and that he was 'unstable'. Throughout his life, he had a way of appearing anxious and ill at ease. From the time of his psychiatric treatment at the age of fifteen or sixteen – a period which he always reckoned to have been one of the happiest of his life – right up until the moment when he felt unable to spend two consecutive full days at the monastery at Osera, in spite of the admiration and warmth he felt for the monks and their lives of silence, there was always this restless side to him.

However, this aspect of his character never in any way affected either his complete clarity of judgement, or the aptness of most of his decisions. It is true that some of these were taken, as he put it, 'after the dangerous third Martini', but Graham Greene's extraordinarily balanced judgement is evident from the way in which the main characters in his novels speak and behave. I can often remember seeing him sitting in his armchair, his head resting on his open hand, deliberating on some delicate matter or other; then, unwillingly as far as I was concerned, leaving the final decision to me.

Perhaps this lack of 'steadiness' manifested itself in his frequent need to travel, in his sudden impulses and, above all, in his occasional outbursts, which were so untypical and were usually delivered without any serious intent. I don't believe I saw him in this frame of mind more than ten or fifteen times in all the years of our friendship.

The nervous anxiety he displayed was that of the great artist, and it was made all the more acute because of his tireless work and because of the serious problems with which he became involved throughout most of his life, in particular during the years from 1979 to 1985, on account of the cursed mafia in the south of France.

It should also be said that Graham slept badly practically all his life and had taken sleeping pills since his youth, and that he could sometimes feel enormous remorse. Furthermore, he dreamed a great deal, and since he had always attached a great deal of importance to dreams – ever since his psychoanalysis – he used to make notes of these dreams the moment he woke up, switching on the light to jot down a brief summary before he forgot the dream. This meant that sleep was never a great comfort to him.

Because he never rested sufficiently, his nervous system was not nourished as it should be by the essential hours of sleep, resulting in his relative instability and comparatively mercurial changes of mood.

All these factors help to explain why Graham Greene was someone who so cherished his freedom, who hated feeling 'claustrophobic' and loathed 'feeling he was protected'. He said to me one day, on the road from Burgos to Logrono: 'I don't feel as if I were free.'

What had gone wrong? The trip in question had actually been planned by a third party, because it had been necessary to make hotel reservations in advance and these had been paid for beforehand. Graham appreciated all this, but nevertheless he felt as if he were not free. He could not bear to feel that things had been programmed for him. It was not his fault; that was the way he was. He was made to rebel and protest whenever the shadow of the most trivial imposition 'threatened his freedom'.

•

Graham's sudden outbursts could be disconcerting. His mood changes lacked any basis of reason and would normally occur at hotels and *paradores* at the end of a meal or after a late dinner. We might arrive feeling hungry and thirsty and drink at least half a bottle too much between us. It was the half bottle that would do the damage! On our picnics in the country there was never any unpleasantness. The breeze from the trees and the murmur of the water provided balm and peace.

The first time Graham truly lost his temper was on 2 July 1981 in the Restaurante Valencia in Salamanca. We arrived there for lunch at about three o'clock in the afternoon. The meal had begun well, with each of us convincing the other that the man standing watching us on the corner was a secret agent. Then we began to discuss all sorts of things, among them the business of arms dealing. It was a subject we had spoken about frequently just like anything else. The timing was unfortunate ... Two contradictory ideas suddenly came to Graham's mind: the priest of peace and the weapons of death. Graham made many unfortunate remarks, some of them rather insulting, about the priest and the weapons. I listened to as much as I could in silence, but he had gone too far. It was clear from the expression on my face that I took it seriously. Time and again he would ask my forgiveness. 'I drank one glass too many...' The remorse he suffered for what had happened affected him very seriously. He took the blame so much to heart that he called me a few days after he had returned to Antibes, still very upset by what had happened. I had to talk to him very seriously in order to persuade him to forget this unimportant incident.

The worst discussion for many years took place on 16 August 1984 in the *parador* at Segovia. It was after three o'clock and we were eating some delicious little lamb chops for lunch. We were exhausted. We did not drink much wine, but perhaps the effects of gin on Graham and whisky on the 'Third Man' may have been partly to blame. Or maybe I was being too serious.

We dined at the same *parador* that evening and asked for more of the lamb chops that we had eaten for lunch. At dinner, the conversation grew even more inflamed; I believe it was the only really overheated conversation we ever had. The subject: the Pope's involvement in the political situation in Central and South America. Graham attacked the Pope very strongly: his meeting with Reagan on the eve of the American elections; the Pope's treatment of the priests who were members of the Nicaraguan government; the fact that he had not publicly condemned either the assassination of Archbishop Romero or the attacks on the North American nuns.

I defended the Pope stoutly. It was not true, in my view, that he had not condemned the murder of Archbishop Romero publicly. How foolish I was! Had I burst out laughing, it is likely the other two would have reacted similarly, but because of some morbid scruple on my part, I got angry. I ruined everything.

It had been a grim evening and we bid each other good night fairly stiffly. When I went to call on Graham the next morning, I found him looking very odd indeed. He opened his arms to me in a gesture.

'We drank too much last night', he said.

'That's true, but don't worry. Alegría!'

'Alegria!' said Graham.

I knew two Grahams: one belonged to the period before 1979 and the battle with the mafia; the other, to the period afterwards. The struggle against the wretched mafia affected his nerves and his sleep more than ever. It was not that Graham was particularly difficult during that time, far from it, but one had to bear in mind the colossal mental and psychological pressure on the man during those ghastly years. He was very tired and he would get upset much more easily.

Was Graham Greene a difficult man? Many of those I have asked, including those closest to him, say he was. I sincerely believe I never saw him in that light. He could be difficult at particular moments when human injustice tested his nerves and his strength to the limit. At such moments a certain tact was required and, in my case, rather more silence than is my wont. And rather fewer photographs . . . .

HIS DARKER SIDE

WAS GRAHAM GREENE a depressive? He reckoned that he was, but he added that his depressions had been more frequent and more serious during his youth and adolescence. He used to say that with age he got less and less gloomy.

When we talked about this, Graham recalled the well-known occasion when he had fallen in love with his sister's governess, and his subsequent suicide attempt. He decided he would be rid of this life, and so he swallowed between fifteen and twenty aspirins with a glass of whisky. He fell asleep and woke up feeling more comforted and alert than ever, after one of the best sleeps in his life. As luck would have it, there was a telegram waiting from an old girl friend asking him how he was.

'Because of the happy coincidence of that telegram arriving at that particular moment and after that sleep,' Graham concluded as he recounted the episode to me, 'I began to feel happy again.'

The depression that led to his three-month drinking bout had been an unfortunate start to his Oxford career. Fate came to his rescue in the shape of his tutor, who helped him resolve to be patient.

Graham and I often spoke about his periods of depression, especially those in the years following his adolescence. His fits of temper were sudden, but always sporadic and momentary. On the other hand, it is obvious that a psychiatrist might well have noted certain aspects of his behaviour which were abnormal. There were the telepathic phenomena which he told me about himself, and which were also associated with his mother and older sister; the nervous hypersensitivity that could affect him for no reason at all; his fits of boredom tinged with sadness. But these were all passing afflictions. I never saw Graham Greene affected in these ways for very long. His moods were relatively mercurial. As Graham told me, and as the wife of the psychiatrist who treated him in adolescence told his biographer, Norman Sherry, 'it was a pity he decided to write novels, because he would have made "an extraordinary medium".'

I am no psychiatrist, but there were certain moments during the course of our friendship which caused me considerable worry; in particular one seriously alarmed me and suggested that Graham may have been the victim of occasional depression.

•

Madrid, 25 July 1980. Our journey through Spain and Portugal had been a happy one. Graham was flying back to France that evening. As everyone knows, Graham spent a large part of his life travelling in aeroplanes.

We went over to my house that morning. I observed that Graham was much more emotional than normal. He was feeling somewhat weighed down, as he always was, by the thought of the quantity of mail that would await him whenever he got back to Antibes after a few days' travelling. It was worse if he had spent weeks away. These piles of correspondence were like some sort of constant bloodless martyrdom which seemed to haunt him throughout his travels. They seemed to be saying: you can go away and forget all about us, but when you stop, as stop you must, you'll have to return here!

The battle against the mafia over Martine's marriage had already begun (see pp. 247–59). Graham carried a letter from Martine, the daughter of his good friend Yvonne Cloetta, in his wallet. It had been written when she was nineteen when he was experiencing a variety of personal problems, some of which were very serious. Martine told him that he would never be alone; that she would always be with him; that she prayed for him . . .

At lunch, he had been reminding me of the beauty of the Vietnamese woman, the wife of an American diplomat, who had been at the reception at the Retiro gardens, before we started on our journey through Portugal. Graham had fallen in love with Indochina almost by chance, without quite knowing why. It may have been to do with the beauty of Phuong, the Vietnamese heroine of his novel, *The Quiet American*, among other things.

Quite suddenly and without any warning, Graham seemed to have momentarily forgotten those matters that were usually on his mind – but which at last were no longer urgent – and moved on to another much more serious subject: 'If I die today in a plane crash, I charge you in all seriousness with this request: there are a number of things

I want you to tell Elisabeth concerning what should happen to the money from the manuscripts that were sold in London the other day.' And Graham went on to list the recipients and the amounts.

At first, naturally, I did not know how to react or what to say. Graham said that he had been speaking perfectly seriously.

When I had pulled myself together, I said the sort of things I might have said to anyone: what on earth gave him the idea that there might be an accident in this day and age, given the safety of modern planes? In the unlikely event there were one, I would do exactly as he asked me. We spoke for about an hour while I did my best to dispel these notions of Graham's. But there was nothing to dispel. He was not afraid of death, only that it would catch up with him one day. That day might come this very day in the form of an aeroplane accident.

It was the first time Graham had introduced this subject and it took me totally by surprise. Although there had been no secrets between us for many years, the extraordinary and unexpected request revealed a hidden side of Graham Greene's nature.

I have already said that the battle against organized crime and the mafia on the Côte d'Azur had begun. It was this that brought to the surface many of the half-hidden, subconscious facets of this man's mysterious inner being. I will cover it in detail later.

8 June 1981. Graham and I might have called June 1981 the month when we went 'from heaven to hell and back again'. Our moods ranged from joy to disillusionment, and all because of our journey that summer.

On this particular day Graham telephoned to enquire after my throat and to find out whether it would be possible to start our travels at the beginning of July as we had originally planned. We talked for a long time. My throat operation had been postponed until the twenty-third, but the difficulty was not my throat so much as the problems affecting our 'Third Man' on this occasion. A member of his family was ill and he had to be at home. We agreed on 3 July as the date that Graham should arrive in Spain, for Antibes became so noisy when the tourists arrived that it was impossible for him to live there. Furthermore, he needed to go to Anacapri later on, and he wanted to continue writing *Monsignor Quixote*. It was just as well that Aurelio and his wife, Pilár, were so understanding and that Aurelio and his car were always at our disposal.

16 June. At ten o'clock the telephone rang. It was Graham calling from Antibes. We were like two children imagining and looking forward to our next journey: first La Mancha, then Castille, then Galicia and Portugal ... Graham had already planned our route. This time we would set out on the road to Valladolid to visit Cervantes' home. (All this was in connection with *Monsignor Quixote* which was by now almost finished.) Then, on the return journey, we would stop at the *parador* at Oropesa which had long been one of our favourite places. Naturally, we would not fail to pay a visit to the Cozinha de San Humberto in Evora. We had made a promise to the Holy Ghost, who had been most offended at being equated to a half-bottle of wine in the original proof of the Trinity in the first draft of the novel, that we would emend our theological error and use three equal bottles at dinner that night.

17 June. Graham called again at the usual time. The reason for the call was this: he now thought it would be impossible to make both the Monsignor Quixote journey as well as the visit to Maria Newall in Sintra. I had to leave for London on 19 July, for my throat operation. What he proposed was that we should set off on the Monsignor Quixote journey now, and wait until the end of August to see Maria. In this way, he could go to Anacapri in the interim, where he would be able to finish the novel fresh from his experiences in the Mancha, Cervantes' house in Valladolid, etc.

The conversation was entirely based around these imaginary adventures of Monsignor Quixote's. It was agreed I would book a room for him at the Mindanao Hotel.

29 June. Less euphoria. Judgement in Martine's case had had to be adjourned because the 'Devil's advocate' had had one of his marvellous brainwaves which knocked the enemy's hopes sideways: he had been given insufficient warning that judgement had been brought forward. Martine was very depressed. The 'Devil' was now attacking 'Martine two', another girl, also called Martine, who was her bosom friend – he had struck her with the butt of his pistol. But there had been no witnesses and now he was denying everything.

We tried to cheer each other up. Summer would soon be over, and then, with God's help, we would celebrate the triumph of truth over the forces of darkness.

30 June. Bitter days! Graham was very distressed when he called at the usual time this morning. He told me that Martine's problem had reached crisis point, that the 'Devil' was now desperate, that I should please pray for the lives of Martine and her child at Mass. The police had washed their hands of the attack on 'Martine two'. He had sent a resumé of what had been going on to the British, French, German and American press. Graham continued: 'In this situation, I feel psychologically incapable of leaving Antibes. I couldn't survive. I need to have the telephone by me at every moment. If you don't mind, I would prefer to delay the whole trip until the end of August or the first three weeks of September.'

He apologized over and over again. Naturally I said that all that mattered were his peace and happiness and, above all, the safety of Martine and her child. I would cancel our lunches with Enrique Tierno Galván and his wife, and with Esteban Pujals.

Graham told me that I should go to London; that he would come to see me after the operation as soon as I could speak again; that his closest friends kept telling him that he ought to go away to Spain with me. But we both agreed that he could not leave at present.

I sat where I was, not knowing what to do or what to think. After a while, I decided to wait until the next morning before cancelling our engagements.

I said Mass as if I were sleepwalking. Not only did I feel sad, I felt shattered. I asked God to help us.

30 June. There's light and hope once more! Graham telephoned again. He said: 'Your prayers have been heard very quickly' ... Martine's lawyer had just spoken to them. The case was to be heard on the tenth, thank goodness, as originally arranged. Her lawyer was extremely optimistic. Apparently he had all the evidence he needed.

Graham sounded delighted. He asked whether it was too late to rearrange our journey; whether I had cancelled our engagements. I answered: 'No, I haven't cancelled anything. Let's go ahead with the trip.' And I told him how I had mulled everything over in my room.

We felt so overcome with emotion that we were unable to continue the conversation. We said goodbye: 'See you on Friday, Leopoldo.'

'Until Friday, Graham! Give my love to Martine.'

1 July. After telephoning Crowborough to speak to Elisabeth – Graham's sister and factotum – on an urgent private matter, I rang

Graham in Antibes. I found him upset and almost gloomy; he was not at all pleased. I remembered the words of the poet: 'All that can happen between yesterday and today!' We spoke very briefly. What had happened to Graham?

2 July. At ten o'clock in the morning, Graham called from Antibes. He was upset and apologized for what had happened yesterday.

'After two days of good news about Martine's problem,' he explained, 'Yvonne and I have been sticking at each other.' He laughed. 'But please don't give a moment's thought to these little matters.'

However, Graham is always ultra-sensitive and considerate and does concern himself about such matters. He took the opportunity to ask me what he should wear for our lunch with the Mayor. I am not very expert on such matters, but I do know Don Enrique and his wife, and I told him there was no need to bring a formal suit.

Graham was upset. But I managed to cheer him up a little. So . . . a big hug! see you tomorrow, God willing, in Madrid.

Next day he arrived at Barajas airport in a very good mood. Graham was happy.

•

Madrid, 1 August 1985: Graham Greene's ideological will and testament.

At about eleven o'clock in the morning, we set out in the direction of Alto de los Leones. We were unable to find any English newspapers. We were chatting about all sorts of things. Graham spoke about the problems of the teaching profession in France. Catholic schools had been in difficulties for twenty-five years. And now Mitterand had made Jean-Pierre Chevènement Minister of Education. He was a member of the left wing of the Socialist party, and had sided with the Catholic teachers and restored Catholic teaching.

Our picnic took place among the pine woods. When we had finished, Graham and I went for a walk through this silent, beautiful scenery. There was a magnificent view through the woods to the distant horizon. It was very hot and the 'Third Man' (this time it was our dear friend Octavio) was taking a siesta. Just before this, he had been reading us these words spoken by Salvador de Madariaga in a programme broadcast from Paris in 1954: 'Graham Greene, who is considered to be England's leading contemporary novelist . . . . This excellent writer . . . is a literary artist whose output is distinguished by the profundity of its conception, always the result of mature and careful thought.'

It was the first and last time I ever saw Graham Greene pleased when listening to something said in praise of him. Yet his pleasure was an act of humility: Graham had a very high regard for Salvador de Madariaga. The passage had been read out by Dr Octavio Victoria Gil, in my opinion the foremost living authority on the life and work of Madariaga.

As we walked, we both held a small glass of Señor Antonio de las Regadas' white wine in our hands. Graham suddenly stopped, looked me in the eye, and spoke the following heartfelt words: 'If Reagan should be President for another four years, something which is most unlikely, I may become a Communist. Being a Communist is not the same thing as being a Marxist. This does not mean I am giving up the faith.'

And he continued: 'Tomorrow I am leaving by plane for Antibes. One never knows whether a plane will crash. Should that happen, I entrust your conscience, in all seriousness, with these words which I would like you to make known: Should Reagan continue as President for a further four years, Graham would probably have become a Communist.'

On an earlier occasion, Graham had also said to me: 'Supposing I were seriously ill and in danger of dying. I would summon you to be with me at that time. I would try to make a good confession. And at the end, I would say: "I entrust you with this message which I want you to state very clearly in public". And he said the same words he had just spoken about becoming a Communist. "I seriously believe", Graham continued "that there is no reason why a Communist should renounce his Catholic faith, and that Communism was one thing and Marxism another".'

I stared at him, wondering whether he was being serious or speaking half in jest. But he said emphatically: 'I am being perfectly serious.'

I felt very moved when he said this. In that lonely place and in that lonely atmosphere his words seemed to be spoken so earnestly that I needed all my strength not to show that my eyes were moistening.

'For God's sake,' I begged him earnestly, 'let us change the subject. Only God knows who is going to go first – you or I.'

And, indeed, we did change the subject. But nothing will ever erase Graham's solemn words from my memory. Even then, he continued: 'For God's sake, Leopoldo, broadcast it to the four winds that I died wanting to be a Communist, but without wishing to abandon the Catholic faith.'

Graham's voice sounded totally natural and calm when he spoke. It was quite clear to me that he was not feeling depressed or even melancholy. Thank God, he arrived back in Antibes safe and sound. Reagan was elected President for a second term. Graham did not become a Communist – nor did he remind me of this most serious of conversations.

•

On 22 March 1986, Graham and I met at Nice airport as we had arranged. He was arriving from London where the Order of Merit had just been conferred on him; I was flying in from Madrid to spend a few days with him in Antibes. I don't remember a single occasion when I saw Graham pleased about an honour being awarded to him, and he did not seem in the least excited about the Order of Merit.

That evening, contrary to our usual custom, we did not dine at home. We ate at 'L'Auberge Provençale'. Our meal was excellent, but, as always, what really mattered was the conversation. Graham told me how very depressed he had felt before receiving the Order of Merit. As the day when he was to receive the award approached, Graham felt as if he was about to be crushed by some vast weight. Her Majesty Queen Elizabeth II did her best to arrange matters so as to please Graham, and the ceremony could not have been simpler. There were just the Queen and he in a small room, furnished with two or three quite ordinary chairs and that was all. How well Her Majesty knew him! Nevertheless, that day, when Graham told me about the ceremony and the wretched days that preceded his audience with Her Majesty, he quoted the grim words of a poet whose name he mentioned but which I cannot remember:

> *All honour be to the skeleton, to the destroyed man,*
> *to the corpse.*

Graham Greene's darker moods were sometimes connected with the telepathic phenomena I mentioned. On his first journey to Panama after Omar Torrijos' death, Graham experienced a terrible depression as he flew over the ocean. Did he have a premonition of how much he would miss his friend when he landed in Panama? He had to fortify himself with a double gin to make the journey tolerable.

Something similar happened in August 1984 before leaving Antibes for Spain. A premonition of something terrible came over him, to do with his plane crashing into the sea, and it came with such force that he entrusted his Panamanian diaries to an acquaintance. What is more, he left instructions on top of his desk for his son Francis, in the case of his unexpected death on this journey to Spain. When he recounted these things to me at supper on his arrival in Madrid, I read him a marvellous passage from St Augustine which relates what a much beloved person who has recently arrived in Paradise has to say to those who mourn: 'Don't weep for me, if you had truly loved me when I was living among you . . . .' When we telephoned Maria Newall in Sintra, our eventual destination, from the *parador* at Oropesa, we were told that she had died. Greene commented on these coincidences. Similar things had happened frequently throughout his life.

THINGS OF THE SPIRIT

AT THE TIME of Graham Greene's death, Paul Gray wrote the following in *Time International*:

> Greene never took his religion lightly, and the
> Catholicism that would come to stamp his fiction served
> both as a stern gauge by which to measure the behaviour
> of fallen mortals and as a powerful source of divine
> mercy.

And on the same page, the magazine introduced Paul Gray's article with these words: 'Graham Greene . . . invaded and shaped the public imagination more than any other serious writer of this century.' (15 April 1991, p.62) These are the most accurate words I have ever read about Graham Greene.

It was Graham Greene's obsessive faith, and the problems it engendered, that provided the basis for our friendship. Without this obsessive faith, which was constantly at war with itself (in this sense he was the English Unamuno) and the fact that I was a priest, such a relationship would never have been possible.

To show what I mean, I have selected three occasions on which Greene's faith appeared to consume his whole being and overwhelm him.

During our first conversation, Graham Greene put this surprising and unexpected question to me: 'Do you think I have true faith?'

Now Graham knew that I had spent several years studying his work. I stared at him with a look that was part questioning, part disconcerted. After a few moments' silence, I replied: 'You know as well as I do that there is no effect without a cause. Reading your books, I notice that the name of God appears constantly. But that's not all. Your work hinges on the existence of that Being . . . . I genuinely believe that your faith is greater than mine. I have no doubt about it.'

Graham Greene was astonished at this reply. 'Thank you very much indeed. Your answer is very comforting.' He was clearly delighted and moved by what I had said.

He had, incidentally, already said something similar in a letter he wrote to accompany my doctoral thesis at King's College, London, which was later published in Spain. This is what he wrote:

> Dear Father Durán,
>   I have read your thesis with great interest and I am glad to have your theological support . . . Thank you very much for spending such time and patience on my work. I have received a great deal of encouragement from your thesis.

We went on talking. In the course of that first conversation – which I refer to in Chapter 1 – we got along so well that we might have been old friends, and when Graham asked me quite openly about my own faith, I answered truthfully and succinctly: 'I do not believe in God, I touch him.'

I am absolutely convinced that this remark was providential in my whole relationship with Graham Greene. It was something that just came out; I did not think about it. Yet for Graham, it remained cleaved to his heart. As time passed, I began to see it was a crucial phrase for him, and the only one he needed, as will become clear at the end of this chapter. The dialogues between Monsignor Quixote and Sancho have the remark at their core, once it has been spoken by the monsignor. At first, the priest uses the phrase literally; later he changes it somewhat: he believes he touches God. Greene wanted *Monsignor Quixote* to be a book about doubt, not certainty. It was to be an autobiographical book to some extent. Father Quixote tells Sancho that he too has his doubts like any other mortal. And Sancho is rather bemused: he had sought the priest's company because he thought that in his company all doubt would be removed.

In *The Other Man*, Greene immortalized that casual remark when he confessed to Marie-Françoise Allain, 'I am inclined to find superstition or magic more "rational" than abstract religious ideas such as the Holy Trinity. I like the so-called "primitive" manifestations of the Faith.'

'What are they?' asks Miss Allain.

And Greene replies: 'Oh, the ones I've been telling you about, and others which are harder to describe. For instance, one comes across people endowed with a strange aura. I'm thinking of a friend of mine, Father Durán [the French words, *le père Durán* were omitted in the English translation], a Spanish priest with whom I go travelling every year. He has a faculty for bringing people to life. He is not a conventionally pious man, but he is possessed by an absolute faith. When I asked him to describe it, he modestly replied, "I do not believe in God, I touch him."'

What follows took place in Antibes on 16 December 1982. We were discussing Graham's faith and some of the difficulties he encountered. He can quite readily accept heaven as a purely active state, and purgatory as well. But hell is not the same. How can one reconcile eternal damnation with the infinite mercy of God who is our father? Graham argues his case rationally. With the help of faith he can believe in hell, but his reason rebels against this truth. We discussed these problems slowly.

'God is not only merciful', I added, quoting St Thomas Aquinas. 'Furthermore, his infinite mercy can supersede his infinite justice.' I tried to say something of these tremendous, fathomless mysteries about which our human reason can only stammer and stutter. Later, I spoke of the joy and simplicity of my own total faith.

Graham replied more or less as follows: 'When you speak of faith, I feel reassured and happy. Our visits to one another are my peace, and they mean everything to me.'

I can only say that this was not Graham's normal style of response, for he was usually so restrained, considered and profound. Nevertheless, I feel sure that even if these words are not his literal words, they give the exact sense of what he said. Providentially, the steadfastness of my own faith was the overriding argument. He was delighted that I should talk about my faith. He was happy to see me happy. My self-assurance made him feel at peace – he who always seemed to live in a state of war in his own hidden world.

It is quite obvious that Graham never saw anything unusually spiritual about me. I simply said my daily Mass – the absolute basic essential for a priest who has faith – and tried my best to say the rosary. I did try to pray in the back of the car after each of our midday picnics, but I usually fell asleep. How Graham laughed when he saw me asleep with my rosary in my fingers! Whenever the engine started up, he never failed to say: 'Time for your rosary.'

And when he noticed that I had woken up, he would ask me, trying not to laugh: 'Have you finished your rosary?'

I did laugh. We understood each other well. He probably took pleasure in remembering the words of Jesus: 'The spirit is willing, but the flesh is weak'.

•

It was 8 July 1987 and we were in Vigo. I wrote in my diary: 'After breakfast, we remained chatting at table for over an hour. A far-reaching discussion about his faith'.

'Each day I have less and less faith,' said Graham.

And I replied: 'Yes, but you have often told me that with every passing day you find you have less "belief", but more "faith".

Graham was silent. He suddenly came out with the most perfect remark on this subject. 'The trouble is I don't believe my unbelief.'

No more precise sentence could have been uttered to define the faith of this man, to describe his spiritual life.

When I heard him make this remark, which I later described as 'his life's formula', I asked him: 'Do you mind writing down that wonderful phrase for me?'

He replied: 'Best not to write it down. It's a private remark between ourselves.'

The phrase is beautiful both from a literary and a theological stand-point. Like some precious, tiny jewel, it sums up and contains in essence all there is to know about the embattled faith of this man whose simplicity was so like that of a child.

I can testify that Graham Greene's faith was in a state of constant inner struggle with itself and that it obsessed him. He would say that his conversion to Catholicism, to being 'baptized again, conditionally' imprinted on his faith a certain character which would never leave him. Did he not once call it a malign virus from which one could never be cured? I know very well that this illness provided him with some of the high points of his life, and it was the reason, as we shall see, why he died so happily and peacefully. Far be it from me to identify Graham Greene with the character of Brown in *The Comedians*, as so many have tried to do, wrongly, with others of his characters. However, when Greene writes of Brown struggling with his faith, in the way that young boys struggle against masturbation; or when Brown is unable to find peace because of the splinter of ice in his heart; or when Brown complains about the sense of guilt which the priests at the College of the Visitation instilled into his conscience when he was too young to give his consent, it is clear that in some way Graham was thinking of the demands his own faith made on him.

I think it may be sensible to propound a few ideas about Graham Greene's unquestionable faith. Immediately after we had first met each other, he told me on different occasions that each day he found he had less 'belief' but more 'faith'. By 'belief' he meant the kind of faith that is based on reason, or better still, on the reasons that support one's faith – in other words, to use the language of theology, faith assisted by 'motivation for credibility'. His short story, 'A Visit to Morin', deals directly with this matter of 'faith' and 'belief'.

My reaction was straightforward: 'You are very fortunate. What matters is plain, unadorned faith. Those reasons which make our faith credible are worthless.'

Throughout his life Graham worried that he 'did not believe enough'. The constant purpose of his prayers – and he never, even in his most forlorn moments, stopped praying a little every day – was to ask God that he might 'truly believe' and that 'his faith might be increased'. When he told me that he asked God for 'belief', I argued, using the words of Pascal which Greene puts into the mouth of the Father Superior in *A Burnt-Out Case* when he is talking to Doctor Colin about Querry's faith:

> You remember what Pascal said, that a man who started looking for God has already found him.

Eventually, I only began to take his obsession with his complete lack of faith half-seriously.

'You think about death much more naturally than I do, and you're less frightened of it', I said to him one day, half in jest.

'Perhaps because I only half-believe, and I don't think about the next life as much as you do', he answered.

●

Graham was keen that I should meet Alec Guinness, and I agreed.

'He is a rather devout Catholic', he used to say to me.

'Even more than you?'

Graham laughed out loud and said with his usual restraint: 'Much better than I.'

On a certain occasion, when he was recalling one of the more delightful moments of his life, he said: 'Once, during the war, near Euston, I experienced a very profound feeling of faith.'

Charles Moeller, the Belgian scholar, has called Graham Greene 'the martyr of hope'. I don't know whether it would not be more appropriate to call him the 'martyr of faith'. His collection of *Catholic Essays*, published in Spanish, is the religious testament of a totally committed believer.

One afternoon, in the restaurant in Oporto which I mentioned earlier, he became particularly concerned about the subject.

'I speak on behalf of those almost lapsed Catholics', he said to me.

Without really thinking about what he had said, I replied: 'It's just as well you say "almost lapsed". Your faith is greater than mine, in that I think very little about it.'

Graham was not an obviously devout man, but he did say his prayers with great intensity. I think that his favourite prayer was the simple words of his friend François Mauriac, which he always carried in his wallet: 'O Jesus of the evening.'

On one occasion he had actual proof of the efficacy of his prayer. Graham always prayed very intently for whatever he was asking. In this case, it concerned two women friends of his. The one he had originally been closest to was jealous and hated her new rival. Graham went into a church and prayed: 'Lord, could you not do something about this business?' He later invited his former friend to dinner and spoke to her. The result was that both women eventually became friends.

At those moments when his faith seemed to have disappeared, he told God: 'Lord, I offer you my unbelief.'

Graham had a great affection for the Virgin Mary. He never understood why in the old days Protestants, or anyone else, had attacked the Virgin. 'We need a Mother', he would say. On several occasions, we went to Bejar, to visit the shrine of the Virgin at Castanar. He loved the site of this shrine, and the face of the Virgin, and wanted to see an image of her dressed in actual period clothing.

He told me how once, in Malaya, he had experienced an extraordinary feeling of love for the Virgin. It was a moment he would never forget. When Graham spoke of her he nearly always added the name Mary.

On one occasion he had a curious dream. He dreamt that he had a small piece of gold and that he was going to spend it on a prostitute.

As he was walking along, he saw a white wall. Behind it there was a young woman with a child, and three kings who were offering her things. He also gave his lump of gold. Later, when he was reading the Gospel, he realized that the gift had been intended for the Virgin Mary.

We would sometimes take part in the singing of the Salve Regina, the hymn with which the Cistercian monks take their leave of the day and of the Queen of Heaven, offering up their brief repose to her. The first time we heard the Salve Regina sung, Graham uttered in a low voice: 'Very moving', and in the corridor that led to our rooms, I could hear him mumbling 'O Jesus of the evening'.

No, Graham was not what one might call a devout person. But I can testify that for the last third of his life there was nothing of importance that was not mentioned in my daily morning Mass. He would warn me about whatever it was, and, whenever possible, he did so a few days in advance. It is amazing how much faith Graham set on his friend's Mass, as I never tire of saying. If only I could emulate him!

On the question of the liturgy, Graham was distinctly traditional. Why simplify the liturgy to such an extent? he wondered. Why omit some of the words spoken by the centurion, for example? The passage from St John's Gospel which used to conclude the Mass has true greatness. It is badly missed. We often used to say it on the occasions that I said Mass in Latin.

As far as the sacraments were concerned, there was only one occasion when Graham kept away from them. His close friend, Father Martindale, once wanted him to go to confession, but Graham gave his reasons for not going and he was extraordinarily sensitive and delicate about the matter. I will say just this: during the last ten years of his life Graham received all the sacraments with normal frequency. It was not something I ever mentioned to him. I was absolutely sure he would raise the matter himself one day.

Metaphysical proofs mattered little to Graham. He found other kinds more helpful. The scene when Peter and John race to the tomb in Chapter 20 of St John's Gospel was of great help to Graham's tortured faith throughout his life. He often talked about this chapter to me. For him, the passage had all the indications of absolute veracity. I loved to watch him analysing it. He read it often, even though he knew it by heart.

He was very interested in the most recent scientific studies relating to the Turin shroud. For him, the discovery that there was no sign on the shroud of Jesus having had a navel provided proof of the virgin birth. These points of scientific evidence helped to alleviate some of the agonies of Graham Greene's very real but tormented faith.

•

We spoke continually about the Roman Catholic Church and it was the subject of some of our most heated discussions. I have already mentioned Graham's two audiences with Pius XII and Paul VI. We always came to the conclusion that when one spoke of the Church one had to keep in mind its two constituent elements: the divine and the human. Unless one did this, it is impossible to talk about the Church without talking nonsense.

Graham had some strange views on these things. He was a liberal-minded person, and he sometimes disagreed with the directives of the hierarchy on contemporary matters, or with Vatican policy towards certain parts of the world, particularly Central America. He would voice his disagreement in letters to the press or by writing in one of the Catholic journals. Despite the fact that he admired Paul VI, he very much regretted that the Pope appeared to disregard the opinions of most experts when he published his encyclical *Humanae Vitae*. I suggested that perhaps the last pages of the document did provide a little hope: there, the final decision on certain fundamental points is left to the conscience of the individual. If Catholic historians disagree with these authorities when they are dead, why not do similarly when they are still alive? Because he loved the Church, this is what Graham sometimes did in some of his articles, though never in his books.

Nevertheless, I do remember very clearly the polemical newspaper correspondence that Graham had with a certain American writer when he poked fun at his adversary with delicate irony and told him that he was unable to appreciate the English sense of humour. Yet his opponent was making some very serious assertions about the Roman Church, alleging that it always sided with the most powerful. Giving a series of examples, from Archbishop Romero to Cardinal Segura, Graham proved that this was not the case. He read out to me his most recent letter to *The Times* on the subject, and we both agreed that one had to be proud of the role the Church was playing in Central America, in Haiti, the Philippines and elsewhere.

One of the things we both most regretted was the abuse of the

Church's authority, especially that of the Vatican. We also regretted the Church's treatment of so many distinguished theologians, from Karl Rahner to Congar, who had been silenced by Rome for no reason whatsoever. These were men who were providentially being made into martyrs by poor Cardinal Pizzardo or someone. We spoke of the deposition of Cardinal Mindszenty in Budapest, and the way in which Cardinal Wyszynski had been more or less abandoned in Warsaw. This was the human element in the Church! We were grateful that the Church had recognized its errors by asking these men's forgiveness and by raising them to cardinals. To see John Paul II kneeling in front of Mindszenty's tomb struck us as a great act of contrition on behalf of the Church.

At the time that Graham wrote his letter to *The Times* mentioning Cardinal Segura, we had a long conversation about him. Graham admired him greatly. I had known him personally and had spoken to him on several occasions in the seminary of San Pablo in Cuenca where the Cardinal Archbishop of Seville had come for a rest. He had always been grateful to the Vincentians. They had given him a small amount of financial support at the time of his exile in France, where he lived in the utmost poverty.

Graham was extremely interested in this man and asked me to tell him all I knew about him. I told him that this man led a simple and austere private life. As a defender of the rights of the Church, the Cardinal was another Mindszenty; a man of steel. He had been Bishop of Coria, a small rural diocese, at the time King Alfonso XIII went to visit the poverty-stricken community of Las Urdes. The Bishop accompanied him, said Mass and preached a simple homily. Alfonso XIII was so moved and impressed by what he saw and heard that day that he recommended to the Holy See that this good man be made Cardinal Archbishop of Toledo, Primate of Spain. And so he was.

Tedeschini was the Nuncio in Spain at the time, and he stood poles apart from Cardinal Segura. He was an elegant, rather vain man who even had his hands manicured at his residency, and apparently his conduct left much to be desired. One day he was summoned by the Primate of Spain to Toledo and told without further ado that he was not pleased with the rumours he had heard about the Nuncio.

Cardinal Segura, being Primate, was close to the crown, and when the Republicans seized power he was expelled. But he was not in the least interested in human politics, only in God's politics.

When I told Graham this he interrupted me. 'At the hour of his death, he will be glad that he acted in the way he did', he said forcefully.

During his exile in France, Cardinal Segura received orders every month or two from the French Government to move further north.

When he became ill, he begged the Vatican to give him permission to go and live in Rome. The authorities took a long time before giving their agreement, but at last they consented because his health was so delicate. The Cardinal sent his chauffeur ahead to Rome and asked him to meet him at the railway station. When he arrived in Rome, he discovered that Cardinal Pacelli, the Vatican Secretary of State, was also there, waiting to receive him formally and with all due protocol in an official car. Along with the Secretary of State there were reporters from the glossy magazines, ready to provide irrefutable evidence that the Cardinal had been treated with all the necessary honours on his return from exile. The adamantine Cardinal Segura shook hands graciously with the Secretary of State and, having greeted them all appropriately, without further ado he stepped into his own car, ignoring Pacelli and the reporters. He had suffered a great deal in France and the Vatican had ignored his appeals. The Spanish Government's requests had carried more weight than the poor Cardinal's distress.

While he was in Rome, Cardinal Merry del Val fell seriously ill. Cardinal Segura went to visit him every day. A few days before he died, Merry del Val told his friend and compatriot: 'I am going to tell you something, Pedro, which may surprise you, though you are also a cardinal, and being a Cardinal yourself. I have spent all my life here in the Roman curia and I believe I have the authority to tell you this. Having spent twenty-two years at the Holy Office, and been Secretary of State during an entire pontificate, I have reached the following conclusion: There are two elements to the Church, the divine and the human. As for the divine aspect, I have tried to do what little I could; I would give my life for it a thousand times over. But as for its human side, my dear Pedro, how miserable it is. Nevertheless, we must carry on if that is God's will.'

After the end of the Spanish Civil War, Cardinal Segura was made Archbishop of Seville. The Falangists had daubed their symbol of a yoke and arrows on the walls of many Spanish cathedrals, including Seville. Cardinal Segura publicly condemned this act. Later, he personally refused to receive Franco as head of state under the pallium

at the entrance to the cathedral. Either the Vicar General or the
Capitular welcomed him instead.

One Christmas Eve, when the Cardinal was staying at his residency
at Cuenca, the Rector of the seminary of San Pablo and I went to
wish him a happy Christmas. We spent a long time in conversation
with him. We were Vincentians and, as well as being fond of us, he
put great trust in us. Every week, someone from our community
would go to hear his confession. That day he spoke to us about his
latest pastoral letter which he had brought with him. In it he condemned a series of propositions put forward in a book about the
Virgin Mary which had been published in France, for which a Foreword had been written by Cardinal Tisserand, the Dean of the Sacred
College. Was it *The Virgin Mary* by Jean Guitton?

Storm clouds kept gathering over Cardinal Segura. He was
regarded as a tiresome man and in due course an auxiliary Archbishop
Bueno Monreal, was appointed to succeed him. Cardinal Segura was
gradually being forced into a corner.

And we must not forget that the Nuncio, Tedeschini, had returned
to Rome, by now a cardinal and a close friend of Pius XII. We should
also remember Tedeschini's summons to Toledo by Primate Segura
and the serious warning he had been given. Cardinal Segura was
absolutely right and the proof of what he said is incontrovertible.
Needless to say, this did not reach me via Cardinal Segura. If that
were the case, I would not affirm it here so categorically. I would say
nothing. And while we are recalling these events, let us not forget
the meeting at Rome station between Cardinal Segura and Secretary
of State, Pacelli.

This is a summary of the conversation Graham and I had about
this man of God. It was one that Greene would never forget.

We continued to discuss the human aspect of the Church. Graham
told me about some old philosopher's stone, which apparently Cardinal Tisserand used for turning ordinary paper into dollars. And I told
him about the life and times of Nuncio Lari out in La Paz in Bolivia.
An acquaintance of mine, Father Gil, a Vincentian priest, had had
the misfortune to be his secretary and adviser. He was well informed
on Canon Law and Nuncio Lari made full use of him. But this
Nuncio was up to no good and sank to the worst degradations. When
matters had become unbearable for those around him, a number of
distinguished people decided to inform Rome about the continuing
scandal. Nuncio Lari came to hear about this but he was not worried.

'My cousin Maglione will throw all those letters in the waste-paper basket', he said calmly.

Apparently, he was telling the plain and simple truth. Cardinal Maglione was the first and last Secretary of State appointed by Pius XII. But one day, during the time German troops under Keyserling were occupying Rome, Secretary of State Maglione was assassinated in his carriage on the orders, so it was said, of Keyserling. A little while later, without warning, Nuncio Lari was summoned to Rome by the Pope, and it appears that His Holiness did not even meet him on his arrival. It seems that the Pope had sent him to a convent to do penance for his sins. After Maglione's death, someone had discovered the letters sent from Bolivia denouncing Lari's calamitous life. In future, Pius XII was only to appoint Prosecretaries, not Secretaries of State. Reliable sources say that Maglione's covering-up of Lari influenced the Pope's decision. But as to Pius XII's real motive . . . we must leave that to one side.

I remember that when we discussed these dark deeds perpetrated by our Mother Church, I said to Graham: 'If tomorrow someone were to say to me that the Pope in the Vatican led the same sort of life that Lari did, I would feel absolutely appalled, but my faith would not be affected in the least. Why? Because my faith is based on one thing alone: Christ said he was God and showed that he was God. Nothing else matters as far as my belief is concerned.'

We dismissed sensationalist books, such as *The Vatican Empire* by Nini de Bello, which had nothing to commend them, but on several occasions we did discuss Andrew M. Greeley's book *The Making of the Popes* which, according to Graham, was 'fascinating'. Even if it had little literary value, it had all the suspense of an Agatha Christie thriller. The sub-title itself is revealing: 'The Politics of Intrigue in the Vatican'. Any believer, on reading it, may feel that his world is collapsing around him, and that the divine aspect of the Church is nothing but an illusion. But anyone who does feel like this must lack any real grounding in these matters. Such people – though they may never have heard of St Thomas Aquinas nor understood any of his teaching – are convinced that bishops and cardinals are men who 'take it for granted that they have indeed acquired virtue', and are considered to be saints already; at the same time monks, priests and believers everywhere are still fighting 'to acquire' this virtue, this sanctity, however remote it may be. The truth is that bishops and cardinals – and Father Salaverry, the Jesuit theologian, virtually said that on some occasions bishops were infallible when they spoke as pastors! – are generally poor ordinary mortals like everyone else, who are doing their best to live a godly life that leads to salvation. And that is all there is to it! The ideal is one thing – all those fine Thomist doctrines – and the prosaic truth is quite another. Of course I do not deny that there is a vocational grace; that actual grace which we all possess as human beings, and which we all need to accomplish our obligations. But the weight of a bishop's or a cardinal's views depends on his intellectual training, on his wisdom, on his advisers, and on the hours he spends at prayer each day. All the rest is celestial music.

We also spoke about David Yallop's book, *In God's Name*. A marvellous title. How did John Paul I, that smiling saint, die? The book is a serious one. Its hypothesis – that he was assassinated by some of the highest authorities in the Church, those closest to the Pope – seems a little exaggerated. He puts forwards conjectures, even probabilities, but they are not convincing reasons for murder.

While on the subject of books, Graham told me about a manuscript he had just read which the author had lent him before sending it to his publisher. I do not recall the title or the author (though it may have been Peter Nicholls), and I am not even sure whether it has been published. In Graham Greene's view, this book was perfectly documented. The author had obtained express permission from the Pope to consult whatever papers he needed in order to clarify the death of his predecessor .... The conclusion which this author reached was not that the Pope had been murdered, which did not really seem likely, but that, rather sadly, there was an atmosphere of constant political manoeuvring and intrigue within the Roman Curia. Among that army of monsignors, all that mattered was getting on and ascending the promotion ladder.

Graham returned to the same subject on another occasion. 'I have just re-read X's book in typescript', he told me. 'The Pope had given the author permission to make investigations and to ask questions of anyone in the Vatican or in the Church. He reaches a conclusion that is even sadder than the assassination of a Pope, which is probably not even mentioned here. It derives from his experience of the intrigue and false wisdom in those circles, in which people refused to reply to questions despite the fact that the Pope himself had given permission for the author to ask them. In other words, he has observed that dark side of human nature that helps one to move up in the hierarchy. That lack of simplicity and clarity.'

And he added: 'The author of this book had three interviews with Archbishop Marcinkus. Marcinkus is not the sort of man who would commit such crimes. I do not like him, but in this matter he is innocent.'

•

We frequently referred to the Jesuits and Dominicans in our chats. Graham had had good friends among both Orders and I had been taught by them. We both regretted that the traditional discipline of the Jesuit fathers was going through a crisis. The Church greatly depended on this discipline, and so did the world.

'After all,' added Graham, 'the life of a priest is supposed to be a hard one. That's what he undertook when he made his vows.'

•

As has been mentioned, Cardinal Pizzardo condemned *The Power and the Glory* 'because it was paradoxical and dealt with extraordinary circumstances', and Cardinal Griffin, at least 'by implication', condemned *The End of the Affair* in a pastoral letter.

How did Greene react to these incomprehensible condemnations? With a breadth of understanding that only he possessed. Listen to his own words:

> The price of liberty, even within a Church, is eternal
> vigilance, but I often wonder whether any of the
> totalitarian states, whether of the right or of the left, with
> which the Church of Rome is often compared, would have
> treated me as gently when I refused to revise the book,
> on the casuistical ground that the copyright was in the
> hands of my publishers. There was no public
> condemnation, and the affair was allowed to drop into
> that peaceful oblivion which the Church wisely reserves
> for unimportant issues.

•

There can be no doubt that the problem of celibacy and chastity was the subject we discussed most frequently. Over many years, we came to realize that it was one of those topics of conversation to which we would constantly return.

Graham greatly admired priestly celibacy and he was a stout

defender of the notion that religious ideals require a chaste life. He was fascinated by chastity. For him, it was one of the most interesting subjects to talk about. Graham had a strong yearning for lost purity. He was a great idealist, and although his own life did not always live up to his ideals, he would often contrast passing sensual pleasures with the eternal ideal of purity.

Augustine of Hippo assures us that purity is a thousand times more satisfying than 'the gratification of flesh and blood'. And he should have known! In the 'Song of Alborada' in his *Confessions*, he wrote:

> How delightful did it instantly grow to me to lack the delights of those vain things; yea it was now a joy to me to be deprived of those joys, which formerly I had feared to lose. For thou, O Lord, didst cast them out from me, thou true and supreme delight, thou didst cast them forth, and in their place didst enter in thyself, more sweet than all earthly pleasure, though not to flesh and blood; clearer than any light, yet more hidden than any secret; higher than the highest honour, but not to such as are high in their own conceits. Now was my mind free from the biting cares both of honour and of riches, as also from weltering in filth, and scratching the itch of lust; and I prattled childlike unto thee, my light, my wealth, my salvation, my Lord and my God.

Graham and I read this short, sublime chapter out aloud. It is hard to think of any aspect of it that did not come up again and again in our chats. Graham reckoned that those priests who had married showed very poor taste when it came to choosing wives. After marriage came divorce. I made light of it all and joked to Graham:

'Perhaps they will get tired of flying up to the stars and will decide to travel by donkey again.'

'Exactly!' exclaimed Graham.

One day, shortly after we had first met, he told me that 'he would be very sorry if I were to marry'. I was still quite young in those days. Graham assured me that priests did not realize how fortunate they were not to be married. That freedom could not be compared with any amount of wealth! We agreed that the man who had the mind and the dignity to be a priest gave up certain pleasures of the flesh, but received a thousand graces in exchange.

Graham and I used to relate our most intimate experiences to each other. He never tired of hearing me talk about girls I used to know and his eyes would sometimes moisten when we spoke about such matters.

Everything I ever told Graham always centred on the one great human experience of my life: the prize of celibacy and priestly chastity. For to be celibate without being chaste is worthless. Graham understood perfectly what I am now saying: the overwhelming human joy of being the recipient of so much boundless trust; the young people who pour out their whole being and place themselves – their true selves! – in your hands: their feelings, emotions, proclivities; everything, large or small. Graham was fascinated by the notion.

Without mentioning names, I spoke of friendships I had known in Villafranca del Bierzo, in Cuenca and in Madrid. I assured him that it cost one nothing to behave decently with a woman, as long as she also behaved herself properly. All that was needed was purity and idealism – the idealism of truth – a great deal of respect, and a genuine longing to exalt that person. And, of course, the grace of God! Here are my exact words:

'I'm even selfish about it. I'm interested in a friendship that never dies. If you behave well with women, a "love" is born which is eternal and cannot be expressed in human language. I have always been infinitely more interested in the tender eyes of my female pupils than in those other aspects that are hunted by beasts of prey. If you really do love them, their feminine intuition tells them so at once. And you can be sure that you can count on their undying affection and friendship. That is something quite sublime. The heart of a pure girl is worth the world. Are all discriminating girls able to sustain such a relationship? Those that I have come across have certainly been able to do so.'

I once related a simple anecdote to Graham about a certain woman friend. The last thing I ever expected of her was to be rewarded. On the first occasion that I had met her after her wedding, two or three months previously, she and her husband had come to collect me and take me out to dinner. At a certain moment, she took me aside and said: 'How well you always behave with me.'

Later, I thought about what she had said, and I understood what she meant. But won't it always be like that? It would be a terrible thing to destroy a friendship that might have been immortal . . . just because one didn't know how to dream a little.

This was an endless subject with us, yet it was one in which Graham scarcely ever intervened. The conversation used to turn into a monologue from me. And it often continued after we had dined in the *paradores*, enlivened by a drop of excellent wine.

'Perhaps only a priest can dream up such nonsense. The ideal girl deserves to be put on a pedestal. That makes her happy. And you will also be fortunate because, without even trying, she will help you to be truly happy yourself. I repeat, no special qualities are required. All you need is to read and experience as much poetry as possible; always study a lot; and pray a little every day. Perhaps it is rather like being a priest with a vocation!'

Graham never interrupted me in my pipe dreams, although I see that in my diaries he once said: 'I have never seen anyone dream in this way. But I am delighted, because I know that your dream has been your life. And it continues to be.'

I once mentioned that many people might take me for a bit of a simpleton; a lost romantic. Graham Greene's steady gaze did not accept this. How wonderfully he sustained me on this path over so many years! Did he not call himself my 'spiritual adviser'?

We were in Tordesillas. The 'Third Man' had just been swimming in the pool at the *parador*. Evidently, he had been very smitten by three pretty girls he had seen there. He talked and joked about them and the conversation became a little 'sexy'. I told him again that for me what was most satisfying and inspiring in a woman was her face, especially her eyes, and her soul. I could see that he did not agree. He tried to make a joke at my expense. He declared that on an average day he scarcely ever saw a girl who he thought was really beautiful. I smiled to myself and added: 'You don't know how to perceive purity. There are masses of marvellous girls.'

I advised him to take a vow of chastity, even if it were for a few months. But he did not seem much inclined to take my advice, for he laughed . . .

●

If the question of his faith obsessed Graham Greene, so too did theology. Theology was nothing more that that same faith 'trying to be understood' – *fides quaerens intellectum*. Before Graham became a

Catholic, he devoted himself to reading theology in order to know what he was going to have to accept. After his conversion, he never stopped reading the subject or thinking about what he had read. He had a need to study his beliefs and his doubts in depth in order to be able to understand a little more. 'Theology is the only form of philosophy which I enjoy reading', he tells us in the epitaph to his play, *Carving a Statue*. And in the Introduction to *Brighton Rock*, he writes: 'In my spare time, I read a good deal of theology – sometimes with fascination, sometimes with repulsion, nearly always with interest'.

Graham did not study any systematic theology, but he was an intuitive theologian. In *The Honorary Consul*, Father Rivas speaks of the 'night-side of God' and the 'day-side of God'. According to Greene's priest, there is a continual evolution with God himself, so that 'with our help' the dark side of God or Christ overcomes the darkness. In this way, the evil in the world will come to an end. And God or Christ will be total light. This is a brief synthesis of Father Rivas' reasoning.

Is there a better way of expressing the doctrine of Christ's mystical body? This was what I told Graham and he was very surprised.

Later, he said in *The Other Man*: 'Well, listen: in *The Honorary Consul* I did suggest this idea, through the guerrilla priest, that God and the devil were actually one and the same person – God had a day-time and a night-time face, but that He evolved as Christ tended to prove, towards His day-time face – absolute goodness – thanks to each positive act of men. I thought I had invented a new theology for my dissident priest, so I was a little disappointed when my friend Father Durán told me that this was perfectly compatible with Catholic doctrine.' Graham Greene is so orthodox that he wishes to invent a 'slightly' heretical doctrine for his guerrilla priest, and he doesn't succeed!

It is quite impossible to study Graham Greene's major works in any depth without a substantial knowledge of theology, both vocational and intuitive. For he was born to live in conflict with his beliefs. There is a world of theology in *The Power and the Glory*, in *A Burnt-Out Case* and in *The Honorary Consul*; in plays like *The Potting Shed* and *The Living Room*; even in a straightforward short story such as 'A Visit to Morin' or 'The Hint of an Explanation'.

We spoke frequently about Hans Küng, most of whose books Graham had read. On 19 December 1979 we were told that this theologian had been condemned by the Church. Graham reflected: 'It is now that Hans Küng must give the greatest proof of his "gentility". Not say a word against the authorities; continue writing, and nothing else.'

But, regretfully, we were obliged to retract this and say: 'This greatness must be left to Rahner, de Lubac or Congar', for in *The Times* that day we read that Hans Küng had defied the Vatican. Graham was reminded of Don Quixote's wise remark: 'You've run into trouble with the Church, friend Sancho.'

Above all, we discussed Newman, one of the men who had most influenced Graham Greene's thought, as well as nineteenth- and twentieth-century thinking. He may well have been the true father of the Second Vatican Council. I have already mentioned Graham and Newman. He liked his novel, *Loss and Gain*, and he admired *The Dream of Gerontius*.

We spent a greater part of one afternoon discussing suicide. We agreed that it may not always be a sin of despair, but rather a sin against hope. Sometimes it comes from depression and weariness, or an incapacity – real or imagined – to bear the burden of life.

Adultery: was it first and foremost a sin against justice, or against purity? It was against both equally.

We compared St Augustine with St Thomas Aquinas. The latter was more academic and systematic. Augustine had genius and was more original, more of a poet.

For a time, Graham was particularly interested in the work of the Belgian theologian, Schillebeeckx, although he did not share his ideas on the Resurrection.

We often discussed moral theology. Graham was unable to comprehend the crucial distinction between mortal and venial sin. Graham thought that for a sin to be considered mortal, it had to be an act done deliberately to offend God. I believe he later came to understand the distinction more clearly.

Graham never stopped laughing, and making me laugh, with his strange tales of Father Heribert Jone, the German moral theologian immortalized in *Monsignor Quixote*. In particular, what he had to say about *coitus interruptus*, which Graham (with the help of Señor Marquez's stratagem) also perpetuated in his novel.

This paragraph should really be subtitled 'theology in bed'. The phrase may strike some as rather suspicious, but this is what happened. I had the devil of a cold. Graham and Aurelio (our 'Third

Man' that year, and my faithful nurse) were making me an efficacious grog. I swallowed it down and, tucked up in bed with my head wrapped up, we were discussing the subject of confession. It appeared that neither of them, at that time, had been to confession for a while. As I sweated out my cold, I tried to insinuate a little catechism into the conversation.

My two friends were anxious to cure me by giving me concoctions and telling me stories. They kept me there, in fits of laughter, until one o'clock in the morning. We had lunched that day in a restaurant called 'Estalagem Muchaxo' in Cascais. Graham had observed a young English woman, and her little daughter, who had picked up some Portuguese man and was trying to make herself understood with the help of a dictionary.

Years later in Antibes, after dinner one evening (19 December 1982) when it was already quite late, Graham walked with me as far as my hotel. But we were unable to say goodbye to each other because we were collapsing with laughter. It was all on account of the moralist, Heribert Jone, and his very curious book. We went on chatting at the door of the hotel and came to the conclusion that moralists must have rather lewd thoughts to write the things they did. I told Graham about another moral theologian who advised readers to kneel when they were studying the Sixth Commandment. This was enough to set Graham laughing all the way back home, while I climbed the stairs to my room hoping I would not meet anyone who might think I had been drinking.

•

Graham always felt a certain attraction towards the priesthood. There is a marvellous gallery of ecclesiastics in his work, some of whom are the principal characters in his novels, while others are secondary figures. 'When the priest is the protagonist,' an American academic wrote, 'the novel invariably turns around this character. When he is not, the priest influences the work proportionately more than his role would seem to merit.'

I do not know of any convert to Catholicism who does not feel a special affection for the priesthood; perhaps because, in the majority of cases, it was a priest who inspired his or her conversion.

I do not believe this was the reason why Graham liked certain priests. Strangely, I do not ever remember us speaking about Father Trollope, the Redemptorist who instructed and baptized him. The fault is mine for never having asked him, for I would have liked to know his opinion of this priest. Rather, since faith and theological problems were continually on Graham Greene's mind, he needed to have as a friend a priest whom he could turn to at any moment.

I have mentioned Father Gervase, to whom Graham dedicated *The Power and the Glory*, and in Graham's view it was his advice that saved the novel from being a disaster. Father Gervase was a Dominican, the brother of Bishop Matthews, an extremely distinguished man and Graham's counsellor on many important matters, particularly when he needed to discuss Cardinal Pizzardo's decision to condemn *The Power and the Glory*. According to Graham, this bishop was both a wise man and a saint.

Graham told me of the pressures he was put under by a great many priests. It sounds absurd, but they turned to him with their own problems of conscience as they would to a spiritual adviser. Graham did not know what to do with the letters he received from priests from all parts of the world.

One of the priests of whom Graham was most fond was the Jesuit, Father Martindale, a man well known throughout London for his wisdom and virtue. When he was old, the Jesuits sent him to another community, away from Farm Street, and used to keep a watch on what he drank, and other trivial things. Graham went to see Father Martindale at least once a month to take him out to dinner, and afterwards, when he brought him back, he always left a bottle or two of whisky hidden among the bookshelves. He used to speak to me about him with great affection.

After Father Martindale's death, Graham had other friendships with priests, some of which had sad memories for him. I shall only mention two of these priests, without giving their names or the Orders to which they belonged.

Father X had spent a long time living in a married state with a girl whom he referred to as 'his friend'. He told Graham all about this affair, but he had no intention of changing this wretched situation. He insisted that Graham should get to know the girl and that he should speak to her about the matter. And so he did. The girl was not a Catholic, but she opened her heart to Graham. She was very upset. She thought it was appalling that a priest should go to bed with her and yet say Mass every day. She was very sad and very confused by the situation . . . .

Graham spoke about this to Father X – who was very well known

– as the girl had asked him to. He told X: 'For God's sake, either marry her and quit the priesthood, or leave her alone.' Unfortunately, there was nothing he was able to do. It was a most hopeless business to start down that road.

The case of the other friend was even more painful for Graham and it affected him very personally. Apart from anything else, I would call it a betrayal. It happened many years ago. Graham had a mistress who was married. The husband did not mind but, at the same time, he had to protect his reputation. Graham and the lady decided not to see each other for three months. Because of this, Graham went to live in Paris, though there were two occasions on which he and his friend deceived the husband and she came over to France. However, a priest, Father Y, got to hear of something and told the woman that she should not trust Graham. He assured her that he had other women friends in Paris. She then wrote to Graham, very upset, and he was completely stunned by her letter.

She was a Catholic. When Graham returned from Indo-China, he told her everything. He arranged a meeting among the three of them and said to Father Y: 'You told A . . . that I had been with a woman before I left for Indo-China. The woman I was with is actually here in this room. You have upset her greatly and you have told her a lie. You must go to confession.'

Later, he told me: 'From that day forth, I kept him at bay.'

When Graham had finished relating this sad story, I told him about something that had happened to me with another priest. A few days before I left the Vincentians to move to the diocese of Astorga, the Father Provincial and another priest came to Orense where I was staying. I had been one of this priest's professors and I had helped him in various ways. Given that he was very young, I reckoned it opportune to tell him about the step I was going to take. We went for a walk on the banks of the River Mino. It was an unforgettable walk! I told him that I wanted to explain my decision to him; that I would always continue to be a priest, and that my life would be much more strict than it had been. I hoped that he would continue to live and work happily as a Vincentian, and that, naturally, everything I had told him was secret and highly confidential.

Before going to bed that night, the Father Provincial summoned me. It was quite clear that he had been told of the entire conversation. He advised me 'to volunteer for the foreign missions so that he could answer for me before the Father General of the Order . . . .'

Graham was dumbfounded. He asked how old this priest had been. 'About twenty-seven,' I replied. We both agreed that he had been old enough to know how to keep such a vital secret.

PART TWO

CHAPTER I

OUR JOURNEYS

GRAHAM AND HIS brother Hugh used to play a strange little game: one of them would mention an unusual, faraway place which he knew, and the other had to respond with another until they discovered a place that the other did not know. I don't remember who the winner usually was, but what is certain is that both brothers were born to be constant travellers.

Deep within Graham, there was some angel or demon constantly urging him to be on the move. I doubt if there is any aspect of Graham Greene's life as a traveller about which he did not have an anecdote to recount.

Graham Greene was allergic to 'official' tourism, with its organized visits and places of artistic interest, its timetables and, of course, its guides. If ever he visited a cathedral – or on the rare occasion he entered a museum – and he heard the voice of some knowledgeable guide, he was strongly tempted to postpone the visit. Where art was concerned, Graham's tourism consisted of walking into a gallery and stopping in front of a particular painting very briefly to admire and consider it on its own merits. We once visited the Prado where he only wanted to see El Greco, his favourite painter. Then we went to Toledo. He didn't care for Goya. However, when we walked past the Goyas, something unprecedented happened: Graham could not stop looking at that line of straight muskets, vomiting death and other graphic paintings by Goya. As we left the museum, he said to me very positively: 'You have converted me to Goya.'

Who knows the reasons why Graham decided to set out on a journey? On occasions, we might visit particular places purely for the sake of a new experience.

'A novel could come out of experience like this,' he once told me on the way to Vigo. 'The first sentence of the novel might be this: "I never knew or met him, but he was dead".'

Herein lay the subconscious aim of all his journeys, I think.

Subconscious, because Graham never travelled in search of any particular experience. That particular 'something' just seemed to happen to him along the way.

I believe Graham suffered somewhat from claustrophobia. On the first or second of our picnics, before I knew his tastes and his little habits, we were staying at the hostel of San Marcos de Leon, near San Isidoro with its paintings and artistic treasures, and we decided to tag on to a group of tourists who were going to visit that gem of a place. The group was enormous, the heat was stifling, and the guide was using a loudspeaker in order to make himself heard. All of a sudden, Graham said to me in a rather unsteady voice:

'Let's go, let's go . . . Let's get out of here.'

The people around us could hear perfectly well that he was saying something to me in English. I had to ask for the door to be opened. They obliged, but I felt sure that if we could not manage to get away something serious would happen to Graham. I was quite frightened.

•

Our trips through Spain and Portugal had nothing to do with tourism. They were something entirely different. We described them as 'picnics': delightful jaunts in which we took our food with us and ate it in the fresh air of the countryside. Graham christened these excursions 'picnics' from the very first day.

We would decide beforehand on the route we would take from Barajas airport. Galicia and Sintra (when our good friend Maria Newall was alive) were places we had to visit. Rooms would be reserved at *paradores* for the first two nights of our 'picnic'. Everything else would be arranged as we went along, up until the time we eventually returned to the same two *paradores* where we were expected at the end of each journey.

It is incredible how little is required for two people to travel through the country in this way. Our crockery was absolutely basic and we would buy our food anywhere we could. We always set off with a few bottles of something drinkable, some biscuits, a thermos flask for ice, paper napkins, small and medium-sized glasses, knives and forks, and that was it. The daily newspapers served as our tablecloth.

I had only four things to pack: my washbag, some basic crockery, the box containing what I needed to say Mass, and the camera.

What was essential for our picnics was that they should take place under the shadow of some trees, by a stream, and not far from the road.

Once we were on the road, we had the feeling that we had forgotten all the inevitable pressures that so sap the freedom of modern man. The soft, caressing July breeze floating through the car windows reminded us time and again of Anna-Louise's words in *Dr Fischer of Geneva*: We are free, free. Say it aloud after me. Free.'

For Graham, those picnics were something quite incomparable, especially in the period before the fateful war against the mafia. He felt free and full of humour, and he always had a joke on the tip of his tongue. I had the impression that he had lost all his inbred sorrows; his cares seemed to have vanished. Peace seemed to return to him. Even faith became a much more straightforward matter!

Between eleven and twelve o'clock we would drink a small glass of Señor Antonio de las Regadas' white wine, with a little ice, and a few biscuits. It was usually very hot. Our picnic would last until two o'clock. For our joy to be unconfined, the place was very important; good shade and cool water were essential.

After lunch, we would sometimes take a short siesta. Our conversations, interrupted by a nap, became more like confessions and for a few moments, we were freed from all our inhibitions. No secrets remained.

Those picnics, and our after-dinner conversations at his home in Antibes, are among the most unforgettable moments I spent with Graham Greene.

We were usually expected at the *paradores* at between six and seven o'clock in the evening. Our routine was to take a shower, followed by 'whisky time', conversation over dinner and, quite often, a further chat in our bedrooms before going to sleep.

●

Graham was always delighted by Spain's national *paradores* and they contributed a great deal to the enjoyment of our journeys together. According to Graham, in no other country did one find anything quite like this type of hotel. Their cleanliness, simplicity and the family ambience made him feel entirely at home there. There were often rooms available, even in July and August, but we were advised that they should ideally be booked a long time ahead, especially in our case, since we required three separate rooms.

Thereafter, we always tried to plan our next holiday with sufficient time to reserve rooms in the *paradores*. Once we had decided on our destination, it would be my job to make the reservations. I always booked in my name for the sake of discretion, but the management always knew perfectly well who we were. I usually secured my three rooms without any difficulty whatsoever.

Graham always appreciated the absolute privacy of the *paradores*. There were only three occasions that the press discovered us, and then it was always the fault of those whose job it was to keep our whereabouts secret.

Quite frequently, the *paradores* were situated exactly on our routes, which is why we visited them so many times. Those at Puebla de Sanabria, Oropesa and Tordillas were the ones we knew best. Then there were those at Siguenza and Salamanca, Soria and Segovia, Guadalupe, Merida and Cambados. I must not forget the Mindanao Hotel in Madrid, and the Canciller Ayala in Vitoria, which I shall mention again later; or the Hotel Don Cesar on the road from Burgos to Vitoria, and so many others. I can never be sufficiently grateful for the countless charming gestures Graham, our 'Third Man' and I received in these places over so many years.

•

My camera was a great trial for Graham Greene, especially during our first picnics together. I did not know that Graham was absolutely allergic to being photographed, and yet I had set out on holiday with two ideas in my head: to try to remember everything Graham said by heart, and to take photographs of him from every angle. Poor Graham!

Many years ago I had bought a good camera, but I had only ever used it once. Some mechanism inside had been damaged and the camera only worked once in every ten occasions.

On our first journey, we had arrived at Salamanca and I was keen to take photographs of Graham in every one of the squares of that wonderful city. He had been in a very good mood until then, for he fell in love with Salamanca from the very first moment. But I was asking too much, even though he was letting me have my way; he did not yet have the confidence to tell me to go to hell. Because I did not understand how my camera operated, Graham was obliged to wait for ages for every snapshot to be taken. Eventually, I had my camera repaired, but even then we still could not hear the 'click'. It is one thing to write about this, and quite another to think of the misery I must have put Graham through that day. Years later, when we returned to the rose-coloured city, the camera really was working properly, but I could only recall the awfulness of that first picnic. How did the dear man's patience not crack?

Graham returned to Antibes after a fortnight full of adventures. A little while later, I sent him an album with all the snaps my broken camera had produced. On his return from Anacapri, he wrote me a letter which ended:

'The photographs in the album amused me a lot. It was a complete record of the drinks we took. Almost every photo contained glasses. I hope you are keeping up your new reputation as a whisky priest.'

Next summer we travelled from 13 July until the end of the month. Once we were in the car at Barajas and on the way to Portugal, Graham turned round to tell me that he assumed I had not forgotten the camera. He was happy, and that question was definitely a licence for me to continue with my mania for taking pictures. He seemed pleased at my newly-acquired speed and to see that I no longer needed to be constantly calling in at camera shops. I sent him the familiar album containing the results. His response was encouraging:

> Dear Leopoldo, Thank you a thousand times for the beautiful album of the photographs which arrived today. They are a better lot than last year's I think, and just as much drinking. Sad that we haven't got Maria among them.

It was evident that Graham had formed the notion that my camera was one of the crosses God had sent him in this life, so he had better make a virtue of necessity!

'Watch the photographer!' Graham would say.

The following anecdote was told me by Robert Laszlo, a Hungarian writer and television producer who was a friend of Greene's. Later, Greene confirmed it himself. The two men were in a restaurant in Budapest. A newly married couple came in, and among those accompanying them was the man who took photographs at the wedding. When he set eyes on him, Graham said simply: 'Watch the photographer!'

Later, he was informed that the photographer had been the new wife's former lover.

This anecdote helped me greatly in my battles as an amateur photographer. In order to try to make Graham smile a little, and to prepare him for a new assault from my machine, I would simply call out: 'Watch the photographer!'

It used to bring good results.

Chapter II

THE FIRST AND SECOND HOLIDAYS

As i have mentioned, I kept a diary and notebook throughout each of our 'picnics' through Spain and Portugal. What follows are random extracts which I recorded during the course of those first two trips together.

17 July 1976. From Barajas we drove to the Hotel Don Quijote which certainly made a charming impression on us. It is a pity that oasis in the countryside is now no longer a hotel. It was five minutes away from my house, and it was there that Graham stayed during the first three or four years he came to Spain.

We got off to a good start. At our first dinner in that hotel, there was a North American family at the table next to us – a married couple, another woman, a boy and a girl. The boy, who was about eight or nine years old, reigned supreme over the other four. He had his mother and father dancing in the palm of his hand. Graham had a marvellous time over dinner, observing this little whippersnapper's total command of the situation:

'She is the mother and the other woman is the aunt; they must be sisters, they look very much alike. The aunt encourages the child by laughing at everything he does. The mother is over-ruled . . .', whispered Graham.

After dinner, we went up to Greene's room. On the bedside table was a piece of machinery looking like a small rectangular box. Greene explained to me: 'By introducing a twenty-five peseta coin, the bed begins to move and vibrate gently. It is like a massage which soothes you and helps you to sleep.'

We bade each other goodnight. The following day, when I asked Graham how he had slept, he replied cheerfully:

'Very peacefully. That machine was broken and with a single coin the bed kept rocking away for most of the night.'

Well might Graham say: 'Strange things happen to me in hotel rooms.'

We spent the first day in Madrid. Graham rested, and we chatted calmly about certain urgent and private matters. We ate lunch and dinner at the Hotel Don Quijote. When we went down to the dining-room, we saw there was a wedding feast going on, and, naturally, the newly wedded couple were sitting at the head of the table. There was the usual air of merriment. When we had finished lunch, Graham noticed how merry all those who had been present at the wedding were. Walking towards the door, he said to me:

'The newly married couple have gone already. Everything ends as it always does. It seems that the banquet was going on too long for them. They were consulting timetables for flights to wherever they were spending their honeymoon.'

We set off early for Salamanca, passing by the Valle de los Caidos first. Graham enjoyed himself greatly in Spain and, from the beginning, he liked the country very much; just as I liked England. However, he thoroughly disliked the Valle de los Caidos, or 'The Valley of the Dead' as he called it, and as a result he felt a complete antipathy for this entire memorial. He wrote a cruel paragraph about the basilica there, which I shall mention later. The grandiose setting of the Valle de los Caidos and Graham Greene's taste for simplicity simply could not be reconciled.

I am convinced that he never understood the significance of this building, nor the spirit in which it was built. As a result, he disliked everything about it. For Greene, 'The Valley of the Fallen' (as he also called it) resembled 'a huge Ancient Egyptian tomb in very bad taste'. As we have seen, Graham never understood Franco's political and spiritual ideology.

19 July 1976. We are in Salamanca. It is the first time Graham has visited the city. In the years ahead we would often come back to see it. It is true to say that Salamanca cast a spell over Graham from the very first moment. [He often said that it was the most beautiful of all the cities he had ever seen.]

It was Unamuno's tomb that had brought us to Salamanca. Greene had a deep affection for this writer and suspected that he had been influenced by him, particularly his *Sentimiento Tragico de la Vida*. Graham and Unamuno had much in common: their rebellious natures, and their constant struggle with their beliefs.

The cemetery at Salamanca. At the entrance we ask for Unamuno's grave.

'Unamuno?' replies the person in charge of the cemetery, 'Unamuno is number 340.'

Graham Greene had understood what was said. Nevertheless, he asked: 'What did that man say?'

'He says Unamuno is number 340.'

He turned pale at this. We had been talking about Churchill's grave in a small country cemetery, where his name was engraved on a simple tombstone. Graham Greene did not expect a mausoleum to have been erected to Miguel de Unamuno – he would certainly have disliked that – but for Unamuno to be known by a number . . . First footpath to the left, and down there at the end, inside the wall, is tombstone number 340 with its famous epitaph:

> *Eternal Father, lay me in your bosom,*
> *that dwelling-place of mystery . . .*

We stood by the grave for about a quarter of an hour, thinking or praying. As we left the cemetery, Graham said decisively: 'You should write an article entitled "In Search of Number 340".'

'This article must be written by you,' I replied, 'so that everyone will know what happened in this cemetery today.'

The experience became fixed in his memory and we often spoke about it. At the end of our trip, Graham asked me to translate and write down the whole of the epitaph in English for him. He later wrote several marvellous lines for me, contrasting the tombs in the Valle de los Caidos with Unamuno's resting-place. By then he could not relax until he had finished writing his novel, *Monsignor Quixote*.

Afterwards, Graham Greene wanted to take his time inspecting everything connected with Unamuno in Salamanca: the house where he had lived and the statue that stands in front of it which he liked very much. It seemed to him to convey all Unamuno's rebelliousness. We took a number of snapshots and it was the first occasion that I thought Greene seemed reasonably happy to be photographed.

Later, we visited the University and Unamuno's classroom. It was not possible to take any photographs here, for Graham felt it would show a lack of respect to his memory.

We passed the façade of the Universidád Literária, the statue of Friar Luís and the classroom in which he taught. Graham would always remember the children playing by the side of the statue who were quite ready to tell us all they knew about the frog sculpted into the front wall. These children and their 'frog' gave Graham much pleasure. The friar's famous remark 'As we were saying yesterday' after five years of imprisonment by the Inquisition immediately gave Graham an insight into the greatness of the man. All these things made their mark on him.

•

We travelled on to Orense and its celebrated 'San Miguel' restaurant. We arrived too late, so we ate our banquet at four o'clock in the afternoon.

We went to see Osera for the first time. We were only there for a couple of hours, but it was enough for Graham to be enchanted by the stark simplicity of the magnificent Cistercian monastery. He wrote in the visitor's book:

> *Thank you very much for these moments of peace and silence.*
> *Please pray for me. Graham Greene.*

[We returned every year to this monastery.]

We set off again in the direction of Marin where the Vincentian fathers were expecting us for dinner. The road from Osera had been very bad and it was impossible for us to reach Marin before midnight. It was growing cold, and night was falling over the Alto del Parano. We decided to eat the little we had left. There was a small piece of chorizo, which we divided in three as God asks us to do, biscuits and bread, as well as Señor Antonio de las Regadas' familiar unlabelled bottles. The wine revived us somewhat and we continued our journey towards Marin.

It was one o'clock in the morning when we arrived at the Colegio de San Narciso. We had not been able to warn them of our late arrival since we had not been able to find a public telephone. The road had been wretched, and we had reckoned without the pack of Alsatians that hurled themselves against our car, ready to finish us off the moment we arrived. It was impossible to get out of the car to ring the bell. The fathers, thank goodness, had all gone to bed, assuming we would not arrive. It was just as well that the diabolical noise of the dogs woke up one of the priests and Father Leal came down to open the door to us. He locked up the dogs for the time being and we were able to leave the car. If only they had been locked up for the entire night. They continued their infernal barking until dawn!

I rose very early but Graham had been up already. He had not slept a wink that night.

'If you agree,' he murmured in my ear, 'I think we should set off after breakfast to Santiago. I did not sleep at all because of the dogs barking.'

Our plan had been to spend the day with the community in Marin.

Graham went on: 'We should say that we have to leave now because our time is very short . . . Of course, we are very sorry not to be able to spend the day here with the Fathers, looking at these views over the sea.'

23 July 1976. On our way once more, towards Santiago de Compostela. It is the eve of the Feast of St James, the patronal saint. Before anything else, we wanted to see the cathedral, to say the odd prayer and have a look at the Portico de la Gloria. We knelt down briefly, but it was impossible to say even one Hail Mary. The cathedral was crowded with visitors who had come for the festival and the noise was simply ghastly. It was like a market-place. Although the noise was moderate now, at around three o'clock in the afternoon, the canons would start 'to fire gunshots from the choir' to every liturgical hour. I was perspiring with panic and heat, while Graham was distressed by these noisy scenes inside a church. He turned to me and whispered: 'It's best that we go now, even though we'll miss the indulgences.'

We left and walked around the old streets, then we continued our journey towards La Coruña.

There are days when one's lucky star never shines. We had asked the Vincentian fathers to book rooms for us in a hotel, but on our arrival we were told that it had been impossible to find a single room in any hotel. At that season, and during the festival, it was essential to book in advance. There were two guesthouses which could put us up. They were very ordinary, we were told, but we stayed there nonetheless.

Before setting out to Lugo, we visited the San Carlos gardens where the British general, Sir John Moore, is buried. Graham was particularly interested to see this quiet spot, for General Moore was a distant ancestor of his. Greene experienced a wonderful sense of peace in the silence and poetry of that tomb. He knew by heart Charles Wolfe's poem which was engraved on a bronze plaque in the wall. In a low, steady voice he recited a line or two:

Not a drum was heard, not a funeral note . . .

I translated the first lines of Rosalia's poem for him, which was
also engraved on the other side of the wall:

> *Cuan lonxe, canto das escuras niebras*
> *Dos verdes pinos, das ferventes olas,*
> *que o nacer viron! . . .' 'Cuan lejos, cuanto de las oscuras*
>   *nieblas,*
> *de los verdes pinos, de las hirvientes olas,*
> *que le vieron nacer! . . .*

We left the cemetery garden in silence and set off through Galicia.
We reached Lugo. None of us knew the town. We needed a restaurant. We asked a very fat local policeman. He mentioned one in
particular, but so as to have a choice, we asked another local official,
this time a very thin one. Each of the places recommended were
quite far apart. Graham made the decision: 'Let's go to the one the
fat man suggested. There can be no doubt he knows where to eat
well.'

•

We crossed Asturias, stopping only in a small town for the night.
We were soon in Vitoria, the Basque town Graham really had come
to know and love for its simplicity and beauty over twenty-three
years.

The problem was to find lodgings. We had no hotel reservation
and it was halfway through July. After asking in a number of places
and not finding a single room, we arrived at the Hotel Canciller
Ayala. I went to the reception desk and the girl told me the truth:
there were no rooms available. There were three suites, but she had
orders never to fill every room in case some important person arrived
and might find themselves in an awkward situation. She asked me
how many we were. I told her we were three. I explained that for
the moment I could not explain exactly who we were but if she would
agree to let us have the rooms I would come down shortly and clarify
everything. She trusted me. Later, I came down with three passports
and told her in secrecy that one of my companions was Graham
Greene and that we were travelling incognito so as to avoid publicity.
The girl could not believe her ears and was extremely excited because

she was an avid reader of Graham's work and had a number of his
books in English. Blushing a little, she asked me whether he might
sign one of his books that she had at home. I told her to bring some
round the next day.

When I returned to our rooms, I told Graham what had happened.
He burst out laughing. Of course he would sign her books. Before
we left the following day, he inscribed all the books the girl had
brought. In one of them, he wrote: 'For X [how sorry I am to have
lost the note of her name!] who spoke English so well, and who
looked after us so attentively. With best wishes. Graham Greene'.
He spent a few minutes talking to her, shook hands, and we set off
for San Sebastián.

One passing detail. We were dining at the hotel. When we looked
at the menu, our attention was drawn to 'chicken in a basket'. We
ordered it. It was roast or fried chicken, but it was served in a small
wicker basket, rather like those sometimes used for bread. We
laughed with relief, and embarked upon the chicken, washed down
with some good wine from the Rioja Alavesa. It reminded me of the
story I told my friends of how, when I was in London and making
my first steps in English, I asked for the menu in a restaurant and
read the word 'vermicelli'. I did not know what it was, but I asked
for it just so as to learn the word. What should be my surprise when
I saw appear before me an enormous plate of noodles. I felt as if I
had eaten enough noodles during my time in Rome to last a lifetime.
However, I did not have enough money for anything else and I just
had to confront the noodles.

Graham had very bad memories of San Sebastián. He thoroughly
disliked beaches in summer, and when we visited La Concha, there
was a terrible accumulation of human flesh. We did not stay a minute.
We caught a taxi. I told the driver what we were looking for and we
were dropped outside the Restaurante Arzac. I spoke briefly to the
owner and he served us personally. The man was extraordinarily
friendly and unaffected, the very embodiment of the spirit of Basque
hospitality, and any passer-by should certainly sample the 'Cogote
de Merluza' as prepared by Juan Ma. Arzac Arratibel.

•

This was the only journey we ever made to the Basque Country and
it was many years ago. Thirteen or fourteen years later, a reporter
on a provincial newspaper described it this way: 'The novelist,

Graham Green [sic], a likely candidate for the Nobel Prize, has recently made a journey through the Basque Country. Accompanied by a priest close to ETA (ETA *Euskadi Ta Askatasuna*, the Basque Liberation Movement), he travelled through Basque villages, towns and cities. It is thought he may make use of the experience in a future book.' I have no comment. In an interview given to El Pais, Graham refuted the story with a few cutting remarks.

●

28 July 1976. We set off in the direction of Madrid, but we stopped for one night on the way at the Hotel Residencia D. Cesar at Miranda de Ebro. We were very well looked after and the dinner was excellent. We chatted until the early hours, mainly discussing *The Quiet American*. The last thing Graham expected when he went to Indo-China was that he would write a novel about it. He told me at length about his relationship with the leader of the French forces, De Lattre de Tassigny, who was very courteous, even affectionate, to Graham to begin with. He put a small plane at his service, invited him to dine with him and even conferred a decoration on him. This was still during his days of glory.

But everything had changed when Graham returned to Vietnam a few months later. It was 1951. The General had lost his son in an ambush at Phat Diem. The colonels were tired of hearing him bemoan his enormous sacrifice. Countless French families had under-gone the same suffering without the consolation of seeing their sons taken back to be buried in France.

By that time, De Lattre was something of a sick man, both mentally and physically. Quite illogically, he associated the death of his son with Graham's visit to Phat Diem, and even with the fact that Graham Greene and Trevor Wilson, the British Consul, were Catholics. In his confused mind, he made Greene and Wilson responsible for this misfortune. Trevor Wilson, who was decorated for his services to France during the war, was expelled from Indo-China. 'This expulsion meant that France lost a great friend and the Foreign Office a fine consul,' said Graham.

●

Things did not stop here. Greene felt that he was being watched by the French Security Services assigned to Hanoi. One particular person, who Graham christened Monsieur Dupont, was given the task of watching him. He also spied on Wilson who had been allowed to return to Vietnam for a few days. The poor devil searched every bookshop daily looking for copies of Graham Greene's books so that he might ask for them to be inscribed. When Graham and Trevor discovered what the wretched fellow was really after, they decided to play a practical joke on Monsieur Dupont. They arranged a rendez-vous in a café and made Monsieur Dupont drink more than he could take. The man returned home in a deplorable state. Problems at home worsened because his wife could not believe that an excess of alcohol had been caused by official duties. Graham felt a certain remorse when he told me this. 'We were rather cruel to him', he said. Out of politeness, Monsieur Dupont had to drink as many glasses as his two suspects, and these were not single measures. To make matters worse, Graham Greene and Trevor Wilson had agreed that during these meetings, in order to spend more time drinking, Graham would recount in detail everything that he had done – and what he had not done – during that day . . . Poor Monsieur Dupont! On a certain occasion, the wretched policeman was accompanying Trevor Wilson somewhere. Seeing a sign for Chinese baths, Wilson stopped Monsieur Dupont's official car and announced that he wanted to take a Chinese bath, and so the officer was obliged to do the same in the next-door compartment. Unfortunately for Dupont, the price of the bath brought with it a deep massage. Monsieur Dupont's heart was not strong enough to cope with such an intimate massage, and he fainted. He had to be revived with a strong dose of whisky, something the poor man was not used to. The following morning, he was still suffering from the effects of the whisky, and as an antidote, he was made to swallow some other drink he had never had before, which made him feel even worse. Every day some new trick was played on the poor devil, and all because de Lattre was not in his right mind. Still worse, after Trevor Wilson had left, Monsieur Dupont began to feel a certain paternal responsibility towards Graham; on seeing him smoke a pipe of opium, he begged him, on that night at least, to go home to bed without moving on to further diversions . . .

Graham was invited to the farewell dinner De Lattre gave for his colonels before he returned home to France to die. The General told them that Vietnam would always be French; that he was going away just for a few days and that he would return. As a pledge of his word of honour, he was leaving his wife behind with them. But he was never to return for he died shortly afterwards in Paris.

It was by then early in the morning. In spite of this, Graham asked the General if he might speak with him for a few minutes. He wanted to make it quite clear that he was not an agent of the British Secret Service. He had simply been sent to Vietnam by *Life* magazine who were paying him $5,000 for two or three articles. It looked as if the whole matter was cleared up.

On his death, De Lattre was replaced by General Salan with whom Graham got on very well. They sometimes smoked opium together and the General taught Graham some of the finer points about the art of inhaling. But neither of them was addicted to these pipes. They became friends and later there was some correspondence between them.

. . . I don't know what time it was when Graham eventually said: 'Leopoldo, time to go to bed.'

It was certainly very late but it was a pity to have to go to bed. Years later, Graham would write about some of these things in *Ways of Escape*, and before that in his introduction to *A Spy's Bedside Book*. But that night, in the Hotel Residencia D. Cesar, we had a marvellous time, what with his stories and the occasional sip of our 'Tonico Carino'.

•

30 July 1976. We left Madrid on the road for Avila. We stopped on the way for the ritual glass of Señor Antonio's white wine and some Spanish biscuits, and we then spent the day in Avila, staying in the Palacio Valderrabanos-Gran Hotel.

We visited the Convent of the Incarnation, where a relic of the right-hand index finger of St Teresa is preserved; the finger with which she wrote her wonderful books. Graham admired St Teresa. To him, her many visions seemed to have lent her a sublimity, a certain 'sweetness' and we spent some time discussing what it was we meant by this term. We agreed that in her poems, St Teresa combined this essence of sweetness with the essence of fortitude. Her visions and her informal conversations with God 'in a bewildered manner' made her the great mystical saint; her plain-spoken style of praying, over so many years, had made her a great ascetic and conferred a shining vigour on her. It seemed to us that the spirit of the saint was responsible for the atmosphere of devotion, as well as the sense of inner peace and simplicity that one experiences in Avila. St Teresa's influence in Avila is something palpable. Nevertheless,

Graham preferred St John of the Cross, whose poetry he knew and could recite. We also visited the Convent of St Joseph and other places associated with the great Spanish saint, as well as San Vicente and the Cathedral.

At lunch, Graham spoke of Robert Scott, a friend of his from Oxford days, who fell in love with a beautiful barmaid from 'The Lamb and Flag' public house. Students were delighted when they managed to obtain a look or a word from her, but Robert Scott, who was older than Graham and his friends, and smoked a pipe, intended to procure something rather more substantial from the girl whom the students called Nefertiti on account of her rare beauty. Apparently, Robert Scott managed to persuade her to join him on a punt on the river, and there he read her his translations of Ronsard. One day, Robert Scott called on Graham to ask his advice. Nefertiti had threatened to write to the Dean of Balliol complaining about his behaviour. Graham was worried on his friend's behalf because the Dean was evidently not a man to joke about anything to do with sexual matters. Robert Scott was anxious too, but he was also angry.

'I'm going to invite her to tea,' he said 'and just as she is walking up the staircase I'll throw a glass of water over her from the top of the landing.'

Graham tried to dissuade him, thinking it would only make matters worse. But when Scott saw Graham some time later, he assured him: 'It was effective.'

'What was?' asked Graham.

'The glass of water.'

Apparently, the girl did not complain to the Dean after all. Years later, when *Ways of Escape* – where the story is told much more elaborately and amusingly – was published, I read Graham's account. Robert Scott was then High Commissioner in Nairobi, where Graham met him again many years later, and where he also came to know Maria Newall, the marvellous woman we used to visit regularly in Sintra. When Graham asked Robert what he had done to Nefertiti that she should threaten to go and tell the Dean, Robert replied: 'Nothing.'

'Perhaps that was the very reason she wanted to get you into trouble,' Graham suggested.

One day, when Graham went to call on Robert Scott at his residence, he found him in bed, propped up with pillows and fondling his pipe nervously. He had slipped on the soap dish in his bath, the dish had broken and Scott had fallen over. He called for help, but when his 'boy' saw the blood he thought it had something to do with the Mau-Mau and ran away. Scott managed to get to the telephone and call the doctor who, when he arrived, gave him twelve stitches by the light of an oil lamp because the electricity had been cut off.

15 July 1977 We were in Salamanca once again. Graham thought that neither Oxford nor Cambridge could compare with the city. He was speaking about Oxford as it was when he was a student there; now it was semi-industrialized. I told him that during the sixteenth century more serious theology had probably been written here than in the rest of the world put together.

We spent seven hours visiting the places we had most enjoyed the previous summer: Unamuno's grave and the statue of him looking angry and pensive that stands in front of house where he had lived. Here, we took photographs again, but this time with Graham's agreement and approval. We returned to the Universidád Literária, the Irish College, and to San Esteban where we saw the confessional box used by St Teresa and Father Gracian, and the theologians' cemetery. The cloisters of San Esteban contain medallions to some of the great classical masters, and at the entrance to the convent is a statue to Father Vitoria, the pioneer of the International Law.

All this moved Graham deeply; he became even more withdrawn than he sometimes was. He went round these places in virtual silence, lost in thought, and always speaking in a low voice. I told him that Unamuno used to come down to the Convent of San Esteban in order to talk to the friars because he knew they were interested in intellectual matters. And I added that Unamuno used sometimes to go for a walk outside the convent, meditating or daydreaming. Graham told me that he was rereading Unamuno's *Vida de Don Quijote y Sancho*, and he was intrigued to know whether, as Unamuno said, Cervantes had taken his inspiration from Don Quijote Caballero, at San Ignacio.

It was as impossible to take a photograph of Graham Greene at Unamuno's classroom this year as it had been the year before. I never tried to insist on this again for I knew that as far as Graham was concerned, 'it would be inappropriate'.

We ate at the little 'Valencia' restaurant, just off the Plaza Mayor. It was one we always chose when we came to Salamanca. On one occasion, Graham was convinced that the man sitting beside us was a secret agent; from the look on his face, there could be no doubt about this. During the summer, the restaurant put tables outside in a courtyard. There was a simplicity about the place which Graham found very appealing. At about the time *Monsignor Quixote* was published, our 'Third Man' went back to the restaurant and was told that Señor Graham had made a mistake in his novel because he had situated the 'Valencia' in Valladolid. Our friend explained some of the liberties that the novelist's art permits.

We dined and slept that night in the *parador* at Salamanca. At dinner, Graham told us about the pretty girl, wearing a white hat, who had been sitting behind him in the plane. She was reading a book and Graham was keen to find out, without being seen, what it was she was reading. He was interested in her literary taste, as well as her beauty, but from his position it was impossible to do either.

He was reminded of this by seeing a newly wed couple in the bar of the *parador*. The girl also wore a white hat and my companions both found her very attractive. I promised myself not to pay attention to recently married women.

Graham and Octavio – the 'Third Man' – discussed the political situation in Nicaragua. Graham criticized Cardinal Obando strongly, as well as the Pope for having made him a cardinal. Octavio could not see Graham's point of view. Perhaps the Pope had made Obando a cardinal, he suggested, as a reward for defending the Church and freedom against a Communist government. Neither Octavio nor I thought that the Church was free in Nicaragua. Graham had been there on various occasions but he had never lived there for very long. It may be that what he saw had been carefully prepared beforehand. Graham was highly intelligent, but he refused to accept that Somoza's regime was anything other than an abomination, and it did not occur to him that the Communists were adept at lying. Very few politicians had realized this.

16 July 1976 The cathedral at Leon was illuminated by the sun pouring in through its incomparable stained-glass windows. One has the sensation of floating in another world there, and for Graham Greene it was an unforgettable sight. We spent about an hour imbibing that indefinable atmosphere of spiritual peace. I had thought it would be impossible for Graham to spend so long in a building without feeling claustrophobic, but these were two different worlds. We knelt down for a few moments in the very same place where Alec

Guinness, in the part of Monsignor Quixote, knelt when a scene was filmed there.

In Villafranca del Bierzo, the Vincentian Fathers entertained us royally. We arrived in mid-afternoon and we were taken to Corullon to see the marvellous views over the river. After dinner, we went to the cellar where we were treated to some excellent wines made by Father Perez Forneiro, one of the most devout and friendly men I have ever known. A true Benedictine and Cistercian, he has spent his life making this cellar the principal regional supplier of wines used at Mass. But he also made table wines and had only once made a bad one: a rosé of about forty years old which he kept there as a relic. He offered us the best wines he had from his enormous and beautifully laid-out cellar. If only his treasured forty-year-old wine had not failed him that evening. We tasted a little of it. I am no expert, but Graham was, and he thanked God that no more remained in the bottle for any future distinguished guests. Our sojourn at the farm belonging to the Vincentian fathers was one of the most enjoyable among all the places we visited in those years of pilgrimage. How often Graham reminded me of the unforgettable fathers at Villafranca. 'One really felt among old friends and at home there,' he would say.

On the way to Orense, we stopped for a while by the shores of Lake Carrucedo. This lake and the Templars of Castillo de Cornatel are celebrated in *El Señor de Membibre*, the greatest of Spanish historical novels. I told Graham that the medieval order of Knights Templar, like the Cistercians, had also been founded by St Bernard. The monastery at Carrucedo is now being restored; it is a beautiful spot, full of poetry. We drank a glass of Ribeiro wine with our biscuits, and we took the photographs appropriate to such a perfect place. They came out very badly.

17 July 1977 When we arrived at the 'San Miguel' restaurant in Orense, we were very hungry and thirsty. Julio and Carmucha brought us both food and drink and looked after us marvellously. Graham wrote in the visitors' book: 'The very essence of Spain. The University of Salamanca; the stained-glass in León cathedral; and your hospitality this year and last. Graham Greene.'

On the road to Osera, not far from Carballino, there is a chalet by the side of the road, which Graham and the 'Third Man' rather liked. I told him various things about the owner who is a bachelor and had made his money in Mexico.

'He must be homosexual,' Graham joked.

'I've never heard that he likes making trips to Cadiz,' I replied.

Graham told us that when he bought his house in Anacapri, the town was a haunt of homosexuals, though it no longer had the reputation it once had.

We reached the monastery at Osera at about eight o'clock in the evening. Graham loved the silence of this place, as well as the building itself. The atmosphere of prayer and peace seemed to soothe his soul.

•

18 July 1977 From Osera we continued to Sintra. The view from the top of Mt Tecla, on the border between Spain and Portugal, is one of our favourites. Because it lay on our route, we often went there and some of our best photographs were taken here.

Before we reached Braga, the road went through a pine grove and there we came across three or four young girls who were singing a *fado* as they rode up and down on their bicycles. It was sung beautifully and we all loved its melancholy tone.

In Oporto, we spent the night at a convent of the Holy Ghost Fathers where I knew the Superior, Father Rego. They were infinitely kind, but a chiming clock murdered Graham's sleep as cruelly as it had Lady Macbeth's. We were a sorry couple indeed when we had not slept! However, sleep returned to us at the Hotel Pedro in Coimbra and we were as fresh as two roses when we got out of bed the next morning. I have been as bad a sleeper as Graham since the time I lived in Rome. Graham quoted from memory the hymn to sleep in *Macbeth*:

> *The death of each day's life, sore labour's bath,*
> *Balm of hurt minds, great Nature's second course,*
> *Chief nourisher in life's feast.*

How many times we both longed for a good night's sleep!

Since I mention them in the first part of this book, I must omit details of our continuous conversations. We take a short rest. Today Graham tells me how catarrh can be cured with aspirin and gin. He also tells me how to make bread and milk, the only dish he knows how to prepare. The bread must consist of dough alone, he explains. Crusts ruin it. Next, we discuss good taste; not long ago we were

staying in a house with horrible paintings and rather nouveau riche
wallpaper. We did not enjoy ourselves.

We arrived at Sintra. Maria Newall in her wheel-chair reminds
me of the Duke of Alba who, from his sedan-chair, used to issue
orders that were carried out to perfection. She is over eighty, but
she makes up her face each morning in exactly the same way she
did on the morning of her wedding day. She is an exceptional
woman who combines intelligence with beauty, and she is almost six
feet tall. Her house is like a florist's shop and there are books everywhere. Maria Newall has two maids who are models of efficiency
and obedience. I imagine it needs some patience to be at the
'generala's' every call and command, but she is kindly and maternal
to these two women who are like daughters to her. Maria Newall
is as fervent a Catholic and believer as the Pope himself or an
Ursuline nun.

Now I don't know whether Maria, Graham and the 'Third Man'
had all agreed to make fun of their priest friend, or if what I am
about to recount happened entirely by chance. I am inclined to the
former view. Graham announced that he sometimes doubted whether
men have rational souls. He even mentioned the Council of Costanza
which discussed subjects such as this. I looked at him wide-eyed. . . .
Quite extraordinary things were being alleged and muddled up for
no good reason, and Graham, and then the other two, kept making
dogmatic and totally unsubstantiated pronouncements. At first, I tried
to reply with a certain degree of seriousness and composure, but the
chatter got worse. I began to lose my patience. Suddenly, I came to
realize that they were, in fact, pulling my leg. The three of them
burst into peals of laughter, and all I could do was to laugh with
them – and, a little, at myself.

It was very late. Graham and I went outside for our rooms were on
the far side of the garden. On our way to bed, we noticed a black cat
with three kittens. When the kittens saw us, they ran to their mother,
but she merely glared at us suspiciously and walked slowly and mistrust-
fully away. Next morning, Graham told me that he had had an unusual
dream in which a huge cat had scratched and bitten him.

•

We were going to spend the day in Lisbon. On the way there, I
recounted what had happened to me the previous day in Sintra when
I had asked a man in the street which was the house in which Lord

Byron had stayed. The man thought for a few moments and then asked: 'Is he still living here?'

'No,' I replied, 'I think he has left by this time.'

After seeing something of Lisbon, we set off for 'Michel's' restaurant. I christened it the 'Restaurant of Inspiration', for we came here each year and many of the stories and anecdotes related in this book were prompted by conversations that took place there.

After our lunch, we spent some time in the gardens of the castle overlooking Lisbon before returning to Sintra where we were surrounded by flowers and treated like kings by Maria Newall and her maids who, whenever they heard their employer ring, seemed to know her innermost thoughts. Our after-dinner conversations into the early hours will always remain unforgettable for me. There is only one barometer for assessing social, after-dinner conversation: it is the quality of the ideas put forward. Horace put it well: at banquets, lights and sea lamprey matter little; all that matters is the level of good conversation. Truly, good conversation is like the scent of the rose.

On our way back through Spain, we stopped at Badajoz. It was 27 July and extremely hot. We had dinner in a restaurant and afterwards went back to spend the night at the monastery of the Vincentian Fathers. We accompanied Graham Greene up to his room. We bade each other good night and then I went to have a chat with an old friend who was a former pupil of mine, in his room. At about two or three o'clock in the morning, someone knocked at the door. It was Graham in his pyjamas dripping in sweat. He had been wandering from door to door until he heard a voice.

'My room is like hellfire,' he announced without further ado. 'I've never felt so hot in my life.'

I took him back to his room where the heat really was impossible. What must have happened was that when I had searched in the darkness for the light switch, I had accidentally turned on the central heating for the whole building.

Years later in his introduction to the limited edition of Chapter 1 of *Monsignor Quixote*, 'How Father Quixote Became a Monsignor', Graham Greene recalled the hellish experience:

> The Communist ex-mayor of El Toboso was to have been Monsignor Quixote's companion and the cynical critic of his old books of theology ... There was for

instance the time when he experienced (as I did) the
fires of hell in a monastery in Badajoz, Sancho having
accidentally turned on the central heating one night when
the temperature already stood at 100.

Via the theatre at Merida, Trujillo with its equestrian statue of
Pizarro, and Guadelupe once more, we returned to Madrid, and
from there continued to Toboso. Graham was anxious to see this
town, and to visit Dulcinea's house and the library that contained
the autographs of so many eminent politicians.

Graham Greene's mind is unable to rest. His sleepless nights are
obsessed with one single thought: *Monsignor Quixote*.

Throughout the entire journey, he never stopped interrupting our
conversation with spontaneous questions: about Father Quixote, the
bishop sent by the Vatican, and Father Quixote's own bishop, the
Bishop of Ciudad Real.

During our journey to Cuenca – which he enjoyed hugely! – we
hit upon three points of dogma with which the devil would tempt
Monsignor Quixote: birth control; the idea that the assumption of
the Virgin into heaven only meant her spiritual body, not her actual
material body; and the notion that general or group confession was
sufficient for absolution and that individual confession was not necessary. However, Graham would later alter these points in the novel.

I need to read Cervantes' *Don Quixote* again, he told me that
evening, just before he caught his plane at Barajas airport.

He had decided to write *Monsignor Quixote*.

Chapter III

MY FIRST VISIT TO ANTIBES

From the time of our first journeys together, Graham often spoke about Antibes. He told me that he would like me to visit him there one day. The ancient little town on the Côte d'Azur is very well worth knowing and its atmosphere is well preserved. Graham wanted me to meet his friends, and they too wanted to meet me. I delayed going there for reasons which I now consider to be illogical.

Graham was waiting for me at Nice airport and smiled and waved as I appeared. The flight had been badly delayed leaving Madrid and it was after nine o'clock before we landed in Nice. Once through customs, we embraced as we always did, then caught a taxi from the airport to Antibes. It was Graham's normal routine to take a light supper at seven o'clock in the evening, but we left my baggage at the hotel and the taxi took us on to Chez Félix where I at last met his great friend, the patron of the restaurant. Graham ate lunch here most days and he felt truly at home. Monsieur Félix always treated him with real affection and their relationship was a spontaneous and mutually trusting one.

'He is an extremely nice man and he always keeps the wine for me that I leave in the bottle. I eat here regularly at midday, though I usually make a light supper for myself at home in the evenings.'

Our dinner was superb; our conversation better still. But I must move on. I found Graham as confiding as ever. He seemed happy and pleased that at last I had come to Antibes. But he was worried, very worried. He spoke to me at length about Martine – a woman of twenty-seven years old – and about her artistic interests and her unhappy marriage. Her husband's jealousy and his unbalanced mental state were making her life hell. Little did Graham realize, and I still less, that the ghastly battle against the mafia on the Côte d'Azur was about to begin, though he did have a foreboding of the painful trials that lay ahead.

We spoke of many things, particularly about *Dr Fischer of Geneva*, the novel he was writing at the time, which was about a 'monstrous rascal' who tormented his admirers, who all put up with him because they hoped eventually for a reward.

Graham had been reading Bernard Bergonzi's book about him: 'He is complimentary, but I don't like what he says about *The Power and the Glory*. If the book was based on real and actual events, it cannot be out of date; for neither can its subject: the distinction between a man and his ministry.'

We continued talking about Bergonzi, and about his book on Gerard Manley Hopkins. We liked it, but it did not satisfy either of us. Graham interrupted our discussion because he wanted to ask me please to remember Martine and her problem when I said Mass.

Soon, Graham pointed out the entrance to his apartment building. I felt quite moved when I read 'Avenue Pasteur'. To think of the years I had been sending letters to that address. Graham knew what I meant. We embraced. '*Hasta mañana*.'

I arrived at the Residence des Fleurs at eleven o'clock the next morning. It was an appropriate name because there seemed to be flowers everywhere. I went up to Graham's flat on the fourth floor. It was decorated quite simply with books everywhere. There was his large writing table, and on the table-cloth lay the manuscript pages of *Dr Fischer of Geneva*. In the margin of the top page was scribbled the figure 25,000. Later, he explained that this represented the number of words he had completed. There were three or four paintings, including one of some red flowers in relief which was a present from Fidel Castro. There were a few comfortable chairs and a large sofa with a small table in front of it on which to put the book or magazine he was reading, or the latest newspapers and periodicals. The flat was small: a bedroom, a separate bathroom and lavatory, kitchen and living room.

I liked the simplicity of the apartment. There was a splendid view over the harbour of Antibes and in the background stood the castle in which Napoleon had been imprisoned. The windows faced east and on a clear day one could see Italy and the foothills of the Alps. Unfortunately, a large modern building some distance away, which Graham detested, now blocked his view of the cathedral church of Antibes.

It was the first time I had come to this flat. In the years to come, I would come once or twice a year for about a week. When Graham

had settled here in 1966, the port was very small and everything was
much quieter. When summer came, Graham told me, Antibes became
an ants' nest of tourists, and on Saturdays throughout the year it was
impossible to concentrate on work. The horrible noise of cars hooting
in celebration of a wedding was quite unbearable.

We went to have lunch at the Hôtel de France in Mougins, near
Antibes which I very much appreciated for its combination of
elegance and simplicity. When Graham entered the room, I realized
that everyone knew who he was.

We spoke of many things over lunch, but I believe the main topic
was his refusal ever to appear on television. This was how he explained
it to me:

'When I was a child, and even during my years at public school
and in my first term at Oxford, I was very drawn to the stage and
wanted to be an actor. But I never did anything about it and ever
after I have always tried to avoid the temptation. The writer should
be a somewhat mysterious figure; he owes it to his readers. It is what
he writes that matters, not the personality of the writer.'

When we had eaten, we took a walk around Mougins. The little
town is old and very clean, it smells of flowers and breathes peace and
solitude. Graham pointed out some of the more important features
as we walked along the silent, narrow streets full of small antique
shops.

Dinner consisted of smoked trout, apple tart and some Ribeiro
wine from the cellars of our dear friend Señor Antonio de las Regadas.
Graham had bought the trout that morning before I arrived at his
home. I tried to help him carry things from the kitchen to the dining
area, but he told me that he was used to doing everything himself.

Dinner went on until very late. It was the first of our long conversations over dinner at Antibes. I had slept badly the previous night.
The clear sea light had woken me very early, because the French
window did not have shutters, or so I thought. When I arrived in
my hotel room, I noticed there were some flimsy net curtains and it
did not occur to me to open the window to see if there were any
shutters. When I opened the windows to air the room next morning,
I saw there was a little balcony but nothing else.

That night, before I left (Graham always accompanied me to the
hotel), he asked me about the room. I did not want to mention the
shutters to Graham, but it came out during our conversation.

'What's the hotel like?' he enquired.

'The hotel's wonderful,' I answered, 'all that is lacking are the shutters. The morning light is very bright.'

'What do you mean?' asked Graham, looking puzzled. 'Are there no shutters?'

'No,' I said.

'It's impossible. There are very few houses in Antibes without shutters, but I thought all the hotels had them.'

'Well, I don't think there are any there', I replied.

Graham went with me to the hotel which was three or four minutes away from his flat. We went up to the room. Graham opened the French windows, went out onto the balcony, and there on either side were two shutters that opened outwards and were fastened to the wall.

I put my hands to my head in shame and we both laughed aloud. Graham then told me about Etienne Leroux, who was another hopelessly impractical man. He was a well-known French writer, but he found it impossible to write his signature on a cheque, or on any document, in the presence of other people. There was nothing he could do to stop shaking.

Not long ago, he had been in Naples with his wife. Greene advised him to be wary of pickpockets in Naples for they were everywhere. At the end of their holiday, Etienne Leroux and his wife took a taxi to go to the airport. He kept a small case containing jewellery and articles of value on his lap as a safety precaution. It was hot and so they opened the window of the taxi. A few minutes later, Etienne turned to his wife and exclaimed: 'The little box with all the money and the other things has disappeared!'

A thief had put his arm through the half-open window of the taxi and had stolen the box without Etienne even having noticed.

The taxi driver had very kindly taken them back to Naples without charging them anything and there they telephoned some friends to explain what had happened.

Graham reckoned I was rather like Etienne Leroux.

The next morning I asked Graham if he would lend me a towel for there did not appear to be one in my room. 'But didn't they give you any towels?'

He brought me a towel. That evening we mentioned this to a friend of Graham's who said that it was impossible, a hotel without towels. She drove me to the hotel and, much against my will, asked the manager of the hotel for towels.

Our first holiday in 1976. In front of Unamuno's house and his rebellious-looking statue.

The walls of Avila. For both of us this was a place of peace, simplicity and devotion.

Golden Salamanca was one of Graham's favourite Spanish cities...

...and its Plaza Mayor one of his favourite squares. In 1977, however, the Sunday crowds overwhelmed us.

On the mountain of Santa Tecla between Spain and Portugal. Graham said that his 'third nipple' in this picture (actually his sunglasses) would have attracted the attention of the Inquisition.

With Fr Damián of the Trappist Cistercian monastery at Osera.

Graham Greene inscribes one of his books for me in my study in Madrid.

Graham with our
first 'third man',
Miguel Fernandez.

Graham with 'third
man' Aurelio Verde in
the San Marcos Hotel.

With 'third man' José Ramón Losada at Beariz
(near Osera)

We were frequent visitors to Maria Newall's house at Sintra in Portugal with its immaculate garden. This picture was taken in 1978.

Our official visit to Madrid. Mayor Enrique Tierne Galván is on the right.

Writing *Monsignor Quixote* in Antibes.

Standing in my home village of Penedo de Avion, Orense. Graham loved its quietness.

A characteristic picture of Graham and Señor Antonio Nogueiras, wine grower of Las Regadas, in 1985 under the 'biblical' fig tree. He is Señor Diego in *Monsignor Quixote*.

The three of us in 1986.

Cooling Señor Antonio's wine in the Lérez river.

Osera again, during the making of the television film of *Monsignor Quixote*. Sir Alec Guinness - in his monsignor's purple - is second from left. Fr Damián is on the right with a copy of the book. Greene told me that Guinness was a 'much better' Catholic than he.

Leo McKern - Sancho in the film - with Graham and the 93 year-old
Señor Antonio at Las Regadas.

Graham with 'third man' Octavio,
looking out over the French
Pyrenees from Roncesvalles.

Graham with Father Gustavo, the Abbot of the
Benedictine monastery of Leyre in Navarra.

Making the acquaintance of
my family.

Elizabeth Dennys, Graham's sister, in my adoptive mother's garden in Tottenham, London.

In the Sintra mountains.

Greene and I in Antibes.

Graham with Octavio Victoria Gil - 'third man' in 1986 - in the Burgos countryside.

A typical picnic in Galicia. 'Just as much drinking,' joked Graham when he saw that year's collection of photographs.

Graham writes a summary of our recent journey in my flat in Vigo.

Powerful pictures of an ageing
Graham, taken at Vigo in 1989.

Towels were duly brought, the management apologized and I breathed easily. I had been terrified that there might have been towels in the bathroom just as there had been shutters on the balcony. As far as the towels were concerned at least, I was right.

I arrived at Graham's flat by half past nine the next morning. He had written some charming remarks in my autograph book and in my copy of *Babbling April*, his book of poems written when he was eighteen years old. Then, between us, we wrote six postcards to six special friends. One of them was to Señor Antonio Nogueiras, our good friend from Las Regadas, which I wrote and Graham signed, for Señor Antonio knew no English.

We went for a walk in the old part of Antibes which we loved. It was a rare pleasure for me to find so many traces of Greek influence. Afterwards, we visited the cathedral at Antibes. It is a late-Romanesque building that is intimate, serious and inspiring. On the high altar there is a portrait of Christ which reminded me of one of Dali's.

'A friend of mine discovered this Christ', Graham had told me, before we entered the church. 'He told the priest about it, and it was put on the high altar.'

We approached the sanctuary. Some women were dusting. A mass of flowers lay in front of the tabernacle.

'On Sundays this cathedral is packed. I usually stand over there to hear Mass', whispered Graham, pointing to the back of the nave.

We walked around the side altars with their restrained, gilt plateresque altar-pieces. 'These statues are good ones,' said Graham in a low voice, 'unlike those in most churches.'

As we were leaving the building, he told me a strange story. Some time ago, he had adopted a beggar. He was a man on crutches and Graham always gave alms to him. Some months previously, he had made a promise: if his prayers were granted, he would give a considerable sum to his beggar. His prayer was answered and so he decided to put a 500 franc note in an envelope which he gave to him. With the money, he enclosed a note attesting his donation so as to protect the poor fellow from the police if they were suspicious. For a long time, he did not see the beggar standing at the cathedral door. But one day he did appear, looking terribly emaciated and hardly able to stand upright. He wondered whether the beggar had spent his 500 francs in a discreditable way. Nowadays, the beggar on crutches seemed to have disappeared for good. He had not been seen near the cathedral for two years.

'I fear my almsgiving may have killed him,' Graham said sadly.

'Perhaps you should have borrowed T.S. Eliot's title, *Murder in the Cathedral*,' I replied.

We went outside. We wandered up and down a series of cosy, narrow streets that were quiet and spotlessly clean. There were flowers everywhere, elegant shop windows, and children playing safely without fear of traffic.

We reached a square in the old part of town where there is a sort of obelisk that bears an inscription Graham had never understood. It refers to the valour of the town in repelling the invasion of foreigners; and yet history testifies to the fact that those foreigners were its true liberators.

We walked through the market. It was full of noise and activity. We stopped to admire some attractive displays of flowers at a stall. On touching one, we discovered they were made of plastic. We laughed.

'Let's go and find a stall that has real flowers,' said Graham. There were some beautiful displays. Not for nothing is Antibes known as the Côte d'Azur's 'city of flowers'.

There are two stalls which always attracted Graham, the fish-monger's and another that sold cheeses.

'Look; here you have all kinds of excellent fish', he told me. 'And that stall over there is very well known for its cheeses. It's famous throughout the region; perhaps all over France.'

Our attention was drawn to a fairly young man with a small mous-tache, who was selling watches. He was smiling and looking very pleased with himself, probably because of the effect his jokes were having on the crowd of people who were listening.

We continued on through the market. Graham pointed out a plain-looking shop in the arcade on the square.

'This is where all my suits are made,' he said. 'I've always liked to have a lot of pockets, and this tailor puts them wherever I want them. He made these trousers for me.'

We turned down another street. Graham pointed out a sort of restaurant or small bar.

'The owner is the mayor of the old town of Antibes', he informed me. 'He is not actually the mayor, but according to an ancient tra-dition, the real mayor has lunch once a year with this honorary mayor.'

As we had crossed the square, Graham showed me where he used to rent a flat.

'I've really lived in Antibes for twenty years,' he explained. 'I actually came to live here in 1966, but I used to make frequent short visits before that to what was then a quiet corner of the Côte d'Azur to visit friends.'

As we were walking down one of those streets, Graham stopped for a few seconds to greet someone. By coincidence, he was English, and it provided a good opportunity for Graham to tell a long and interesting story. This is how it began:

'That gentleman put me in touch with the Vatican some years ago,' Graham explained. 'At the time, he thought he was going to be put in charge of the adminstration of the Vatican in which case he would have been a rich man today. Now, I had been told that I had £70,000 in royalties stowed away in Belgrade. When I heard about this amount, I asked whether it was in the old or new dinars. Time and again, I was assured that it was in new currency. It could mean a difference of between £7,000 or £70,000 in my royalties.

'But how was I to get the money out of the country? Through this man's connections, someone from my agent's got in touch with the Vatican and someone there spoke in turn to the Nuncio in Belgrade. When I eventually asked what was happening, my agent told me that twenty per cent of the amount had been offered to the Church in Belgrade, but they still did not accept.

'I told him that that was very little; he should have offered forty per cent.'

Forty per cent was duly offered and accepted. When they had earlier proposed twenty-five per cent, Archbishop Marcinkus had replied: 'That is chicken feed.'

'I was assured in Rome that there was no danger', Graham continued. 'I asked my agent again to find out whether the money in Belgrade was in old or new currency and was told that it was certainly in the new money. So I bought a small suitcase in which to put the money and I went to Belgrade. However, when I got there I was told that it was in old money, the equivalent of £7,000. I took enough money to pay for my air fare and other expenses and gave the rest to the Church in Yugoslavia.'

Later, after he had told me this story and we had returned home, he walked over to the far side of the room . 'That's the famous suitcase,' he said. Graham was convinced that Archbishop Marcinkus was also involved in problems with the mafia at the Vatican.

Although Graham normally walks quickly, we are walking homewards. We are talking about Antibes and life in France.

'By the way, what happened about the French wanting to confer the Légion d'Honneur on you?' I ask.

Graham listens to my question with a look of indifference, almost of displeasure.

'I didn't want to accept it. Neither did I want to go to Paris to receive it. That sort of thing does not matter to me in the least.

It was not a question of his scorning the decoration. Graham liked President Pompidou, but was completely indifferent to life's hollow vanities.

'What I did enjoy very much,' he continued, 'was the time they made me an honorary citizen of Anacapri. Once I had accepted it, I was sorry I had done so. However, I went there to receive the award and found myself in a procession of priests and civil dignitaries. The person who presided over the ceremony was the bishop, or archbishop, of Sorrento. He said some most moving things as he made the presentation. He was extremely kind.'

'You said a few words, of course?'

'Yes, I replied very briefly. But what pleased me most was the satisfaction it gave to the people who look after my house on Anacapri and to two or three of my closest neighbours. I arranged for them to have places in the first row and they were in tears throughout the whole ceremony.'

●

I think that this town of Antibes which I am getting to know is one of the most enthralling places I have seen anywhere in the world. The streets are so clean and there is no traffic in the centre of the city; there are enchanting shop windows; the people seem polite and sensitive; there are hundreds and hundreds of yachts and pleasure boats, white as the snow, moored in the port. In that semi-Greek corner of the world, it is almost as if one can hear the word *kalos* (beautiful) being spoken, advising us to open the eyes of our souls to all that surrounds us.

Today, Graham and I made a rather extraordinary and beautiful discovery; the sort of beauty which only the inner self can detect. It was something we both witnessed with our own eyes. We went into a religious bookshop where, as well as books, they sold small objects of piety. I told Graham that I wanted to buy a little medal from Lourdes. We were served by a 'holy woman' in the true sense of that term. One felt inspired just looking at her face and her eyes. She was short, very pale and thin and looked as if she belonged to another world. It was only the flesh and bones of her slight body that seemed to prevent her spirit breaking its moorings and soaring heavenwards.

She told us that some thieves had broken in and had set fire to her shop, but that the fire had stopped when it reached the boxes of medals . . .

While this extraordinary woman was searching for my medal, Graham whispered in my ear, then looked me fixedly in the eye:

'I don't know what it is, but this woman has something supernatural about her.'

Spellbound, we watched her closely. Graham said to her: 'My friend here is a priest.'

It was all that was needed! On hearing this, the woman could not restrain herself. She exclaimed: 'Oh, a priest, a priest! Father . . .'

She looked at me as if she were trying to find traces of the God she so worshipped.

As we were leaving, Graham asked if she would pray for us. Out in the street, we looked round and saw that she was praying, bowed down low with her face in her hands. A saint praying for our souls!

'Extraordinary, quite extraordinary,' Graham thought aloud. Most unusually for us, we walked home in virtual silence.

I christened her 'the holy woman of the medals'. In future, there was scarcely a time that Graham and I met without his mentioning this good woman. He even referred to her in a number of letters he wrote to me.

This episode occurred in January. In February, I returned to Antibes. It was the only time that I visited Graham twice within such a short time. Graham had not forgotten 'the holy woman of the medals'. He decided that we should go and take her a little present: a copy of his *Catholic Essays* in French. Graham had inscribed it to her. She read what he had written and thanked him with a wonderful sweetness and goodness. She was clearly delighted, but she still did not know who it was who had given the book to her. She had remembered our conversation of the previous month and recognized us when we came in, but when I explained that this man was the author of the book, the expression on the face of 'the holy woman of the medals' was transformed, and she exclaimed:

'Oh, Graham Greene! Are you Graham Greene?'

Graham replied that he was, and he blushed deeply in surprise. How was it possible that someone like this should know and admire his name? The wonderful thing was that he was genuinely astonished by such things.

The woman continued to look as if she had seen a vision and was completely overcome. Graham said he must go. She took his hands in order to kiss them, but it was actually he who kissed the saintly woman's hands. I also took her hands in mine to kiss them.

We remembered this each time we passed her shop in the years ahead, but Graham preferred not to go in for he dreaded another show of reverence.

•

While I was in Antibes, a correspondent from the Italian newspaper *L'Unità* came to see Graham. Needless to say, the interview had been arranged beforehand. Graham introduced me to the journalist and asked that I should remain there during the conversation.

The journalist was a cultured and very friendly young man. The interview was a very fine one, in my opinion, and included a wide-ranging choice of basic questions:

The question of the mafia on the Côte d'Azur followed and why Graham involved himself with such thorny matters. He explained that the fact that a family he knew and loved had become involved made him want to publicize the problem on a broader level. He spoke at length about this, about the situation in that corrupt area of 'what is called the Côte d'Azur', and quoted what an important person had told him in Paris: 'There is a tough wall to climb. There are some lawyers, policemen and magistrates who have been corrupted. But one day that wall will be breached, the bricks will start to crumble, and then . . .'.

He was asked about his conversion. Graham replied that it was an intellectual conversion at first. His future wife was a Catholic and before getting married he wanted to learn about her faith; or, rather, he thought that marriage might be easier and happier if they were both Catholics. His emotional and true conversion came later, in Mexico.

Graham spoke at some length about his political views. He told the interviewer that he had always had a tendency to the left; that he did not want to use the terms Christian Democrat or Socialist since they had become rather distorted. He said he had always been against totalitarianism of any kind, and that right-wing totalitarianism of the Argentine variety, rather than left-wing Communism, may have been responsible for more people disappearing in recent years.

He was asked about the historical background to his novel *The Comedians*. The journalist pointed out that despite what he had written, little had changed in Haiti. Graham took out a copy of the booklet* published by Duvalier, read out a few lines and concluded: 'You can see how my book got under his skin'.

The interviewer wanted to know the part politics played in his work. Graham assured him that politics played an essential role. He referred to *The Quiet American* in particular.

He was asked which he considered to be his best books. Graham reckoned on *The Honorary Consul, The Power and the Glory* and *Travels with My Aunt*. Later Graham told him that he should ask my opinion. I was inclined to choose *The Power and the Glory, A Burnt-Out Case* and *The Honorary Consul. Monsignor Quixote*, which along with *The Power and the Glory* may well be the two best books Graham Greene wrote, had not yet then been published.

He was then asked about Israel and the Arab world. Graham tended to favour Israel. He said that the pressure under which the Jews lived could not continue. He illustrated how small the occupied zone was by comparing the size to areas of London.

They then spoke about Christ. The Arabs gave more importance to him than the Jews. 'He was Jewish because his mother was Jewish'; and because he was born, and died, in Israel. Later, Graham and I commented on the fact that in the case of Christ the role of the mother was more important than with other men because it was responsible for his entire human nature, whereas for the rest of us it is shared between the father and the mother.

Graham then apologized, quite sincerely, for having forgotten to offer him anything to drink. When the journalist left, we both agreed

---

* *Graham Greene Demasqué*. Published in French and English by the Department of Foreign Affairs, Port-au-Prince, Haiti 1968.

that he was a delightful and extremely cultured man. It had been an interview conducted on the highest level.

●

We were walking by the sea at Antibes shortly before dusk. I asked Graham to explain to me carefully what had gone wrong on that occasion when we were due to meet in Madrid when *El País*, his favourite Spanish newspaper, had asked for an interview.

'*El País* are proposing to send two reporters here to interview me. If you have a few days free, I'll tell them that I am coming to Madrid and that they can have the interview there.'

'Marvellous,' I replied. 'Whenever. Come when you like.'

'Before your competitive examination or after? Perhaps it would be better afterwards.'

'Later would be better,' I replied. 'Then we can celebrate the great event together.'

Little did I know the snares and pitfalls that lay ahead! Alas, what sort of clergyman is roaming about, even in universities!

'They wanted a television interview which I refused absolutely', Graham continued. 'Then they asked me again if I would not agree to this. I said no. Then they telephoned my agent in Spain to ask if I would not agree to a press conference. "No", I replied, "all I will do is talk privately to two journalists at my hotel".'

When they persisted and suggested that other newspapers would be upset, Graham grew angry.

'Then, quite seriously, we will cancel everything,' he said. 'I will not agree to any interview of any kind, either public or private. Everything is cancelled once and for all.'

We went on chatting. It was one of those moments when earth and sky seemed to blend together in a haze of blue. Graham could become quite violent if he were photographed when people were around, but this was a rare moment. We were at the highest point on the path that surrounds the old part of Antibes, the Greek quarter next to the sea. A group of tourists were feeding the pigeons that were eating out of their hands.

'How about a photograph with this marvellous view?' I ventured.

It was a great mistake to suggest this to Graham on my first visit to Antibes.

'As you like,' he replied reluctantly, ' but I really don't like to have photographs taken of me in public.'

'That's fine, Graham,' I answered, as if the matter was of no importance to me. 'Let's forget about photographs.'

And we continued chatting and walking beside the blue of the Mediterranean.

CHAPTER IV

A DAY OR TWO IN GALICIA

FROM THE VERY first moment we visited Galicia, this part of Spain became engraved in Graham Greene's heart. There was no question but he fell in love with the province in the way he fell in love with Indo-China.

In his foreword to the limited, numbered edition of *Monsignor Quixote*, he wrote: 'Every year we take much the same route: up to Galicia, Father Durán's homeland, by way of Salamanca . . .' A part of his great novel is also set in Galicia and reaches its conclusion in the Cistercian monastery of Osera.

To illustrate what I mean, here are some extracts from the notebooks and diaries I kept that relate just a few of our adventures together in Galicia:

13-14 August 1984 We are setting out from the *parador* at Oropesa en route for Galicia. It is half past ten in the morning. We shall eat our picnic on the way, we shall dine at the 'San Miguel' in Orense, and we shall stay the night at the Hotel Residencia Padre Feijoo. On Sunday we plan to eat beneath Señor Antonio's fig tree. Historic fig tree! Señor Antonio de las Regadas is Señor Diego in *Monsignor Quixote*. God willing, we shall spend that night in Osera.

Graham, like St Augustine, is 'a restless flame'. Two days in the same place are enough to make him feel almost intolerably bored.

On the road to Osera, we spoke once again about the European Common Market. Graham cannot see any great advantages in it as it is presently constructed. He reminded us of the vast salaries pocketed by all those selfless patriots. He asked us what we felt about Spain joining Europe. We replied that it could well become a political platform for the Socialist Party, but that for Spain the effect of joining would probably be prejudicial, at least for some years. On the other hand, if she did not join, she could not participate in conferences that concerned the future of Europe. We wondered how a chiefly agricultural producer such as Spain could compete against the larger industrialized nations of Europe. Graham pointed out that Spain would have to raise the price of its agricultural good within its own borders so as to conform with Common Market prices.

•

Graham had often told me that his friend, the writer Maria Couto, and I should correspond with each other. Graham had a very high regard for her and for her views on the political element in his work. Later, she would publish her book, *Graham Greene: On the Frontier*. Maria Couto showed that Graham's political vision was much clearer than that of the political leaders of the nineteen thirties and their successors. It was a book he much admired.

We dined magnificently in the 'San Miguel' in Orense. We drank a Bradomin wine and it was devilishly good. As the dinner progressed so did the level of conversation. We spoke of the attempts on the lives of Reagan and the Pope and what they represented politically; about the ways the Trinity could be explained. Graham returned once more to his obsession with 'faith' and 'belief'; he also explained his method of getting to sleep. He said that he always kept some strong sleeping tablets, prescribed by his brother Raymond, in case he ever felt like taking his own life ... Graham had never seriously contemplated doing such a thing, nor did I believe that he would. I looked at him gravely, almost angrily, but he smiled at me.

'To do so would not be against my conscience,' he said.

I took no notice.

The effect of those bottles of Bradomin can be very contradictory. On the one hand, they could inspire one to great heights, on the other hand they could instil absurd ideas in the minds of Graham Greene and the 'Third Man'. We always look forward to the 'San Miguel' when we are tired and hungry at the end of a long journey. The head waiter tells me in a low voice that there is a journalist who wants to have a word with Graham. I reply that it is out of the question. The man left.

It is now very late. Yes, wine can be the very devil. Graham and the 'Third Man' are talking complete nonsense. They are trying to suggest that the exceptional courtesy we are always shown at the 'San Miguel' is really only a bribe. It is done just to impress the author. The 'Third Man' was agreeing with everything Graham said, just as if he had claimed that two and two make twenty-seven. Our good friend, the driver, then pointed to Graham:

'And it's not just the author they want to impress, but the chauffeur too', said he.

I could scarcely stop myself wanting to laugh, but at last I decided to intervene:

'All that you are saying is the result of drinking three bottles of "Bradomin", preceded by that whisky.'

Perhaps the notion of 'impressing him' occurred to Graham because they had asked him to sign the visitors' book. They asked him to do so every time we ate at the 'San Miguel'. Of course, they had also asked him to autograph one of his novels in Spanish. Yet Graham had only drunk half a glass more than usual . . .

However, Graham is admirable. He is apt suddenly to realize the errors of his ways. The following day, as we were leaving our wretched hotel and walking along the street, he said to me: 'The "San Miguel" is the only worthwhile thing about Orense.'

He was in a reasonably good mood despite having spent a bad night in a bad hotel. The bed had been narrow and far too short for Graham, and the heat had meant that he had had to sleep with his legs protruding.

At ten o'clock that morning we set off for Osera. We were simply going to leave our baggage at the monastery where our rooms were already prepared. I said Mass in the little Gothic chapel there, and Graham and the 'Third Man' both assisted.

After a few words with our host – 'the happy Trappist', as Graham called him – and with Father Damian, we set off again for Señor Antonio's house. On the way, Graham told us about his great new plan: to bequeath the Spanish rights in *Getting to Know the General* to the Trappist monks at Osera. This was his reason:

'If Sancho [meaning himself] bequeaths the Panamanian and other Latin American rights to the guerrilla fighters in El Salvador, then it is only right that Monsignor Quixote should donate his Spanish rights to the Trappists in Osera!'

A meal had been prepared for us at the 'San Miguel' which we took with us to Las Regadas. On the way there, we discussed the influence of Chesterton on Borges. Graham often spoke to me about the blind Argentine writer.

Our meal eaten beneath Señor Antonio's biblical fig tree was one of the great feasts of Graham's life. There was a fine show of mutual affection between him and Señor Antonio. The warmth and personality of this pastoral poet and philosopher are hard to describe. Graham greeted him effusively and it was clear from their eyes that both men felt an affection and tenderness for each other. Graham wrote a note for Señor Antonio on a half-torn piece of paper addressed to 'the President of this banquet' saying that 'these moments beneath the fig tree will always remain unforgettable to me' and that he looked forward to coming back one day. The 'Third Man' and I would take it in turn to sit between the two friends and interpret, but we soon realized that this was unnecessary. Señor Antonio and Graham understood each other perfectly. How, I never knew, but a glance, an expression or a gesture seemed to be sufficient.

[On a later visit, in 1989 it was pouring with rain and so, unable to eat beneath the fig tree as we had been longing to do, we invited Señor Antonio to lunch in a restaurant. When Graham promised him that he would return again soon, Señor Antonio turned to me and begged me to make sure that his 'English friend' understood just what he was saying: 'Tell him to come back quickly, because if he doesn't, he may not find me here.' As it happened, they never did meet again after this. It was Graham who preceded his friend on the ultimate journey.]

We spent that night in Osera, and the next day in the town where I was born, which was about forty kilometres from the monastery. The greatest gift I ever made to my home town, Penedo de Avión (Orense), was to take Graham Greene there on various occasions. We ate in my parents' home, and only one thing bothered him when he came there: he was always obliged to eat more than he wanted. That is the danger with peasant hospitality. And there was one occasion when he did not feel too well at night.

My parents' home is a large, old-fashioned house on the outskirts of the town, with some fine views over Galicia and it dates back to the time when they used to thresh rye in those parts. From the house you could look out beyond Ayuntamiento de Avión, and it was a view that Graham adored. The silence was absolute; it was a silence he sought all his life, and he found it a few months before he died in Corseaux, Switzerland. How often did he urge me that not a single detail of my parents' house, apart from the odd improvement inside, should be touched!

Some inhabitants may perhaps have observed a very tall man with me at the time, gazing at 'Pena Corneira'. Yet nobody there would ever have heard of the name of Graham Greene. With the sweat of their bodies, the people there spend their time mining gold from stones rather than from books.

We visited a number of hamlets around Avión, for he wanted to get to know the land that those 'Mexican' emigrants came from, people who had had to travel to another world in order to find a crust of bread for their families. I told Graham the tragic and heroic story of those emigrants, and he immortalized it in *Monsignor Quixote*. In some ways the novel is a hymn of praise to those emigrants from Avión and its region who left home and managed to triumph over hunger through sheer hard work. Not everyone has understood the true message of what was written about the emigrants from Avión in *Monsignor Quixote*. At Graham's request, I personally corrected all the pages of the novel that deal with that emigration.

When he saw the houses and streets of those hamlets, and the bleak landscape where few men could subsist with dignity, Graham Greene began to understand the homeric epic of my Galician peasants. I even recited for him in English a few verses of Rosalia de Castro's addressed to those Galicians overseas, so that he could penetrate deeper into the great sacrifice they made. Of course, Graham understood!

●

The Mexican Connection
There are few families here who have not had some relation or other who has emigrated to Mexico. Many families left altogether and there were countless marriages between Spaniards and Mexicans. The youth of my province emigrated to Mexico to forge a future for themselves and their work and the thousands of buildings they left are their great contribution to that country which is also known as New Spain. Some remained forever; the majority returned to Spain with the fruits of their savings and built new houses for themselves in Galicia, for they wanted to retire and die in their native land, often leaving their children in Mexico to continue running the businesses their parents had created.

The emigrants from Avión took the example of their sacrifice to Mexico. Their pockets were empty but within their hearts they took with them a determination that was ready to transmute the stones of the pathways into gold. With the inevitable exceptions, each Galician emigrant to Mexico – or wherever else it might have been – stood as an heroic example of the determination and sacrifice required of men in their search for work.

'You must write a book entitled *The Mexican Connection*,' Graham said to me one day. 'I promise I'll write the introduction. You have material for a wonderful book here.'

How often did he remind me about my duty to do this! According to him, the world should be told about these people. He had seen for himself the bitter poverty of this rugged region around Avión, and he had seen the enormous progress that had been made, thanks to the emigrants and their martyr-like vocation. He really did long for such a book to be written. And I promised him I would write it.

•

14 August 1984. After breakfast and some fond farewells, we left Osera en route for the *parador* at Cambados. We would have our picnic on the way.

We stop at Carballino. We go to Mr Suso's 'Garriga' agency to confirm Graham's Air France flight to Nice, and walk straight into the manager's office since there is an enormous queue of people waiting. On seeing Graham Greene's name on the ticket, Mr Suso stands up in amazement and looks at Graham.

'It is a great honour for me to be able to shake hands with the famous writer, Graham Greene,' he said.

I translate; as usual, the highly sensitive and modest Graham blushes.

Mr Suso immediately calls Santiago and spells out Graham Greene's name.

'Is it spelt like the well-known writer?' he is asked.

'It is Graham Greene, the writer, who is here.'

They also seem to be rather amazed in Santiago.

Suso summons his brother Ramón and introduces him to Graham. Ramón is quite taken aback and turns to Graham:

'How happy I am to meet you! At home I have all the books of yours that I have been able to obtain. If only I had one of them here so that you could sign it for me.'

I translate for Graham who replies: 'Of course I would. Perhaps another time.'

We say goodbye. Graham, as always, is a little embarrassed on such occasions. He never realizes that people recognize him; that people in the street may have heard of his name.

Cerdedo, the next place we travel through, resembles a film-set. Near this village, on the banks of the River Lerez, we had one of the most delightful picnics, the first of many that we were to enjoy there over the years. That first occasion, we found the ideal spot for our picnic, about two hundred metres out of the village, and with shade and running water. I think it was the best of all the places we found over the years in either Spain or Portugal. A eucalyptus tree had been felled by the side of the river, and it provided ideal seats as well as a table for our frugal repast.

What delighted us most was the sound of the gently murmuring waters of the River Lerez as it flowed past us a few feet away. Even on the hottest days of summer the water on the river is very cold and so we were able to cool Señor Antonio's white wine.

[That oasis on the River Lerez was so perfect a spot that the day we discovered it became etched in our memories, and whenever we were near that road, we always sought it out.

On one of those happy occasions, Graham imagined it as a film-set. I was to go and collect the bottles of wine from the river and look as if I were fishing; the 'Third Man' would take the photographs. Graham contemplated the scene:

'Let's go over there. Leopoldo can be the actor; Aurelio, the cameraman; and I'll be the director.'

Unfortunately, the photograph only shows me fishing for the bottles. Next year, we would exchange roles: Graham would be the actor fishing for bottles, and the cameraman took two or three excellent photographs.]

Once our riverside picnic was over, we set off for Cambados. From Pontevedra as far as Cambados, the whole of the magnificent coastal landscape was covered by mist. Graham would not be convinced that the scenery was actually very beautiful and neither would the 'Third Man'. I assured them that it was a great pity they were unable to see the wonderful view from the *ría* of Marin as far as the monastery of Poyo.

'The famous library belonging to Rey Soto is there in the Merced-arian monastery,' I told them, 'and it is one of the best for Galician subjects. There are thousands of volumes bound in white leather, or so I have heard, and they are apparently immensely valuable.'

I told them how this library came to be at the monastery of Poyo. Apparently, Rey Soto had originally thought of bestowing it on the seminary at Orense. As it happened, Rey Soto decided to go and live in the priest's house at the seminary, but the passing years had made him even more eccentric than he had been hitherto. They grew rather tired of him at Orense, and so he took his library and went to live with the Mercedarians. It may have been for the best. The Mercedarians at Poyo probably knew how to look after and make better use of this magnificent library, and they would ensure that Poyo became a centre for Galician studies.

I told them how the philosopher Manuel Garcia Morente came to this monastery of Poyo to make a long retreat after his apparently miraculous conversion in Paris. Later, he became a priest, but died shortly afterwards. It was he who had begun the great work on St Thomas Aquinas' *Summa Theologica*.

All this interested Graham enormously.

Cambados. We remember Alvaro Cunqueiro, the poet of Galician legend and a twin soul of Rosalia's. I told Graham something very important: here in Cambados they celebrate the wine feast of Albarino, that used to be celebrated both by Alvaro Cunqueiro and his friend Castroviejo.

We are outside the *parador* of Cambados (the 'Parador del Albarino'). I wonder whether it was Cunqueiro who gave it this name. Before we go in, we take a look at the house where the Spanish novelist Ramón del Valle-Inclan lived. There is a plaque on the wall.

We enter the *parador*. The golden stone reminds Graham of the gold at Salamanca which so impressed him. We go up to our rooms for a rest. At about six o'clock it is 'whisky time' for Graham and the 'Third Man'. Cutty Sark is one of Graham's favourite blends and he liked it more or less as much as J&B which he made famous in *The Human Factor*. Incidentally, with his agreement, I once mixed a drop of J&B at the end of a bottle with some Cutty Sark. 'There's something really rather special about this whisky,' Graham remarked. 'Perhaps you should patent the mixture.'

Throughout the whisky ceremony (almost two hours), Graham talks about the Catholic Church's condemnation of birth control and how he disagrees with Pope John Paul II. I give him a knowing look. He smiles knowingly back.

The 'Third Man' is also theologizing a bit. I am not drinking whisky. I feel calm (a rare thing for me) and simply listen. Their conversation reaches metaphysical and abstract heights. In the end, I congratulate them on their theological speculations, which would not exactly please Cardinal Ratzinger, and we all laugh heartily.

Graham suggests we go and eat somewhere other than the *parador* 'just for a change'. We decide on the O'Arco restaurant. We order skate, fresh from the sea, and as an hors d'oeuvre a Galician pasty made from tuna. The three of us agree that these dishes are first rate. We order two bottles of Marques de Murrieta 1971, but do not understand how they manage to sell this wine at such a low price: 250 pesetas a bottle. Perhaps they bought it some time ago, or it may be that they are not often asked for wine of this quality. Cambados represents the apotheosis of Albariño the Gallician, who Cunqueiro immortalized in his writings, and who wept when he heard of the death of his minstrel.

For dessert there was a Galician cheese, some special patisserie, and, for me, my apple tart. The 'Third Man' finished off his meal with a local liqueur.

'That was one of the best meals we have ever had in Spain,' commented Graham.

On our way back, as our metaphysical capacities reached new heights, the moon shone over the *parador*. As someone said, it was like 'a midsummer night's dream'.

•

At half past nine in the morning we set out for Villagarcia de Arosa. Only God knows where we shall go, but the map shall guide us. I said a Hail Mary before we set off, as I always do, and Galicia lay before us.... Graham is not happy with the French translation of *Getting to Know the General*....

... La Estrada, Lalin, then we passed through Somoza. We spoke about Galicia as being the 'Mother of Presidents'. Fidel Castro's parents were Galician; so were those of Alfonsín, who was then the President of Argentina. Perhaps Somoza, the dictator of Nicaragua, also had Galician blood.

Jokingly, I added: 'Galicia has given some great men and women to the world. The greatest of all is Francisco Franco.' Graham realized the jibe was directed at him and, quite unusually for him, burst out laughing.

Graham loved these small roads we travelled on. 'There is less traffic and more peace and silence,' he said. 'Galicia's inland landscape is wonderful. I much prefer it to the sea and the beaches ... no tourists, nor press to molest one ...'

We had our picnic about twenty kilometres from Lugo, in the

countryside, where we found another river in which to cool Señor
Antonio's wine. It's nearly always white wine on our picnics.

A short rest under the trees, then off we go in the direction of
León. Graham told what is evidently a well-known story about an
Irish Catholic boy who fell in love with a girl in a brothel. He married
the girl and took her to his parents' home.

'Well, my girl, what is your profession?' the girl's mother asked
her new daughter-in-law.

'I was a prostitute.'

'What did you say?' asked the distraught mother-in-law.

'A prostitute.'

'Oh, thanks be to the Blessed Virgin! I thought you said Protestant.'

CHAPTER V

SELF-PORTRAIT ON THE ROAD TO RONCESVALLES

O F ALL OUR excursions together, perhaps it is the journey we made to Roncesvalles 23–31 July 1985 that best serves to show Graham Greene as he really was. It is why I have entitled this chapter 'Self-portrait'.

Graham's plane arrived at Barajas airport one hour late. I don't know of any serious theologian who would support the notion that we each have a particular devil to plague us just as we each have a guardian angel to protect us, but on this journey some mischievous imp had put Graham Greene in a bad mood. It had begun when his plane was delayed for more than an hour on the Côte d'Azur, and without punctuality Graham is like a man adrift. I might add that he always arrived at airports one hour before departure.

We set off for my home where we had supper and talked with all our old intimacy. We heard on the news that Eden Pastora had disappeared. Graham was reminded of the mysterious attempt on Pastora's life, his earlier meeting with him on one occasion, Eden Pastora's frustrations, and the chance interview he had with the Swedish journalist who had been with Eden at the time of the attack and who had been injured. Nicaragua was an inexhaustible subject for Graham.

The battle with the mafia on the Côte d'Azur, which was to be the subject of Graham's pamphlet *J'Accuse* and the cause of immense anxiety to him, was looming on the horizon. We talked about 'Cosa Nostra' and I related the following anecdote. A Dominican priest from Naples, a man of standing at the Vatican, was returning home for a few days' holiday. It happened that a young girl, a niece of the Dominican, had been molested for several months by some wretched fellow who kept following her. The family had tried every means they could to stop the man, but with no success. Someone had a brilliant idea: why not put the matter into the hands of the Capo (the mafia chief) in Naples? So the Capo then rang up the young man and told him, in so many words, that from this moment on he must forget the girl forever. 'If he didn't . . . well, then he himself would make sure he did.' It was a miraculous solution. This 'supreme justice' had the desired effect and the girl was left to live her life in peace. When the Dominican priest arrived in Naples, he called, as he always did, on his local parish priest. The priest asked him whether he had also paid a courtesy visit to the Capo. No, he replied, and he wondered why he should, for he knew nothing about the favour done to his family.

'You ought to go and see him. Take my advice', the parish priest told him. 'And don't forget to thank him for all he has done for your family before you go back to Rome.' He then told him what had happened.

And the Dominican went to see him. And the Capo was much obliged. And when the priest thanked him on behalf of his family, the kindly Capo made light of what had happened. 'Little things like this will always go on,' he said simply.

And he presented the priest from Rome with a donation for the poor.

That night we went to bed promptly. We had an early morning start.

●

We set off early on the road to Covarrubias the following morning. A visit to the monastery at Silos and its library was essential. We were travelling incognito as usual, but unfortunately a student of mine from Complutense University greeted me in the famous pharmacy of the monastery and, of course, he recognized Graham Greene. That devilish imp must still have been with us when we entered the monastery!

Our private visit to the monastery had come to an end. The librarian arrived to put himself at our disposal. He showed us around the cloister and invited us to partake of some wine in the refectory where the monks had eaten and drunk for a hundred years. Then Father Abad arrived, and Father Enrique. They invited us to have some Benedictine, which Graham does not like at all. He never drinks liqueurs, though on this occasion he took a sip or two just because I did and he did not want me to drink alone.

The monks at Silos very kindly tried to book rooms for us in the Hospederia de Leyre, but the telephone was constantly engaged. They would try again later. We could set off in the certain knowledge that we would have rooms.

We ate our picnic between Aranda de Duero and Caleruega in a beautiful poplar wood. It was delightful. 'I was very hungry when I arrived here,' I said. 'I was very thirsty,' Graham replied.

It was at that moment that Graham said something that was to be of crucial importance to me. 'You should keep a diary of our travels,' he said, very seriously, almost solemnly.

I replied that I had done so on various previous occasions. 'I keep a few notes', I said.

But he persisted: 'You really should keep a diary of our travels.'

We rested for a while, lying on the ground beneath the shade of the poplars. As the car started up, Graham turned towards me in the back of the car and, as usual, joked: 'Time for your prayers.'

We admire the simplicity and isolation of the convent at Caleruega. This was where St Domingo de Guzman, the founder of the Dominican Order, was born. The peaceful atmosphere touches the very soul. Like certain other places I have mentioned, it is a place for meditation, not photography.

We had supper and spent the night at Arlanza, in the Parador Colaborador de Covarrubias where we much appreciated their very special cold apple tart. It was served in an earthenware dish and was quite different to all the others we so often ate elsewhere.

Graham tells me that he does not want to go to Nicaragua now. 'They are trying to do something formal and public, and those things don't suit me, I prefer these things to be private. Endo, my Japanese friend, is going there.'

I ask Graham which of his plays he most likes. He replies: *The Complaisant Lover*, *The Return of A.J. Raffles*, and another which was a failure, *Carving a Statue*.'

'More than *The Living Room*?'

'Well . . .,' he says.

We ate our picnic the next day just before we reached Najera, beside a brook and not far from the river. It was hot. The only irritation were the flies and other insects. We had two types of chorizo, York ham, cheese and fruit. Graham rarely eats fruit, apart from strawberries with cream.

At 5.30 p.m. we were at the *parador* of Olite. Graham and Octavio drank their whisky while I took a restorative bath. Afterwards, we had a long conversation: the Politburo and the Vatican; power, politics and corruption. The Polish Pope: Graham talks about him today with gentleness and understanding. And we also chat about one of our usual topics: Nicaragua and Central America.

'In Nicaragua,' Graham stated, ' Catholics and communists fought together against Somoza. That is why there are people of both persuasions in the government. Ortega is not a communist, though various members of his government are. Ortega visits Russia and asks for Soviet aid in order to survive; the United States refuse him all aid.'

Octavio and I make some objection. Graham tells us: 'Like you, there are many things I loathe about Communism. But I think of Somoza and Baptista, and I see the positive things that Ortega and Castro are trying to do for their countries; especially where culture is concerned.'

Greene turns to Octavio: 'My friendship for Leopoldo is one hundred per cent, even though we disagree about various things; for example, the Pope's political attitudes.'

I feel sure Graham is thinking about Franco too. Perhaps he sees nothing wrong in the political behaviour of Castro and Ortega. Octavio, on the other hand, mentions some of the appalling things he witnessed at Havana airport. In any case, I have never been particularly convinced by Graham's ideas on what is happening in Cuba and Nicaragua.

We had lunch and took a siesta. Later that afternoon we went for a short walk in the town and we were surprised to see neighbours sitting outside the doors of their houses on the pavements, chatting to each other as they only do now, unfortunately, in small towns and villages. As we got up to go, Graham sounded happy and surprised as he said: 'For the first time in my life, I slept for nine or ten hours at a stretch last night. I have never slept so long.'

•

We set out in the direction of Leyre. I feel sure that Graham's demon must have preceded us, probably regretting that it had left Graham in peace the previous night.

We ate our frugal lunch near Castillo de Javier, beside a small stream, and Graham made the most of the good night's sleep he had enjoyed at the *parador* at Olite by making us laugh and telling us hundreds of stories about Chuchu.

We arrived at the famous Benedictine monastery of Leyre at about three o'clock in the afternoon under a burning sun. The monastery stands at the foot of a high mountain and it was the burial place of the Kings of Navarre. On that July afternoon the sun was the only king.

We rang the bell of the lodge, a rather ill-timed moment for some of the monks, who get up at dawn for their morning office and take a little siesta in the afternoons to regather their strength. I had not wanted to ring the bell until a little later for I am used to the time-tables of religious communities. There is no answer. We try again. Silence . . .

In the meantime, we go and look at the 'Fountain of the Virgins' about 250 metres away from the monastery. The blinding sun could not penetrate the deep shade where there was a statue to Our Lady. The water was icy and wonderful and though Graham never drinks water, he rinsed his hands in the stream.

We returned to the monastery at about four o'clock and rang the bell again. We could see monks at the first-floor window and we made signs that we wanted to be let in.

Father Gustavo came down immediately. He is the Abbot, a simple and most kindly man. They were expecting us because their fellow monks at Silos had telephoned to reserve rooms for us at the monastery boarding house. However, the rooms there were fully booked and so at the request of the monks at Santo Domingo de Silos, they had made up rooms for us inside the cloister.

The Abbot recognized Graham Greene immediately. He showed the 'Third Man' where to park the car in a safe place. He then took Graham and me into a small ante-room and told us something of the history of the abbey. It is a history that goes back many centuries and he spent some three quarters of an hour recounting it. It was a miracle of compression, but for Graham those three quarters of an hour seemed like an eternity. Such explanations – just like official guides – usually bore Graham exceedingly. In this case, he is not bored, but the 'Third Man' had gone to leave the car and Graham presumes he is searching for us . . .

He was right. Octavio had no idea where we were and had spent the whole time wandering around.

The three of us were eventually reunited. Father Gustavo showed us to our rooms. Graham's was truly magnificent; it was the 'bishop's room' where he and other eminent people retired to pray.

Graham tends to be upset by grandeur, and when we were on our own I could see that he really did not care for it at all and wanted me to swap rooms.

'You will celebrate Mass in here and so it is quite reasonable that you should occupy the best room,' he explained.

Naturally, I did not agree. I told him that Jesus was born in a manger in Bethlehem and that the same should apply to the Mass. Later, however, when he, I and Octavio were conversing, we thought he seemed quite depressed.

'I hate having to be made a fuss of', he said a little gloomily. 'Being welcomed by abbots; this bishop's room or whatever it may be ... I like to go unnoticed.'

He really did look sad and dejected, and I tried to cheer him up a little.

'I understand what you mean, dear Graham,' I said, 'I really do. But they have heard of you and they want to make as much of a fuss of you as they can.'

It is very difficult to convince Graham that he cannot pass unnoticed. People recognize him through photographs, although very few of those are people who have read his work. Furthermore, these abbots are cultured men who admire his books.

Graham does not understand this because he loathes publicity and discrimination. In one of his regular bouts of bad humour at that time, he told me that I did not realize how much work Octavio did, driving all those hours, that a man of eighty-one years of age gets tired sitting in a car, whereas I sit comfortably in the back, sleeping whenever I want to.

The 'Third Man' interrupts. He tells Graham that the cause of his bad mood is the Benedictine he was given yesterday at Silos and that in fact it was not very comfortable for me sitting in the back of the car in the full glare of the sun.

I laugh. 'I listen and I say nothing,' I then said. But I continue laughing.

Then we discuss whether we should spend one night or two in Leyre. Graham insists on only one. He says:

'I would rather go to Santo Domingo de la Calzada to see the cock and the hen in their cage than see another Virgin.'

Then he laughs. 'You don't mind me joking a little?'

'Good Lord, no,' I say. 'I prefer you to be making jokes all day. Make us laugh a little.'

•

Graham continues to seem rather dejected and in low spirits. Octavio and I try to cheer him up with the suggestion that we go to Ronces-valles tomorrow and spend two nights at Leyre. We can see this may be difficult.

After we have left Graham in his room for a little while, Octavio says:

'It all depends on how well Graham sleeps tonight. If he has a good night we can stay here tomorrow.'

•

We had an unforgettable dinner of garlic soup, trout and salad, and watermelon that evening at Leyre, but Graham hardly tasted the soup. He changed his spectacles to take out the bones of the trout one by one. He had no pudding and he never eats bread. In a word, he did not eat.

'That was the worst meal I've ever had in Spain', he whispered to me as we were leaving the dining-room.

It was just as I had feared.

Yet when the Abbot spoke to us a little later, Graham assured him it was the best meal we had ever eaten in Spain and he praised the peace and beauty of the setting.

I stared at him, my eyes wide open. 'I'm telling you the truth', he said. 'We must certainly spend another night here. That's for sure.'

•

We all sit down for a few moments together. Graham insists that the Roman curia has a negative influence on freedom of thought – proper freedom both for lay Catholics and for the religious orders. Graham is absolutely convinced that Cardinal Ratzinger's influence on the Pope is a harmful one. The Abbot believes that the curia and Ratz-inger may have to act very cautiously; perhaps a little too cautiously, given the times we live in.

I accompanied Graham up to the bishop's chamber. Once the door was closed and we were on our own, I threw myself on Graham's bed and tried to contain my laughter. Graham had clearly not enjoyed his supper in the least. I laughed until I could laugh no more. It was contagious, and then Graham, who understood my amusement, began laughing too, although rather more restrainedly.

Tiring at last, I glanced round these episcopal sleeping quarters. As I looked and stroked the magnificent curtains, I tried to imagine what Graham's thoughts must have been at that moment, and I exploded with another burst of uncontrollable laughter.

I asked him to forgive me for that mad outburst. He laughed too. 'Good night', he said and we embraced warmly.

'I will leave you here to say your wordless prayers in this chaste silence', I said.

The thought of keeping 'chaste silence' in the bishop's chamber of that Benedictine abbey caused Graham to laugh this time. And so I left him. For a few moments at least, that unpropitious demon had been defeated

Octavio and I chatted in my room for a while afterwards. 'The miracle of the trout,' he commented. And I recounted what had happened in the bishop's chamber.

'Schubert has a song about a happy, capricious trout,' Octavio mused. 'Perhaps once this trout had arrived in Graham's stomach, it felt happy to be swimming around in the Benedictines' garlic soup. But it really is a miracle.'

Nevertheless, neither I nor the 'Third Man' can keep Graham happy all the time. It would only take a mischievous mosquito to destroy our happiness by giving Graham a bad night.

What a great man, but what a child this famous friend of mine can be!

•

Yesterday Graham suggested that we should celebrate Mass in the marvellous crypt of the monastery, so we did so today at seven o'clock in the morning. After a frugal breakfast with the monks, the Abbot accompanied us to our car.

The road from Leyre to Roncesvalles is truly beautiful. It goes through magnificent woods which Salvador de Madariaga compared to the Black Forest in Germany.

Graham mentioned the Basque resistance fighters. I tell him that it would be a curious thing if they kidnapped Graham, or both of us, and locked us in a cell without whisky or wine – just water, or perhaps a little of that Benedictine liqueur whose name Graham does not want to hear mentioned.

Octavio interrupts: 'Kidnapping Graham would be a serious problem for the Government.'

'Plenty of photographs in the newspapers', was Graham's comment.

We talk, as we often do, about the human and the divine; but we don't say much, for the beauty of those woods and the song of countless birds seem to invite us to proceed in silence.

We are in the town of Roncesvalles. We drive to the top of the hill, as far as cars can go. The view to the horizon is truly imposing and difficult to describe. Over there in the distance we can see France. I recall the poem of Juan Ramón:

> On yonder side of the mountain
> lie the fields of Spain.

We take photographs, which, given the expertise of the photographers, will certainly turn out well! We remain there for a long time just gazing silently in the direction of France. For us, this view from Roncesvalles is the best sort of museum we could hope to visit. There is no guide. Only our eyes, which absorb the beauty, and our hearts and minds, which dream and meditate.

It was some time past midday. Everything had turned out wonderfully well. I thought to myself: Graham Greene's demon has not accompanied us today. Perhaps it never woke up. Or else it fell asleep at Mass.

Later, we visited the Valle del Roncal, but we took no more photographs here because Graham's mood had changed. (The wretched demon had returned after all!)

We have some difficulty finding a suitable spot for our picnic, but eventually find somewhere by the side of the road. A couple of young *guardias civiles* join us for a glass of the Galician wine from Las Regadas. They are delightful lads. They tell us that whenever they enter a bar they always salute, but many people do not bother to respond. It is astonishing how surly some people can be. Graham is very interested in all these details and very soon we are getting on so well that there may as well have been five in our party.

●

On our second night at Leyre, we have a bad omelette for supper and some rather greasy white rashers of bacon for breakfast. I write this with the greatest respect, knowing how mortified the monks would be. They are so kind and hospitable, and worthy sons of St Benedict, whose Rule obliges them to welcome anyone who comes to the abbey as they would Christ himself.

From Leyre, we plan to set off in the direction of Santo Domingo de la Calzada, but before leaving we take a few photographs at the request of the Abbot, who is a wonderfully good man. And now, very soon, we shall be able to see the cock and the hen in the cathedral at Santo Domingo de la Calzada again.

At Liedena, the first town on the way down from Leyre, we buy provender for our picnic: chorizo, cheese, fruit and bread. We already have enough water, ice and wine. We eat our snack not far from Logrono in a reasonably shady place and everyone is happy.

Graham talked to us about what life was like for a well-known writer when he first went to live in France.

At Leyre, the inn had been fully booked, which was why we stayed in the cloister. The kind monks had telephoned the parador at Santo Domingo de la Calzada to reserve rooms for us, but it was impossible, they were fully booked. It might have been different if only I had been allowed to telephone myself and mention Graham Greene's name. Having ascertained the *parador* was full, they called St Teresa's Hostel for Cistercian nuns, and that is where we are bound.

During our picnic, Graham is concerned about our lodgings. 'Too much of Church on this journey', he announces somewhat solemnly.

We go directly to the cathedral. And there they are, the cock and the hen in their cage. Graham loves looking at this cage and hearing the origin of the miraculous legend.

At St Teresa's hostel, we are received by a very attractive young nun.

'What a beautiful woman!' Graham whispers in my ear.

When we go into the dining room, it is quite clear that the demon has returned. Nearly everyone there is an elderly woman guest. Quite clearly, the place is a summer home for old age pensioners.

Graham is seated opposite a very fat woman who is devouring her food voraciously. He is so appalled that, time and again, he looks to one side with an expression of near horror on his face. I make a supreme effort to contain my laughter and say to him as seriously as I can:

'Try to imagine that you are not looking at her; imagine it is the pretty young nun we met when we arrived.'

Graham had a horrible supper.

To make matters worse, there was a loudspeaker that made a very unpleasant noise and which kept blaring out and summoning such and such a lady to the telephone. Every time he heard it, Graham would hunch up his shoulders as if protecting himself from some imminent danger.

The only compensation that evening lay in contemplating the spirit of charity with which these good old ladies smiled at each other, as well as the charming and very pretty young girl who attended us with sweetness and an angelic smile. Graham was enchanted by her. He is always captivated by feminine beauty and he found it hard to take his eyes off a pretty young face. It is not a question of sensuality. It is something purely aesthetic. He is extraordinarily sensitive to beauty. Noticing Graham's obvious satisfaction, the 'Third Man' commented:

'In these small towns, you still find young girls whose innocence and purity of soul is reflected on their faces.'

I think the girl must be a postulant for the Cistercian convent.

Graham has another curious anecdote to relate on this occasion. He told us how he once made a journey to the Congo with his friend, Mario Soldati. They went to call on a religious community where Mario Soldati fell madly in love with a beautiful young nun.

'And what happened?' I asked Graham.

'Nothing. There wasn't time.'

●

Graham slept badly. The bed was too narrow. His demon had not deserted him. We went to change French francs at the Banco Zaragozano in Santo Domingo de la Calzada. We were kept waiting for over a quarter of an hour.

'Absurd, this is absurd,' grumbled Graham, and he would have walked out if he had had his passport and money in his hands. To make matters worse, the rate of exchange was low: eighteen pesetas to the franc.

Graham's patience appears to wear out easily today. At breakfast, I was frightened in case he got up to go because we had to wait ten minutes before we were served. The breakfast was disappointing.

'It would have been better to go to a cafeteria,' he muttered.

We ask the pretty young girl who served us last night if she could put some ice in our thermos. She returned immediately with the thermos so full that we could not close it, but she looked beautiful and wore her angelic smile. For Graham, this was equal to half a night's good sleep. It was the moment for my great friend's soul to awake. I felt certain that the girl was hoping to become a Cistercian nun and I am sure Graham and the 'Third Man' thanked God for the need to ask a favour of her. I was reminded of a scene in Sterne's *A Sentimental Journey*. I happened to have the book with me, and later I read the chapter entitled 'The Pulse, Paris'.

The Cistercian nuns had been extremely kind to us. We had come on the recommendation of the Benedictines at Leyre and we were setting off in good humour. For the time being, Graham's inauspicious demon was not very happy.

●

The best picnic of the entire expedition! Beside a stream, a few kilometres away, we cross into the province of Soria. We eat beneath a dense copse of trees, our tablecloth a rug on the ground. Photographs are taken. Enthralling conversation about Bruce Howard, an American collector, who bought some of Graham's documents concerning the war against the mafia on the Côte d'Azur.

Graham tells us that he has no aptitude for speaking in public formally. He prefers to answer questions from the audience. I make the point that replying to questions is somehow more immediate and natural.

We discuss second-hand books and first editions in particular. 'They are big business nowadays', Graham says. How is it that a shabby and stained book in its original binding should be more sought after than a handsome, nicely bound modern edition? The world of second-hand books and first editions is a very strange one . . .

Someone mentioned the pretty young girl at St Teresa's hostel. We then speak about virginity. The 'Third Man' does not attach much importance to it.

'The world would soon come to an end if too many girls offered their virginity to God', he objects, though he may be biased.

I laughed at this objection. I tell him not to worry; this will not be the reason why the world will end. It is already obvious that man's instinct for mischief will continue and the world still go on turning. Graham laughed and seemed persuaded by my argument.

We continued to dwell on the theological aspects of this subject. I pointed out that for a Catholic there was no room for discussion; virginity was superior to the married state, and that was an article of dogma. Later on, to be more precise, the lives of each priest or nun, and each married person, would show who had been the more perfect. It could well be that a married person might lead a semi-chaste life, and a religious person behave like a cuckoo.

Graham can be a devil. Whenever we get involved in a serious discussion about doctrine – which almost always originates with him – he produces some anecdote that defuses the situation. This time he sent us into fits of laughter by elaborating more fully on the scarcely virginal propositions, he had mentioned to me before, made to him by the woman, who was a professor at a certain American university, who made the pretext of his eightieth birthday her reason for coming to see him.

'Like me, she was not someone exactly drawn to virginity', he concluded.

●

Our journey to Madrid will put the finishing touches to the self-portrait.

We had dinner and spent the night at the *parador* at Siguenza where there is an ancient and enormous castle that dominates the historic city. Over dinner, a serious discussion between Graham and the 'Third Man': Graham accuses him of machismo, quite unjustifiably. Graham's wretched demon is in fine form, but his conscience is pricking him and he sleeps badly.

'I slept badly', he said when I called on him next morning. 'I feel guilty about last night. I get upset by machismo. That's why I said what I did.'

From that moment on, he was perfectly delightful with the 'Third Man', otherwise known as Octavio Victoria Gil.

The battle against the Côte d'Azur mafia, which led to the publication of *J'Accuse*, had begun by now. There were clear links with the Italian mafia: power, money, drug trafficking.

Today, Graham reminds me of a saint. Few people are so conscious of their behaviour towards others, and what takes place in their hearts and minds. I tell him that it was not as bad as all that; that he should forget about the matter. I tell him something about our friend and companion, Octavio, and how during a protest by some of my students in the English Literature first year course at Complutense University, he had been my great supporter. A contemptible fellow professor, lacking in knowledge and conscience, had been the *eminence grise* behind the insurrection and, backed by his cronies, he had chosen a ringleader to organize a written petition against me and declare that they would never set foot in my class again. A small number of heroic third year students stood up against this libellous farce, however, refused to sign, and did not miss a single class.

When, after three months of not attending classes, the ringleader, whose name was Mena, explained to the *eminence grise* that he was frightened they might fail and lose all support, the wretched professor in his very own English Literature department, tried to urge him on by saying, in a whisper that could be heard by everyone: 'You must all persist. If you are united, you will triumph in the end.'

The rebels, having been instructed what to say, asked for a meeting of the Department. The Dean, Antonio Ruiz de Elvira, in a gesture of courtesy, called to tell me that the meeting depended upon my being there. He was not very happy about it, and I, being a real novice in such matters, told him I would be quite happy to attend. The meeting took place. I would describe it in the terrible words of Paul Claudel: 'Death to the Christ and long life to the bull!' A good number of the dissatisfied students disappeared from the University (I am not sure why) either that same term or the following year.

The fourth- and fifth-year students were entirely on my side. After all, they had more reason to judge me for I had already taught them for two or three years. Octavio was in his fifth year. Along with two or three others, he was the very soul of reason.

Graham was very moved by this story and could hardly believe it. A number of years later, when I was already living here in Vigo, I would tell him another story about university life, but an altogether crueller and more shameful one. It also has to do with two professors from the English Department, but I don't want to describe it now since it deserves half a book to itself.

'But what was going on? Do the parents of the students know about this abominable act?' he asked.

I did not reply. I only added: 'The *eminence grise* fled, when he realized that he had failed. He had lost all credibility and was covered with shame, or fear.'

Anything to do with student life fascinated Graham.

●

... This was the way Graham and I used to confide in each other; there were endless general confessions of this kind. On the way to the airport we talked about Aurelio Verde, another 'Third Man'. Graham never forgot that Aurelio came to stay with me here after I had had a throat operation. We talked about how Aurelio had been both cook and nurse, and much else, during my recuperation. Graham and I felt both encouraged and moved by acts such as this.

The miserable moment always comes when we have to bid each other an effusive farewell. On this occasion, I don't know whether that cursed demon that preyed on our happiness went with him or decided to stay in Spain, but it certainly played its part on this journey – on all our journeys – in providing the brushstrokes to this self-portrait of Graham's most hidden world.

CHAPTER VI

SILVER JUBILEE OF A
FRIENDSHIP

F OR SOME TIME Graham and I had planned to commemorate
the silver jubilee of our friendship with a double celebration in
Vigo as well as in Antibes. The day that I had received my first letter
from Graham Greene was 30 June 1964. That was when it all began,
although our first meeting was not until 1973. It is not easy to describe
in a few lines how much the occasion meant to us. For me, the
meeting has been a key event in my life; Graham said much the same,
although I never believed it.

Four months before these celebrations, Graham telephoned from
Antibes, rather earlier than normal. Knowing how punctual these
chats were, I did not imagine it could be he. Speaking with his characteristic self-control and as if there was nothing out of the ordinary,
this is how our conversation began:

'Leopoldo, did I wake you up?'

'Oh, Graham. No. What is it? Has something happened?'

'Very bad news.'

Naturally, I was alarmed and asked what it was.

'Elisabeth had a stroke.'

And Graham described what had happened and how the police,
who happened, providentially, to be following in a car behind hers,
had taken care of everything. He had rung me at this time so that I
might remember her in my daily Mass. This was always something
to which he attached great hope, and he knew that I usually said it
at about half past nine in the morning. Our telephone conversations
took place at ten o'clock, after he had written his daily ration and
dealt with correspondence. To ring at any other time, only ever
meant that there was urgent need for prayers.

It was a long conversation. Graham was always in total self-control
at difficult moments in life, but what had happened to Elisabeth was

extremely grave. Firstly, he adored her, and secondly, she meant almost everything to him. Her foresight, her good sense, her wise advice, were irreplaceable.

'I don't know what to do', he said.

This conversation, a significant one in Graham's life because of what had occasioned it, took place on 25 February 1989 on the dot of nine o'clock in the morning. This is not the place to repeat what we said, but I mention it none the less to show how grievous the shock was for Graham – and, of course, for me as well – before relating how we marked our anniversary.

●

Three weeks later, on 21 March 1989, Graham telephoned again at seven o'clock in the evening. He had rung in the morning at the usual time but I had been out. After the usual greeting, he said in a well-disposed, happy tone of voice:

'I'd like to spend a few days with you.'

'But how splendid, dear Graham.'

He went on: 'For some time I've been meaning to come and see you so that we can start our anniversary celebrations, but I've been very forgetful. I don't suppose one of our friends would be available to drive us.'

'Don't worry. Everything will be arranged. When are you thinking of coming?'

'The 25th would suit me, or the 26th.'

'Call me tomorrow afternoon, if you can, to see if I've been able to find anyone who can be our 'Third Man'.

It was agreed. But a few hours later I telephoned Graham back to let him know that everything was resolved. We now had a 'Third Man', Miguel Fernandez, a friend who had accompanied us in the early years. His father had just been operated on for cancer, but he was already much better and Miguel was happy to drive us.

'Don't forget to ring up the little *parador* on the way, the one we liked so such.'

Graham was referring to the *parador* at Puebla de Sanabria where we had stayed several times and where we were always well looked after.

It was the beginning of Holy Week. There was no time to lose. I telephoned the *parador*. Every room was booked. I explained the situation to the Manager who was as courteous as ever and told me he would ring back in half an hour. He did so, and we were given three single rooms. Everything seemed to be running smoothly.

But man proposes and God disposes. The following morning Miguel telephoned from a hospital in Segovia. His father had taken a turn for the worse and he could not leave his side. It was impossible to get hold of any of our other friends for everyone had left for the holidays. To make matters worse, my telephone was out of order . . . On the radio I heard that in the past two or three days more than sixty people had already been killed on the roads. I felt really alarmed. Was it prudent to drive to and from Madrid to meet Graham, tour round Galicia, and then drive back to Madrid again? In this case it was not the impish demon of the previous chapter, but my guardian angel who gave me my instructions: cancel the rooms at the *parador* at Sanabria, fly to Madrid, and then travel to Vigo and back to Madrid again by plane. Driving around Galicia was less of a problem.

I obeyed my guardian angel, told Graham the reasons for my decision, and everything worked out wonderfully.

•

On Holy Saturday, 25 March 1989, Graham arrived at Madrid on an Iberia flight. My friends, Amancio and Sylvia Lavandeira were with me at the airport to meet him, and we spent the three hours between the arrival of the plane from Nice and the departure of the flight for Vigo at their home. They organized everything perfectly and Graham was delighted. Sylvia is English and highly intelligent, and Amancio is a most amusing man. The four of us had already made several journeys together, to El Toboso, Cuenca, and the mountains around Madrid. What with vodka and all the things we were offered to eat, our Silver Jubilee celebrations had already begun.

Graham took out of his pocket a letter he had just received from Spain. A newspaper article had been enclosed, written by the mayor of a provincial city, which claimed that Graham Greene had been on the point of visiting the city but that the visit had been postponed. It was all complete nonsense, but it was one of many misleading and fictitious articles published about Graham Greene in the Spanish press.

One national daily published in Madrid wrote about Graham Greene, and his 'occasional collaborator', and published a front-page article that was a synthesis of four pages from a chapter in *Ways of Escape* which, it was stated, Graham had written for that newspaper. The Madrid paper translated the passage very badly, even changing the meaning of certain sentences.

I should like to make one matter absolutely clear. Graham Greene never collaborated with any Spanish newspaper or magazine, at least during the last twenty-seven years of his life. He gave two interviews to *El País*, and that was all.

I could go on mentioning many similar inventions. In *Doctor Fischer of Geneva*, Greene demonstrated that there is no limit to human avarice. Neither is there a limit to vanity, the characteristic vice of the fool.

•

Nevertheless, we were both in a good mood when we sat down to dinner in the kitchen that evening. Graham never wanted to eat in the dining-room in Vigo. 'The kitchen is perfectly adequate. Look at the view we have over the sea,' he would say. How much this man taught me about simplicity and humility! Dinner? It was our usual Spanish omelette, a bottle of Murrieta 1981, and a small cake or other. It tasted marvellous and we talked non-stop as if nothing unfortunate had happened.

From the kitchen we went into the drawing-room and drank two small glasses of 'Tonico Cariño' each. We drank to the 'Silver Jubilee of our Friendship' and chatted without once looking at the clock. The conversation made me very happy: he had patched up his quarrel with his nephew, Graham Carleton Greene. He had been very touched by his nephew's treatment of Sarah, his stepmother, as well as of Elisabeth and her family. He knew that this news would make me very happy indeed. It was something we had spoken about frequently, and I had often told him all about his nephew Graham's many kindnesses to me.

He went on to advise me to beware of an unauthorized biographer by the name of Mockler. He told me was tired of foolish people asking him about the theme or the background to his novels. Graham never used the word 'thesis'; he thought it far too pretentious.

'My intention is clear enough from the epigraph at the front of each book', he said.

We discussed the epigraph to *Getting to Know the General*. Graham preferred Browning to Tennyson, but one day he opened a volume of Tennyson and came across the perfect lines to describe his friend Omar Torrijos.

We continued to talk about epigraphs. The one he used in *The Captain and the Enemy* is also very apt. Without ever having delved very deeply into this novel, I expounded my view about the Captain's 'enemy'. For me, it was both the 'Devil' and the Americans, as Pablo affirms in the novel.

'That's Pablo's view,' Graham said to me. 'It's more philosophical than that.'

I had not fully understood the novel. Later, I did. The Captain had God knows how many enemies; certainly all those whose rights he had infringed ... I praised the moral and emotional qualities of the Captain in respect of Lisa, but I was reminded by Graham that he was a thief and a drug trafficker. Perhaps the positive side of his nature would overcome the negative, but, to return to the epigraph again:

> Will you be sure to know
> the good side from the bad,
> the Captain from the enemy?

'It seems to me that the love between the Captain and Lisa is entirely platonic,' I said to him.

'Who knows?' Graham replied.

I believed that I now understood the book completely. At least, I hoped so. A discussion with Graham Greene about the roots of one of his novels was so illuminating. How superficially people write about his books! At least I never wrote about them without talking to him first.

By now it is well into the night and very late. It seemed to me that Graham was waiting until the last possible moment to tell me about something terrible he had experienced. It had been a terrifying passing temptation, but for a minute, when he heard about Elisabeth's sudden illness, Graham had thought of taking his 'pills' and committing suicide. Thank God, he did not try to do so, as I knew he would not!

•

26 March 1989. It is Easter Sunday. Graham has risen earlier than I. I find him reading Chekhov. He is jotting down notes on the inside back cover. We have breakfast. He continues reading while I go to smarten myself up.

We chat for a while on our own in the drawing-room, after which we prepare the altar for Mass in my study. There are just the priest and the acolyte at our Mass. We both take communion. Graham keeps on talking about the Gospel for Easter Sunday. It is the passage, already mentioned, that so appealed to Graham, about Peter and John running to the sepulchre (John 20, 1-9): 'They ran both together: and the other disciple did outrun Peter . . .'; the linen cloths lying on the ground, and the napkin, 'wrapped together in a place by itself'. For Graham, the scene had all the authenticity of an actual experience, so there could be no doubting its historical accuracy. 'It's like a twentieth-century journalist's account.'

We went to 'La Tahona' (Pintor Colmeiro) to look for food. The wine was 'Viña Costeira', in honour of Galicia. It was one we both liked.

We had forgotten to move our clocks on by an hour. At half past three we were about to take a siesta before going for a drive into Portugal, but it was actually half-past four and our new 'Third Man', José Carlos, was ringing at the door. We first set off along the coast towards La Guardia, then to the summit of Mt Santa Tecla. We returned via Tuy, travelling through woods and beautiful mountain scenery.

For supper we had a perfect Spanish omelette and some Riazan wine. Later, a drop of Señor Antonio's 'Tonico Cariño' helped extend our conversation well into the night. These nocturnal chats are very similar to those we have in Antibes or Sintra. They are conversations that go far beyond good and evil; they go far beyond mere confidences. There is no room for them in my notebooks; just a few hieroglyphics that I drive myself crazy trying to decipher.

●

The outstanding event of the week: our visit to Osera. It was pouring with rain that day. Our 'Third Man' has become a 'Third Woman': Maria José Alvarez, a teacher of English. Her English is perfect and her liberal ideology is akin to Graham's. The monastery was like an ice-box, but at least the monks put an end to our shivering with a colossal banquet and some Cacabelos wine. We slept the night at the monastery.

The next day, we went to Las Regadas to collect Señor Antonio and to take him to a restaurant. The great friendship that Señor Antonio and 'el ingles' (as the 'Gaiteiro' of Las Regadas calls Graham) have for each other is truly wonderful.

Today something that Señor Antonio said remained etched in Graham Greene's heart. He said it in a loud voice so that Graham should understand. 'I now have proof that I am immortal.'

He was referring to what he regarded as a miracle; a miracle which had recently prevented him being killed outside the Restaurante Caravel. It had meant just ten days in hospital.

The rain stays with us all the way back to Vigo. Maria Jose and Graham converse happily about their political philosophy. I sleep in the back of the car on the pretext of saying the rosary. There are some advantages to being a priest . . . .

29 *March*. We contemplate some of the views from Vigo towards La Guia and as far as El Castro. I took a lot of photographs. Graham has resigned himself to being a martyr to this implacable camera of mine.

We travel to Portugal for some grilled *bacalao* and *vinho verde*. The meal was a minor disaster. Neither the wine nor the *bacalao* were good.

There was further conversation after supper. Then Graham inscribed various books and autographed some documents. Not much time for sleep these days!

•

Graham's arrival in Vigo was a happy coincidence for I had been preparing a conference on his work. The Dean of Philology at the Complutense University had organized a series of conferences under the rather solemn title 'Masters of Philology'. In a polite, even affectionate letter, the Vice-Dean of Cultural Studies , Dr Santos Sanz Villanueva, was gracious enough to ask me to give one of these talks. He himself proposed the subject, knowing that as well as being a close friend, Graham's work was a special subject of mine. We agreed it should take place on 13 April 1989.

When Graham told me that he was coming to spend the last week in March with me, I saw it as something of a blessing. We would both be able to discuss my conference and perhaps I would be able to provide the students with a few interesting ideas. What Greene most liked about the notes I read out to him was the title which I had given the talk: 'You Can't Cross the Frontier'. My theme was *The Power and the Glory*. Together, we revised my lecture.

'If I heard that someone who had known Conrad or Trollope for

twenty-five years was going to speak about them,' Graham remarked,
'I would go and listen to them. You have known me since 1964 and
now we're beginning to celebrate the Silver Jubilee of our friendship.'

Half an hour before the lecture was due to start, I arrived punctually
at the conference room. Two friends, both academics, were waiting
for me.

They remained waiting, too. No one turned up. Not one single
student. None of the present lot of students knew me, for in 1986
Señor Maraval had ordered me to rest at home on compulsory retirement. There had been no resistance on their part. I have good memories of my English Literature students at Complutense. The Dean
had done everything that he was capable of doing.

When the time came for my talk that my talk would have ended,
I reported what had happened and even laughed about it. Then I
returned to Vigo. I should like to thank the Vice-Dean warmly for
the letter he sent me: 'You cannot know how much I regret what
has happened, and it says very little for our community. All I can do
is to apologize and thank you for expressing so delicately something
that might have been said somewhat angrily.'

Later, when I phoned Graham to tell him what had happened, the
line seemed to have gone dead. I thought that we had been cut off.
But it was not that; he was thinking. Later, we discussed what had
happened, and I learnt from his wisdom. On my table there is a book
which my great friend knew almost by heart: Unamuno's *Life of Don
Quixote and Sancho*. I opened it and read: 'This is wretched, absolutely
wretched.'

Now, after several years, I have decided to describe what happened
in this book. Perhaps these pages will have a larger circulation than
a university department, and, perhaps, upon reading them, certain of
its members may give up a few moments of their precious time to
reflect on our dear University.

●

On the way from Madrid to the airport, Graham recounts a strange
encounter he once had on a flight to London. The man who had
produced his first play was on the same flight, recognized Graham
and asked him whether he was Graham Greene. They had not seen
each other for many years. The man was now married to a Japanese
novelist, Nobuko. A few days later, Graham received an enormous
packet of manuscript pages in the post. It was a novel by Nobuko.

Graham began to read it: the first pages were very dull, but by the time he had read thirty pages, Graham had been completely won over. It was a book about the quarrels between rival theatrical companies in medieval Japan, full of fighting and murder . . .

Graham wrote to the author and gave her his highly favourable opinion, and told her to get in touch with his American publisher. In due course, the book was published. 'It may well have been a bestseller', Graham added.

After that, the novelist wrote long, rather boring letters to him, and telephoned him every fortnight. Graham had told her to telephone at about six o'clock in the evening. She did so punctually. Nobuko's husband told Graham that he hoped his wife was not being a terrible nuisance. He was not totally wrong . . .

We said goodbye to each other at the airport and looked forward to our next meeting. God willing, I would go to Antibes in July to continue the celebration of our Silver Jubilee.

•

On 21 July 1989, I set off for Antibes. Graham was waiting for me at Nice airport. During our last telephone conversation, he had asked me not to bring anything other than some tins of squid and Spanish biscuits, but I did not do exactly as he asked. We put the luggage in the car and set off for Antibes. Graham showed me to my room in the Hôtel L'Etoile. We both decided we needed a short siesta. At six o'clock, I arrived at his flat and we chatted before going to eat at Chez Félix.

We prefer eating on the terrace. The view from beneath the stone arch just beside the restaurant sets the imagination flowing, especially at this hour of the evening. It is a wonderfully calm and poetic sight.

Graham always seems to be in a good mood whenever I come to Antibes, but this time I don't feel he has recovered from his efforts over recent months to help his friend and British publisher, Max Reinhardt, launch his new publishing imprint. Graham is always extremely sensitive, but constant weariness can make him hypersensitive where his innermost feelings are concerned. I had no idea, a short time ago in Vigo, about what I was shortly to discover.

We discussed the biography that Norman Sherry was writing at some length. Graham thought it was too long and detailed. He again mentioned a book of about eighty pages in which the author would present a portrait of four or five other people. 'Why does he waste so much time talking about me?' he said.

It must have been the devil who brought the name of Mockler, the 'pirate biographer', as Graham called him, into the conversation. A mood of depression or anger seemed to come over him.

'I feel foolish having two biographies written at the same time,' he said. 'If possible, I am going to take legal action against the pirate biography.'

His good friend, Yvonne Cloetta, was with us. Together, we did our best to convince Graham that he had no reason to think himself 'foolish'. Quite the contrary. If various people wanted to write a biography of him, it was because there was something exceptional about him.

Graham was not open to persuasion at that moment. He always listened carefully to what others said, but this was one of those times when a momentary depression, or rather, a sense of total discouragement, would come over him. 'I feel I have come to the end,' he said with conviction.

It was not so. We told him over and over again that it was really not so. His clear mind and his whole psychology were proof of that. But there was no way of convincing him or raising his spirits.

What had been happening? Did Graham no longer feel he had the ability to produce major works as he had done up till now? Yet he continued to write, and to his own standards of perfection too. I tend to think that Graham had begun to be aware of how much his physical strength, which is essential for continuous intellectual creative work, was beginning to fail. Furthermore, that summer he had reached the limit of physical resistance, giving daily interviews to all the media, except television, in order to help Max Reinhardt with his new publishing enterprise. It had been too much and Graham said 'never more'. After all that frenzied activity earlier in the summer, it was now relatively quiet, but I wondered whether Graham subconsciously missed all that intellectual stimulus.

A few jokes helped Graham revive. He and Yvonne accompanied me to the hotel and we agreed to meet at eleven o'clock the next morning.

Next day, he seemed quite happy. He told me that he had fallen over again in the flat and had hurt his shoulder slightly, but it was nothing serious, thank God.

He explained carefully to me what he had told Norman Sherry

about seeing proofs of the second volume of his biography at an early stage. He wanted to avoid any errors in future.

Graham insisted on paying my hotel bill, but I refused. He told me again how pleased he was with his nephew, Graham. 'He is doing everything he possibly can for Elisabeth,' he said. His niece, Amanda, was sorting out all her mother's paperwork and dealing with his affairs. We then spoke to Elisabeth on the telephone before going to eat at the Auberge Provençale. Sirloin, vin rosé, and blackberries and cream, but it was hardly surprising. It was our jubilee, and the only shadow for me was the thought that we would not see our golden jubilee. For Graham, however, the converse was true; life had been quite long enough for him . . .

•

23 July 1989 was a historic day for both Graham's peace of mind and my own. Graham wrote a very important document for me. I have never mentioned it, but I keep the autograph document in case it may be necessary in the future.

We ate on our own on the terrace Chez Félix. Graham was delighted that I was drinking my share of wine. He believes that nobody here recognizes him, but I reckon virtually everyone knows him.

While we are eating, a dark-skinned man stops in front of us, greets Graham as 'Mr Greene' and speaks to him as if he were an old friend.

'He's from Dakar,' Graham explained to me afterwards. 'He's got eight wives and eighteen children.'

The man wore a fine black velvet tunic, covered with what I assumed to be rather expensive appliqué jewellery. On his head, he wore a splendid sort of black cap, similar to what village priests used to wear many years ago. He sold very expensive goods: women's leather bags, belts, necklaces and other finery. Apparently, all these things were made by his family in Dakar, and he earned a living for all of them by selling them in Antibes.

It is Sunday today. Another man, who is young, elegantly dressed and wears make-up, stops in front of Graham. He is dressed in a black suit and a black cravat. He speaks perfect English.

'He used to perform here for the diners,' Graham told me. 'His body went completely rigid when he did his act. It was as if he were made of metal.'

That evening Yvonne came to prepare dinner and, once again, we sat on Graham's balcony and ate magnificently. There was much laughter again, then later that night, before dropping me at my hotel, we went for a drive around the surrounding region.

Eventually, the time came for me to leave. We embrace once more, and then it is farewell to Antibes, to Graham's flat and to those memorable dinners.

●

The dinners at Antibes! My best moments with Graham were always at dinner time, alone, at his home. Lunch was always at a restaurant.

In the mornings, we would set out to do the shopping for the evening meal. Nothing that needed cooking, just food that was prepared beforehand: smoked trout or salmon, cold meats ... Our dessert was usually an apple tart. And a bottle of good wine was essential.

We would eat at about half past seven in the evening. But the meal was the least of it. The conversation, which had hardly slackened all day, now miraculously revived, and the evening would usually continue until eleven o'clock, midnight, or even later ... When I think back on our friendship, it is those conversations over dinner at Antibes that I now remember with most delight and nostalgia.

Of course, we talked wherever we were, but those conversations in Antibes were very different. It may have been the fact that we were on our own. Or perhaps it was the time of day, or the particular quality of the silence at dusk on the Côte d'Azur. Greene was always at his best towards the end of the day. If he was always an unparalleled conversationalist, at those dinners at Antibes he was an enlightened one.

Without being in the least pretentious, Graham would delve into his memory with disarming naturalness and the atmosphere would become almost magical. These were moments one never wanted to end. It was as if all sorrow had been removed. Past and future seemed to vanish; only the present mattered. Everything seemed to come to the surface during those long table discussions: Church and State, politics and the Pope, literature and theology ...

A friend is someone with whom one can discuss anything at any time without ever bothering about having to be careful. I have no idea what the future holds in store for me, but I do know that after those conversations in Antibes it will be difficult, probably impossible, to find anyone who could ever equal Graham's genius for friendship.

CHAPTER VII

A VISIT TO MADRID

T HERE WERE FEW things that my friend hated more than official
honours of any kind, for he had a horror of publicity and official
honours, and I suspect that Graham would have entitled this chapter
'Diary of a Comedy'.

In May 1980, Christian Casanova telephoned Graham from Paris.
He was calling on behalf of the Mayor of Madrid, Enrique Tierno
Galván, who was in Paris with him, and who wondered whether
Graham would agree to travel to Madrid at the invitation of the City
Council. Christian had become a friend of Graham's when he had
visited President Allende in Chile and he had been the person
appointed to look after Graham. (At that time, Graham did not know
the man who was inviting him, but Enrique Tierno was a great man
and a great mayor of Madrid.)

When the suggestion was first made, Graham thought it was a
minor matter that might take up a few hours. We were due to set
off on one of our trips during July, and postponing it by a day or
two would not make much difference. Graham had begun work on
Monsignor Quixote and, who knows, this 'official visit' might provide
some amusing episode for the novel.

Thinking of the two quiet weeks which we would spend afterwards,
Graham therefore agreed in principle. With Enrique Galván looking
after matters, Graham would have been able to accept anything. He
is a delightfully courteous man and he left the choices open to
Graham: the dates he would come to Madrid, a schedule that would
suit him, and everything else. The Council would work out a programme for his visit and would send it to Graham, and he could
modify or adjust it as he saw fit.

After speaking to Christian Casanova, Graham telephoned me in
Madrid. It was to be the first of countless discussions on the subject
of the 'official visit'.

Graham was going to write to the Mayor, but before he did so he wanted to know when I would be free. I told him that apart from the tenth of July, I would be available, and that he should go ahead and make arrangements.

Graham had told the people in Madrid that they should get in touch with me. He wanted me to be with him during the visit and to be his interpreter; they should confer with me about the programme and all other details. He sent me the following letter:

> My dearest Leopoldo,
> I have received a letter from a certain Manuel Ortuno of the Mayor's Office in Madrid and I have replied to him that I would be prepared to arrive in the evening of Sunday 6 July because I would have to be leaving again on the 10th or 11th. I have also told him that I would need an interpreter and suggested that he should get in touch with you and consult with you. What would be nice and what I will explain in the next letter when he has agreed to my plans would be to see you on the evening of 6 July and spend the evening with you in whatever hotel they have put me in. I hope to goodness they don't put me in the Palace.
> How sad about the Don Quixote. I had become very fond of that hotel.
>
> With all our love,
Graham

Meanwhile we laughed and joked, making rather light of the visit in our telephone conversations which continued until half way through June. Unfortunately, I only knew about Don Enrique from hearsay at this time.

●

I was beginning to get a little anxious, for no one from the City Council had been in touch with me. Presumably, Graham would arrive in Madrid on the 6 July, and he would want to know in good time what the programme of official duties would be, and what was required of him. On 13 June I decided to write to him. A series of telephone calls ensued:

17 June. First telephone call. Graham rang at 9.15 a.m. He had received my urgent letter about his coming to Madrid. I had told him that no one at the City Council gave any sign of life. He replied that the whole thing seemed to him to be rather poorly organised but not particularly serious. He did suggest that I might not have been at home when the phone rang. Graham sounded patient and in good humour. As far as I was concerned, the comedy was over but I had the feeling that a rather unpleasant tragi-comedy was beginning.

We agreed that Christian Casanova would accompany me to the airport to meet him. He told me that a lady had rung him about a hotel and suggested the Palace. He preferred the Wellington. Tickets had been booked with Iberia, but he wanted to travel by Air France. He would arrive at Barajas, God willing, at 5.30 p.m. on 6 July.

17 June Second telephone call. The moment I put down the phone to Graham, I had a call from the City Council. They had been unable to reach me; Graham Greene had only given my name and said that I taught at the University. They had asked Mayor Galván, but he had not heard of me. (Poor Leopoldo Durán!) It was agreed that I should come to the Town Hall on the 19th at 11.00 a.m.

17 June Third telephone call. I rang Graham to confirm arrangements. We discussed the hotel. He said that once we had finished with the official functions, we could move to the Mindanao; either then or on our return journey. We agreed that we would leave Madrid on 11 July, without any precise route in mind, but in the direction of Sintra. He had not told anyone where he would be going or who he would be with. Laughing, he told me that I should wear a tie to accompany him at these official ceremonies. I laughed too, for he has a loathing of ties . . .

18 June Fourth telephone call. I telephoned Graham at 8.15 p.m. to tell him about my conversation with Señor X. This man had also telephoned Graham, had been very pleasant and had agreed to the change of hotels; they wanted to pay for the hotel and the flight ticket. Señor X insisted on coming to the airport in spite of the fact that Graham had told him that he would have friends to meet him. He would, however, leave us alone later so that we could have 'a quiet evening'.

Graham and I agreed that my role should be to listen. He was brimming with good humour. He said he still had it in the back of his mind to cancel the trip on account of 'a diplomatic illness'. I told him that that really would be the limit and Graham very decently acknowledged that if they were paying for his ticket and hotel, he should be at their disposal during the mornings as well.

19 June Fifth telephone call We chatted for three quarters of an hour. I had rung to report on the meeting at the Town Hall to iron out the programme of events here in Madrid. Among other things, I told him how Señor X, turning to me, had announced that 'it was time that the world recognized some of Graham Greene's merits . . . that Spain wanted to.' I told Graham that I really felt rather sorry for the man; instructing me as to the merits of Graham Greene was rather stating the obvious. I felt like telling him that I already knew a fair amount about Graham Greene. However, we had agreed that my role in all this was to listen . . .

Graham changed the subject; he would travel from Antibes in casual clothes, he told me.

'And I'll come in my Panamanian shirt,' he joked. 'New adventures await us, Leopoldo, on the roads of Castille.'

Only later did I realize that I had forgotten to tell Graham the most important thing: that they would confer the City's bronze medal on him. I wrote him a brief letter.

28 June Sixth telephone call. I rang Graham to bring him up to date with everything that had occurred over the past few days concerning his official visit to Madrid. I mentioned, in particular, how off-hand, even rude, they had been with me in a certain department of the Town Hall.

'Cheer up, Leopoldo,' said Graham. 'We must treat all this as a joke. When I arrive at Madrid, we shall embrace, as we always do. I shall get into your car, not the official one. They'll understand. Perhaps we'll be able to gather enough material for another chapter of *Monsignor Quixote.*'

Eventually, I started to laugh again. Graham continued:

'This four-day "joke" will soon be over. On the afternoon of the 10th, we'll go to your hotel. On Monday, we'll have lunch with my Spanish publisher. Perhaps you could give her a call in Barcelona. After lunch, if you like, we'll set off for Oropesa. It would be a good idea if you were to book rooms . . . Treat it all light-heartedly. You must come to whatever events you want to be involved with. Don't bother with the others.'

I felt much better. Later, Graham mentioned an anonymous call he had had last Friday from Madrid, at the time he was having his siesta. The voice asked him why he was coming to Madrid, since he was not in the habit of accepting those sorts of invitations. The voice asked him whether he had any friends in Spain.

Graham replied with his usual brevity and tact. We said goodbye effusively, already imagining our forthcoming 'adventures on the roads of Castille'.

•

I had become rather irate about the way I was treated at the Town Hall. It is a great pity that the Mayor, Don Enrique Galván cannot read these lines. Perhaps his wonderful wife, Encarnita de Tierno Galván, may read them. She is a witness that what I have to say is the absolute truth.

After feeling very dejected on the 28 June, and having explained it all to Graham, he spoke to Christian Casanova who got in touch with me immediately. He cheered me up a great deal and assured me that everything would work out wonderfully. He was sure that Don Enrique knew nothing about what had occurred, but he would speak to the Mayor immediately.

I could hardly believe it. Barely half an hour had passed before Señor Ortuno telephoned me: 'The Mayor would like to speak to you for a moment.'

'Kindly tell the Mayor that I am at his disposal at any time,' I replied.

'Thank you. Wait a moment and he will speak to you now.'

And then Don Enrique Tierno Galván spoke. He wanted my address so that he could come and call on me! I was astonished by what I heard. I answered without further ado:

'What do you mean, Your Honour? It's out of the question. I am the one who should call on you.'

Eventually, we agreed that I should call on him in an hour's time. And so I came to speak to one of the men who has most deeply impressed me during my life. I came away from our conversation feeling uplifted. He was a great man. I was to receive many wonderful proofs of his and his wife Encarnita's affection, not just during Graham Greene's official visit to Madrid, but throughout Don Enrique's lifetime. I try to remember both of them in my daily Mass.

To return to the official visit. Once Don Enrique had been informed about what had happened, everything changed miraculously. The whole thing became a pleasure. Instead of being rude, everyone was perfectly polite and it became a pleasure to talk to those connected with Graham Greene's visit. They were considerateness itself. What had happened? What magical power did this man, Don Enrique Tierno Galván, possess?

When I told Graham about the unbelievable change of attitude, he said: 'The "joke" appears to be over. We shall now see how the play is performed.'

'I hope it goes smoothly,' I replied, 'because the stage director is Don Enrique.'

●

Graham Greene arrived at Barajas airport on 6 July. We embraced and he shook hands with the man who had come from the Town Hall to welcome him. There were a lot of reporters there and they tried to ask questions as he walked to the exit of the airport building. Someone asked him, for instance, whether he considered himself a great novelist. Graham smiled and said:

'I don't consider myself a great novelist. Dickens, for example, was a great novelist. I write novels, some of which are perhaps a little better than others.'

We got into our car and set off for the Wellington Hotel.

The four days were very full but were not too much of a strain. Needless to say, Don Enrique had had everything planned to the last detail, and he wanted Graham to be able to enjoy himself as well as fulfilling the various obligations required of him on an official visit like this. I cannot emphasize enough how very tactful, delicate and sensitive Don Enrique was at all times. Sensitivity was Graham's cardinal virtue, and Don Enrique's too, I believe.

Out of all the events that took place over those four days, for the sake of brevity, I will just mention those that I think were most interesting.

On 7 July in the morning, we called on His Excellency the Mayor at his office. After accompanying Graham to the door and introducing myself to Don Enrique, I had intended leaving them on their own. But this was impossible; the Mayor wanted me to be present at all the discussions between him and Graham. After this interview, Don Enrique bestowed the Madrid Medal on Graham and both men made speeches.

The press conference was an important event and there were an enormous number of journalists present. It all passed very easily, with Don Enrique as the chairman, while I interpreted.

At eight o'clock in the evening, the Mayor's office held a reception in the Cecilio Rodriguez municipal gardens at Retiro. Greene enjoyed the occasion because it was here that he met the Vietnamese lady, mentioned earlier, who reminded him of Phuong, one of the most important characters in *The Quiet American*.

The question session at the Casa de la Villa was packed. Don Enrique chaired the meeting again, and I interpreted. There were two hours of questions and answers. Graham was in an excellent mood and there was much amusement, which was reflected in the enthusiastic press comments.

A marvellous afternoon was spent in the British Embassy. The Ambassador and his wife were most delightful people, and we felt at home there from the very first moment. There was something very special about that couple and I shall never forget some of the highly confidential remarks they both made. Both Graham and I were extremely saddened when we heard the Ambassador had died only a few weeks after that enjoyable reception. It must have been a terrible blow to his wife, for they were both young. When we were on our own again, Graham said to me: 'We must come and visit this wonderful couple every year.' Sadly, it was not to be.

I leave to the end the lunches and private discussions Graham and I had with Don Enrique and Doña Encarnita. We ate several times at 'Los Porches' during the official visit and over the summers that followed and it was obvious that a sincere friendship had developed. The charming doctor, Dr Galván, in the novel, *Monsignor Quixote*, was based on Don Enrique, and I believe he is the most elegant of the doctors created by Graham. It was a delightful gesture of homage to the friend he had made in Madrid. Doña Encarnita's cultured and sensitive personality would also remain etched in his memory.

Something amusing or unexpected always occurred during these formal events. One afternoon, Radio Nacional went to the Hotel Wellington to interview Graham. My good friend had asked me particularly to try to be there punctually for the interview. I promised him that I would be at the hotel half an hour beforehand. It was terribly hot at the time and I had been sleeping very badly. I had set the alarm clock especially, but when I woke up it was more than an hour after the radio interview was meant to take place. I had not heard the alarm. There was nothing I could do. I was staying in another part of Madrid and there was now no point in hurrying. I arrived at the hotel feeling totally mortified. Graham was reading. I burbled something as I came in and held my hands to my head. Graham let out a peal of laughter. He was happy to know that, at last, I had had some sleep. He said, simply: 'We seemed to understand each other.'

Graham had been taking his siesta at the Wellington. He had locked the door to his room from the inside. He was awoken by a noise in the lock and when the door opened he saw a camera there. He was in bed and tried to cover his face with a newspaper . . . The photograph was published in one of the gutter press papers, but how had the photographer managed to gain access? Graham told the Mayor what had happened and mentioned it again at his press conference. Everyone was appalled, especially Don Enrique. There was nothing more to be said.

Among the photographs that were taken at the Retiro gardens, there is one of Doña Encarnita, Graham and myself. My left hand is placed between my chest and my jacket, and it looks as if I am holding something I want to hide. This blessed photograph struck Graham as terribly funny and throughout the entire trip he never stopped teasing me, saying that I was a secret agent appointed by Don Enrique to watch over him. He looked at me out of the corner of his eye and said: 'Now I know why you've got your hand there. You were holding a gun. I felt very safe.'

On 10 July, after lunching with Don Enrique and Doña Encarnita, we set off on the road for the *parador* at Oropesa. Graham was in a splendid mood and spent the whole journey making fun of me. Apparently, Radio Nacional had referred to me as 'the *insólito* Durán', and in *El País*, Rosa Maria Pereda had used the term 'the unusual Durán'. These two adjectives were more than enough for Graham to make this a marvellous trip for the 'Third Man' and me. In the end, this official visit which had looked as if it might be disastrous, had turned out very happily. Graham had even added a medal to his collection of honorary awards.

PART THREE

CHAPTER I

THE WRITER AT WORK

G RAHAM GREENE'S LITERARY vocation was inseparable from
his life. He frequently told me how damaging it had been not
to be able to get on with his work when it was interrupted by causes
outside his control. This often happened during the seemingly endless
five year battle against the mafia on the Côte d'Azur. Although his
books continued to be published during those years, it was at great
personal sacrifice. 'I cannot live unless I work normally,' he often
said to me. His pen was his life.

On 15 January 1988, I arrived in Antibes to spend a few days with
Graham. Two days later, walking past the Hotel Royal, Graham
complained, 'I'm worried that I don't have anything serious to write
at the moment.' He had just delivered *The Captain and the Enemy*.
He continued, 'One can only suppress the need to write with sleeping
tablets.'

I looked at him out of the corner of my eye. He changed the
conversation and told me that his next little book would appear at
Christmas and would contain the epigraphs from all his books.

No, Graham was not happy unless he was working. When he was
not doing so, he was depressed and unhappy. 'A writer, like a priest,'
he told me, 'never retires.' And when his good health had finally
deserted him, he saw death as a hope: 'Better to go,' he would say.

When he could no longer write, he died.

How did he work? Graham Greene's discipline was meticulous.
Only one thing was essential to him: silence. The arrival of summer
meant that Antibes became a veritable hell. The tourists disturbed
the peace of the town, and on Saturdays throughout the year there
was the noise of wedding parties and the roar of car engines.

Graham would rise at about half past seven. After the lightest
of breakfasts, he would sit down at his writing-table to compose
approximately three hundred words, which he would carefully count
when he had completed his task. They were two hours of intense

and scrupulous mental work in which he would weigh the precise tone and effect of each word. In the margin of the manuscript, he would jot down the exact number of words he had completed until that moment.

He always wrote by hand, and during most of his later years with an extra-fine black, or blue-black, Japanese pentel ball pen. I have kept one of the ones he used to write *Dr Fischer of Geneva*.

After that, he would sit down to confront the day's post.

Graham Greene worked in the morning, and in the afternoon he would correct whatever he had written that day. He would do that at about four or five o'clock every day, after resting a short time taking a siesta, although he did not always sleep. He would read out aloud what he had written so as to achieve the full euphony of each sentence. He attached great importance to the cadence of a sentence. For him, the highest praise that could be given to a book was that it was 'readable'. By this he meant that the book was interesting, that the ideas were put over with suspense, and that the style had a rhythm. Before he corrected anything, he would drink something to stimulate his inspiration.

Once the book was finished, he revised the whole work. I am convinced that this was frequently the hardest thing of all for him. Sometimes I heard Graham say that he felt as if he were 'blocked' and could not carry on with his work. While he was working on a manuscript, he was carried along on the wings of inspiration; he felt happy – relatively happy, he could not aspire to more! – as he saw his work advance. But when the time came to revise and correct the completed book, it seemed an endless task. With almost all of the books he wrote from the time we first met, he would often tell me that he had finished correcting the manuscript and had had it retyped for a second or third time. Ultimately, however, the only way I could be sure whether or not a book was finished was when I heard that he was going to London to deliver it to his publisher.

Graham was never fully satisfied – the satisfaction was only ever relative – with what he finally handed over to his editor. I do not know whether he ever handed in a book convinced that it was good. Once the book had been published, I did occasionally hear him say that it was 'not a bad novel'. The exacting demands he imposed on himself probably accounted for the fact that some manuscripts were kept in a drawer for years. Some he returned to, and they eventually saw the light of day; others were never published.

To return to the matter of revision. When Graham corrected something, he did so with great thoroughness. At the time that *The Human Factor* had been returned from the printers and Graham had just finished correcting the final proofs, he told me:

'They were not too bad, but I took out Brezhnev's name because I don't believe that his serious illness will allow him to still be in power when the book is published. The book will appear in March, not in January as was first thought, because of commercial reasons. I also changed something about the solutions to African problems. It seems to me that will be very different from what I have described in *The Human Factor*. All that has had to be altered.'

As far as style was concerned, Graham set himself an almost unattainable ideal of perfect simplicity and precision, and he would remove any superfluous words.

When I was in Antibes, I arrived at his flat one morning and there on the table was his novella, *Doctor Fischer of Geneva*, typed and virtually finished. He was revising it at the time.

'It will be half the length of an ordinary novel,' Graham told me. 'I'm checking it now, and I'm only adding a few words and the odd sentence. At the beginning of my literary career, when I was revising a book, I had to cut a great deal of what I had written.'

It had taken Graham some time to reach the level of perfection that a writer can achieve. Here on my table, I have the penultimate typescript of *Monsignor Quixote*, corrected in his hand. On the first page there are no corrections; on the second page two words have been changed; no corrections on page three; on page four he has removed some ellipsis points. In the entire book, some fifty words have been changed. This was in 1982.

Six years later, however, the revision of *The Captain and the Enemy* almost drove him to despair. He did not like it. He never had liked it. He returned to the typescript several times; on various occasions he told me: 'at last it's finished'. And yet, on 9 November 1987, he was still working on this stubborn novel. And to think he had kept it in the drawer of his table for fourteen years!

Something similar had happened with *Getting to Know the General* four years beforehand. The number of typescripts and the amount of corrections! In October 1983 I had been expecting him in Madrid, but on the 21st of that month he said to me on the telephone:

'I'll see if I can come for a few days, but the book awaits me. I've finished the first draft, but it still needs an enormous amount of work.'

On 17 December he told me that he had finished the biography of Torrijos, but that he was not happy with what he had written. He went on correcting and retouching constantly, as he always did. As late as 16 January 1984, he was still saying the same thing:

'I'm waiting for the retyped copy of the book on Torrijos, so that I can do further work on it and make more corrections.'

Many years earlier he had spoken to me about *The Honorary Consul*. There had been four edited typescripts of that novel in all.

•

How did Graham Greene plan a novel? Reading these conversations we had, or rather these syntheses of them, I find that there are certain passages which are of crucial importance in determining the basic elements that Greene needed to begin a novel.

One night at dinner with some of our friends, stimulated by a glass or two of excellent wine and speaking with that wonderful clarity and simplicity, Graham made a number of comments about the novel. They amounted to a brief but profound definition of the genre. This is literally what he said:

> A novel is a work in which characters interrelate. It
> doesn't need a plot. The novelist's own intervention must
> be very limited. What happens to the author of a novel
> is rather like the pilot of a plane. The pilot needs to get
> the plane off the ground. It takes off with the help of the
> pilot. Once it is in the air, the pilot does virtually
> nothing. Once everything has started working, the
> characters begin to impose themselves on the author,
> who no longer controls them. They have a life of their
> own. The author has to go on writing. Sometimes he
> writes things which appear to have no raison d'être. Only
> at the end is the reason apparent. The author intervenes
> to allow the plane to land. It is time for the novel to end.

We were fascinated listening to these remarks and no one interrupted.

Another time, during one of those long nocturnal conversations at Sintra, I asked him how he planned his books. Those nights in Sintra, with just the two of us sitting in his room, were like the nights in Antibes, and Graham was inspired. He replied:

'I plan the broad outline of the book: the theme, the beginning, the end ... possibly some of the main events which will occur. But I frequently let go of the reins and allow the horse to take whichever path it chooses. One shouldn't slacken the reins too much, though neither should one hold them too tightly.'

A particular scene or an experience which impressed him might provide the basis for a novel. After spending a day or so in a particular place, he would announce enthusiastically: 'This could provide the beginning for a novel.'

As time went by, he convinced me of the enormous responsibility that certain people may have had in the making of his novels. People who, for one reason or another, Graham had come across during his lifetime and in whom he had placed some high expectation. A few years after we had begun our journeys in Spain and Portugal, Graham gave me the typed first chapter of *Monsignor Quixote*. In his own hand, at the top of the first page, he had written:

> For Leopoldo, the opening section of a novel which will
> never be finished. It may remind him of our 1977 voyage
> and the flame of Hell in Badajoz. With love from
> Graham.

When I read these lines, a light switched on inside my head and an inner voice seemed to say: 'It will largely depend on you whether this novel is ever completed.' After the publication of *Monsignor Quixote*, Graham made this quite clear in a letter.

Graham often assured me that he had never set out in search of material for a novel, whether it had been in Mexico, Indo-China, or in Spain. It was the theme or subject which came to him and seemed to beg to be brought to life. He neither looked for subjects or for characters; *In Search of a Character* was, simply, a term to justify his travels in Africa.

Whenever a subject suggested itself and refused to go away, Graham tried to describe the effect that subject had had on his life. In his Preface to *The Third Man*, for example, he relates how, years beforehand, he had written the following opening paragraph:

> I had paid my last farewell to Harry a week ago, when
> his coffin was lowered into the frozen February ground,
> so that it was with incredulity that I saw him pass by,
> without a sign of recognition, among the host of
> strangers in the Strand.

Within this paragraph was enclosed a latent life that would later burst into fruition in the script he wrote for the famous film.

Occasionally, an actual scene would appeal to his imagination which he would reproduce almost exactly in order to raise it to a higher emotional plane. This was what happened with the explanation of the Holy Trinity in *Monsignor Quixote*. Graham copied down our conversation, slightly altering exactly what was said by whom. But he created the nagging remorse which tormented Father Quixote throughout his life, thereby introducing a transcendental quality to the scene. It was hardly the time for him to have compared the Holy Ghost to a half-bottle of wine!

•

At the San Michel restaurant in Lisbon, I asked Graham a few more details about how he went about creating his books: the landscape, the subconscious, dreams etc. He replied:

'I'm not interested in landscape, or how a house may be decorated – whether it contains a lamp or a staircase – except in so far as these things affect the evolution of any of the characters in the novel. That is why I am not a great admirer of Sir Walter Scott.'

The subconscious played a crucial part in virtually all Greene's work. This hidden world revealed itself most interestingly in his dreams. I believe that the influence of the subconscious in his work is incalculable. He attached great importance to it and he never tired of discussing his dreams. He would almost always refer to them when we got up in the mornings.

If one asked him about the role of the subconscious in his work, he would sometimes shrug his shoulders, as if it was impossible to be specific. Sometimes he would laugh and say 'who knows whether what we write when we are awake is the same as what we write in the mind when we are asleep'. He could not put it more clearly than that, for the subconscious is a mystery.

What did he have to say about the part that dreams played in his books? Graham was much more explicit about the influence of dreams. He had learned time and again from experience that a dream of great clarity could come to his aid, showing him the right path to take, at times when his mind was blank, or blocked, and he did not know which way to turn. A typical example is the dream that Querry had, which Graham mentioned to me in a letter (31 August 1971):

> It may amuse you to know that the dream you refer to
> on pp.394–5 was an actual dream of my own which
> arrived when I was badly stuck at that point in *A
> Burnt-Out Case*.

This dream dictated the novel. Querry realised that he was risking his last chance of salvation. His selfishness was killing him. And so he decided to become useful to others. This was what the book was about: 'a great parable on Christian charity'. Graham liked this description very much.

In *The Comedians*, four or five of Brown's dreams also play an essential part in the novel. I call them dreams of grace, for poor Brown is saved through these dreams.

Graham dreamed a great deal. When he woke up, he would switch on the light and write down a brief resumé of his dream, so that he should not forget it. He would complete the resumé later in the day. His important dreams were kept carefully in a bound notebook. I remember one volume with an elegant binding which his publisher had given him and which had the title *Thomas Mann*. He intended to write a novel using a selection of these dreams. One day, in Antibes, he read out the prologue and epigraph to this book to me. The epigraph was from Heraclitus:

> The waking have one world in common, but the sleeping
> turn aside, each into a world of his own.

The prologue was also quite delightful. I asked him to read it to me again, but he blushed slightly as usual, and replied: 'Once is enough.'

We went out for a walk by the sea and we continued to talk about the book about his dreams.

'I may write a book with a title something like "Scenes (or Characters) from Another World" without further explanation,' Graham said to me. 'It might begin: "Yesterday I was in Buckingham Palace.

I was standing close to Queen Elizabeth. The Duke of Edinburgh arrived ...".'

The book on his dreams, *A World of My Own*, has now been published. I only regret that Graham could not have prepared it for publication himself.

•

Graham mentioned the enormous difficulty of making a real, known person the hero of a novel. It was a subject he had spoken about before. The hero of his unfinished novel about Panama *On the Way Back* was based on Chuchu, but the real Chuchu kept interfering with the imaginary character he was creating. It was the first time he had tried to write a book with a hero of this type. It turned out badly, and so Graham wrote *Getting to Know the General* instead.

He spoke to me about the need for the characters the author creates always to be true to themselves. Apropos of this, he spoke to me about the critic, Martin Turnell, who had severely criticized *England Made Me*. According to Turnell, the author never developed the characters; they never evolved. Graham argued that it was not he who was preventing them developing or evolving, but the heroine Kate, who turns back within herself because she does not want to appear as if she is in love with her brother Anthony.

On many of his longer journeys Graham had kept a diary. Occasionally he looked at these again later and found passages that could be used for a book. One such passage concerned some characters who were excavating a grave. They were doing so very quietly for fear that the soldier buried on one side might be angry, or that the girl buried on the other side might wake up and discover her condition.

I remember we were once discussing Edwin Muir's poem 'The Combat'. Graham thought it one of the best poems in English literature. He remembered Muir with deep gratitude. As a critic he had been very helpful to Greene at the beginning of his literary career.

I asked him to tell me a little about the difficulties he had had in those early days. He said:

'One day I decided to send *The Man Within* directly to Heinemann, having already made various attempts at other books. I thought I would have to wait months for a response, but after a fortnight the Editorial Director rang up and said he would like to see me. I was in Oxford and I had 'flu, but I set off for London immediately. The

Director told me with great tact that they were going to take a gamble and publish the book. They sold almost 8,000 copies, which was excellent for those times.'

Later, he told me how he was constantly weighed down by economic worries; how, in six weeks, he had written *The Confidential Agent* during the mornings, while at the same time writing *The Power and the Glory* more calmly during the afternoons. He had no money in the bank to support his family. Necessity obliged him to take stimulants when he worked.

'Later, during the war,' Graham continued, 'I had a regular salary and I could write without quite the same anxiety. It's very difficult to live off writing to begin with.'

He was shocked at how many writers produce one or two books and then disappear completely, despite the fact that their early books have been successful. Perhaps those authors resolve their financial problems and then do not bother any longer about literature. He reflected: 'I think that if I had been born into a wealthy family, I might not have written more than one or two books.'

On 24 March 1986, Graham told me: 'No more books now. Just letters. The day must come when one stops writing.'

But I laughed. I knew it was not true. It would be absolutely impossible for him to keep such a resolution and, indeed, he failed to keep it; there were still five more books to come, and Graham continued to write up to his final illness.

CHAPTER II

MONSIGNOR QUIXOTE STEP BY STEP

MONSIGNOR QUIXOTE WAS born in the cemetery at Salamanca. Miguel de Unamuno's tomb would become almost a place of pilgrimage for us on our summer jaunts, but the attitude of the cemetery officials I described there on our first visit had appalled Graham, just as the scant respect of the clowning gravediggers for the skulls they unearthed had shocked Hamlet.

'Unamuno? Number 340.' The cemetery official's casual, disrespectful tone profoundly affected Graham, who had a high regard for the great Spanish writer and thinker. As he stood there in front of the numbered box – 'one cannot call it a tomb' – the idea for his novel entered his mind.

'In front of that box number three hundred and something,' he wrote later, '*Monsignor Quixote* first came to life . . .'

The person Graham Greene had come to visit had simply been put away in a box. It was a *linda mudanza* [a 'fine revolution', *Hamlet*] and Graham had a sharp enough mind to see it.

From that moment on, these ideas would give way to other, clearer notions and, steadily over a period of seven years, they would shape themselves into *Monsignor Quixote*. This chapter, in broad outline, is a diary of how the novel evolved in Graham Greene's mind.

Naturally I refused Graham's request that day that I wrote something myself under the title 'In Search of Number 340'. It was obvious that he would have to write it and, after a few days, Graham had made up his mind that his next novel would have the title 'Monsignor Don Quixote'. He could not stop thinking about that visit to the cemetery at Salamanca. His mind became a volcano and he questioned me over and over again about it.

Graham Greene spent hours inventing scenarios which would bring his hero to life. The principal character would be based on me.

What a way to show his affection! It would, of course, be nothing more than a sketch!

Having decided on the theological issues with which the Devil would tempt Monsignor Don Quixote, Graham seemed to have set his mind on this title and we spent some time discussing the customary Spanish usage of terms such as 'Don', 'Señor', 'Monsignor' etc.

We discussed a number of matters concerning the Roman curia and the Church: its politics, its divine and human aspects and a hundred other things. We visited El Toboso. That morning Graham read Unamuno's essay on Cervantes' poor style. In El Toboso we went to see Dulcinea's house, the library with its collection of famous signatures, the church and other places of interest. He asked me all sorts of details about the imaginary nuncio from the Vatican who would raise the humble priest from El Toboso to the rank of Monsignor. 'This book will be based on material from our journeys,' said Graham.

•

The following year, Graham brought me some good news. He gave me the typescript of the first chapter of *Monsignor Quixote*. And with it was the dedication in his own hand. It was, he wrote, the first chapter of 'a book that will never be finished'.

I do not need to say how moved I was on seeing this first chapter. I read it and said simply: 'Of course you'll finish this book. You must!' He did not deny it and just smiled, but I knew in my heart that his guardian angel would keep him busy.

We continued to talk about *Monsignor Quixote*. How could one justify the Monsignor's journeys? What would the role of Sancho be in the novel? Perhaps the Mayor of El Toboso? But would this friendship not remind people of Guareschi's Don Camillo? I tried to explain that the novels were entirely different. How should Monsignor Quixote die? It is astonishing how various possible passages from the novel keep going round and round in his head.

I felt totally swept up in Graham's enthusiasm, and he never stopped asking me questions. What sort of clothing might Father Quixote wear in El Toboso? Would he use a soutane? Would he have worn a cross on the lapel of his coat while he was travelling? Gradually, the idea of the novel was taking shape in his mind.

We continued discussing these things over lunch one day in London. Graham had just finished rereading Cervantes' *Don Quixote*.

Father Quixote would be born in some non-specific place near El Toboso. There would be a parallel between him and the real Don Quixote.

Clearly moved, he told me about the special de luxe, numbered edition of the first chapter which was dedicated to me. It would be published by Sylvester and Orphanos in Los Angeles, California and printed, he thought, in time for Christmas.

He handed me the charming Introduction to the limited edition. This is how it begins:

> This is the first chapter of a novel which I am fairly
> certain will never be completed, but can I be quite sure?
> Sometimes I think that this is not a bad beginning and
> I am encouraged to continue, perhaps one day when all
> other work has failed me. Then I feel myself a little like
> Monsignor Quixote on the point of leaving El Toboso
> for unknown adventures.

Need I say how precious this two-page Introduction is to me?

●

The third chapter of Part I of *Monsignor Quixote*, 'How a certain light was shed upon the Holy Trinity', came about when we had arrived at Evora one day, tired after a long journey. Having washed and changed in the hotel, we set off to look for a pleasant place for dinner. It had been a very hot day and we were both thirsty and hungry.

Providence directed us to the 'Cozinha de St Humberto'. We ate well and drank even better. They recommended a *vinho verde*, 'Casel Miranda', and we ate some good fish. We needed the rest and we were in no hurry. It was an unforgettable evening.

At dinner, we spoke about the ever-present *Monsignor Quixote*. Graham was joking, imagining how Father Quixote might try to explain one of the Mysteries to the 'Mayor' of El Toboso. Father Quixote, in the novel, is a very simple man and does not resort to metaphysics easily. On this occasion he makes use of three empty bottles which are standing on the table. As a matter of fact, we had drunk two and half bottles of *vinho verde* and this was what Graham did. He stood the bottles in a line and said:

'Here are two large bottles and one small one. The wine in each one of them was of the same quality and the same vintage. This large bottle, the first one we drank, could represent the Father, the origin of the whole Mystery. This second bottle, identical to the first and containing exactly the same wine, represents the Son.

'And now we have this third bottle, a little smaller than the previous ones, although the wine it contained was identical to that in the other two. In spite of the fact that the bottle was smaller, it is certainly the case that it was this wine, the last bottle we drank, that gave us 'the spark of life'. This third bottle could represent the Holy Spirit. Equal in every way to the Father and the Son, God in just the same way as they were, if not quite as well known by the faithful. The Father begot the Son, and the two of them, through their love for each other, inspired the Holy Spirit. The Holy Spirit is eternal like the Father and the Son, but because he was inspired through them, we cannot help imagining him as slightly less important, a little younger. Isn't that it?'

We left the restaurant feeling restored and much more energetic, happier and calmer. The Holy Spirit is all of these things. We walked over to the plaza, next to the restaurant. There was a gentle and agreeable breeze.

Pensively, I turned to Graham and said: 'Your explanation of the Trinity is perfect. There is just one mistake. You have compared the Holy Spirit to a half-bottle, and that sounds a little heretical to me. The Holy Spirit certainly means happiness and peace of mind according to our Mother Church, but he is the equal in every way of the Father and the Son and it was not fair of you to compare him to a half-bottle!'

Graham modestly acknowleged his minor error. He struck his forehead with the palm of his hand in approval.

'Tomorrow we shall correct this doctrinal lapse', he promised me. 'Instead of two and a half bottles, we shall drink three. The error will be corrected.'

Graham Greene had spoken in the name of Father Quixote. The priest had unintentionally been disrespectful to the third Person of the Holy Trinity. The pang of conscience would remain with him all his life, and throughout the novel he bears a terrible guilt for his error. At the most important moments of the book, the burden of his regret makes life unbearable for him. He confesses that he is a great sinner: he has compared the Holy Spirit to a half-bottle of wine.

On the road to Lisbon in July 1977, Graham Greene thought long and hard about his novel. We discussed the classic books of theology that Monsignor Quixote would read, rather than famous books on chivalry. He asked me for the titles of books on morals that the Monsignor might read; for some picture of the seminary in which I had studied; the ideas and moral texts that were in fashion at the time. It was essential to have all these things worked out.

On another occasion Graham said: 'I am Sancho and you are Monsignor Quixote.' And there was one sentence intended for the first chapter, which he in fact omitted. The bishop from Rome was to say to Father Quixote: 'I have in fact eaten like a Spanish canon.' Graham went on: 'This sentence proves that the bishop was chosen wisely for a diplomatic mission in Spain; he knows the country well.'

In Oporto, the next night, Graham did not sleep a wink. We were lodging at a monastery. The noise from a clock on the wall prevented him sleeping and so he spent the night planning a scene between Sancho and Monsignor Quixote for the novel.

Graham had received the biography of Cervantes, *The Life of Miguel de Cervantes Savedra*, by James Fitzmaurice-Kelly, that I had sent him in Antibes. He had read thirty pages and put it to one side. He did not like it at all. The author tries to fictionalize Cervantes' life. 'What we need is history not fiction,' Graham tells me. 'It's unreadable. I'll try again, but otherwise we must look for another of those books listed in the bibliography.'

I told him on the telephone that I had sent a list of the sort of books Father Quixote might have in his library, as well as information about the tonsure. And I told him that I dreamt about Monsignor Quixote myself. Graham laughed, but I know that it is my dreams that encourage him to continue with the book.

At Evora again, at the 'Cozinha de San Humberto', Graham speaks about two further scenes for the novel: one at Villaviciosa, when Father Quixote goes to ask for some ice from a priest in a villa; and another at Santiago de Compostela – this happened four years before as I mentioned – when Father Quixote got angry seeing the scandalous behaviour of the tourists in the cathedral taking photographs and talking, and the canons 'singing horribly in the choir'.

The moralist Heribert Jone, with his surprising casuistry, provides Graham with hilarious amusement. Inspired by this curious figure, he spends hours contriving scenes to do with Señor Márquez's theories on *coitus interruptus*.

Having arrived in Sintra, at midnight Graham reads the manuscript of the second chapter of *Monsignor Quixote* to me. The great work is under way.

July 1978. Today we are going to have lunch at the Cozinha Velha in the Palacio Nacional de Queluz. When we got up this morning, Graham said to me cheerfully: 'There is a room full of pictures devoted to Don Quixote there.'

However, the German President was staying at the palace and we were unable to see the paintings.

'I'm sorry. They might have provided some inspiration', I said to Graham.

'I doubt it. I'm much more inspired by your gymnastic exercises when you get up in the morning and go to bed at night. In any case,' he added, 'we'll see them next summer.'

On his return from Anacapri (25 October 1980), he told me he had completed double the amount I had read in the first chapter. In a postcard sent from Anacapri he wrote:

'Fr. Quixote has nearly doubled in length. The travels have begun! Love, Graham.'

I was overjoyed by the postcard. The exclamation mark, as used by Graham, meant everything.

•

Graham is taking infinite care with each of the details of the book. He asks me the name of the garment to which the Roman collar is fastened. I tell him that in Spanish it is called a *pechera*. He suddenly realizes that in English the word is 'stock', but he likes the word *pechera* and this is the word he uses in the English text of *Monsignor Quixote*.

In 1980, before Christmas, I went to Antibes and Graham read out a large chunk of the manuscript of the novel. He was completely immersed in it. He even mentioned it on the telephone when answering certain questions from an agency in Jerusalem in connection with a prize he was being awarded in Israel for the 'Defence of the Individual'. They had awarded it to Bertrand Russell as well. A little while later, we read in manuscript about the ingenious interpretation which Sancho gives to the parable of the Prodigal Son.

We go out for a walk around Antibes and Graham buys a copy of Marx and Engels' *Communist Manifesto* which he needs for the novel. He outlines a scene in which a cloud hangs over Father Quixote because he has not been wearing his dog-collar, and of an encounter with a member of Opus Dei. I tell him that I hoped Opus Dei would not come out badly in the novel; but Greene assures me that this is the only time that a member of that organization will make an appearance.

There is not a conversation in which Graham and I do not speak about 'Monsignor Quixote'. On 22 April 1981, we were both in London at the same time, and Graham told me that it was now well advanced. He also told me that the last word uttered by Father Quixote would almost certainly be *compañero*. I told him I would be delighted if the last word spoken by Father Quixote were to be a Spanish one. And so it was: "Companero", he said, "you must kneel, *compañero*".' Father Quixote's mission in life was accomplished when he saw his friend kneel to receive communion. How Graham liked the sound of this word *compañero*! He would repeat it over and over again. *Compañero*. It was music and honey to his lips.

Graham feels an urgent need to go to Anacapri to get on with the novel. He is tremendously excited by it and his excitement is infectious.

We discuss slowly those passages in which Father Quixote's bishop and the Guardia Civil appear. Those passages mean a lot to me. The Guardia Civil stand for all that is honourable and orderly in Spain, and Graham Greene's clerical characters are always uplifting. As far as the bishop is concerned, he seems a decent man; but when I defend him, Graham says just three words to me: 'He is Hell'. The mere gesture of using his white silk handkerchief to wipe the slightest trace of dust from the chair on which he was about to sit beside Father Quixote's bed, said it all . . .

On our picnic in the summer of 1981, Graham Greene needed to choose a suitable location; it was to be the place where, in the film made of the novel, Father Quixote and Sancho spend the night. And it would be here that Father Herrera and Doctor Galván would come to make Father Quixote a prisoner.

At the College of the Vincentian Fathers at Villafranca del Bierzo, we had a long discussion about the powers a bishop could have to suspend a priest *a divinis*; whether he could do so, for what reason, and why he might not.

'It's almost certain that the end of the novel will depend very much on this conversation,' Graham announced.

We decide upon Osera. We both wonder about the scene in which Father Quixote is in the monastery after the car accident and is suspended *a divinis* by the bishop.

'Who was it who had the temptations which are sculpted in stone at the main gates of the monastery,' Graham asks, 'St Benedict or St Bernard?'

'Both of them,' I reply.

•

Graham wants to complete *Monsignor Quixote*, but he is anxious about finding somewhere to work during the summer. He is not able to write anywhere. In the end, he decides to go to Brighton, but not until November, to stay at the same hotel in which he wrote part of *Brighton Rock*.

He is totally absorbed in the book and keeps asking me about further details. Yesterday he was bothered about the rhythm of the title *Monsignor Quixote*, for in ordinary English pronunciation the first word has three syllables and the second, two. Today, he has decided to forget about this matter.

'I'm not going to rack my brain thinking about the rhythm of every sentence.'

However, it was a great relief to him when he consulted the *English Pronouncing Dictionary* by Daniel Jones, to ascertain that 'ki'xote' was correct English. So the title *Monsignor Quixote* was euphonious after all.

Our travels during the summer of 1981 were enormously important to the book. We discussed many doctrinal points, with the result that Greene changed the entire ending of the novel. Later, there would be further changes still.

On 26 November 1981, he left for England ready to finish the book, and a month later I received a letter which ended: 'Nearly finished Quixote. Love in haste. Graham.'

Within a few days he told me that he had finished the book. He told me about the epigraph taken from Shakespeare, and we talked about the Spanish publisher of this book: Argos y Vergara.

1 February 1982. Great joy! Today I received a finished typescript of *Monsignor Quixote* sent registered airmail by the Bodley Head. I read it at once and rang Graham to say that the revised ending seems to me to be extraordinarily successful and completely unexpected. We spoke for a long time. He is pleased and I am so thrilled, and as we end the conversation, he says: 'Keep the typescript that I sent you.'

He asked me to read the section dealing with the 'Mexicans' and the area in which they live very carefully and to send him a letter listing any changes that needed to be made. I did so. I sent him a long, six-page letter, and Graham modestly altered everything that I drew to his attention.

1982. I am off to Antibes. The proofs have arrived. At dinner that first evening, when I raise the subject of *Monsignor Quixote*, Graham says: 'Well, the book will be around for twenty years or so, and then it'll be forgotten.'

I did not agree with him.

We speak for some time about Father Quixote's last Mass. Was he delirious? Affected by that overwhelming grace, was it a real Mass? 'For my part,' I told Graham, 'the words you put into the mouth of Father Leopoldo in his discussion with the professor are the most moving and apt in the whole book.'

Graham replied with his usual simplicity: 'I liked them too.'

We discuss the likely reaction of the critics to *Monsignor Quixote*. Graham reckons the British press will not be particularly keen on the book. I think the opposite. Graham said their reaction did not matter.

In fact it was excellent.

●

Marvellous news. *Monsignor Quixote* arrived in his Rocinante! It was the Canadian edition. Two months later, in London, Graham presented me with a copy of the British edition. His brother Hugh was with us and said: 'I'm looking forward to what the critics here will say, for they have never cared for Graham's humorous books.'

Graham says that the book owes a great deal to me; that without me it would never have been written. He would repeat this in a letter, and his generosity and the simplicity of his words greatly cheered his pupil and friend. He suggested that I should write a light-hearted article about the novel for one of the Madrid papers, even though I planned to write something weightier for a scholarly journal. And so I did.

The three of us celebrated publication of *Monsignor Quixote* (25 August 1982) at Bentley's with a magnificent dinner consisting of shellfish and the restaurant's superb white wine, followed by dessert and port. Somewhat emotionally, we recalled some of the actual moments of the journey which are echoed in the novel: our innumerable discussions about theology and communism; the five or six bottles of tonic water that I drank in Talavera; the spotless Roman collar that I wore when I first met Graham, which would be worn later by the rather unpleasant Father Herrera; the inedible Spanish omelette that I cooked in Madrid one night, which was a prelude to the foul dishes served by Father Leopoldo in Osera; the volume of Descartes which Graham discovered on my table, and which would lead the young Leopoldo into a Trappist monastery ... There were many other memories, but above all we remembered those countless meetings we had with Señor Antonio de las Regadas (Señor Diego in the novel), the picnic lunches under his fig tree, and his excellent 'unlabelled' wine which we took with us everywhere.

Father José, incidentally, Señor Diego's nephew, is based on Don Vicente Pereiras, the actual parish priest of Barbadanes (Orense), and previously parish priest in the district of the 'Mexicans'. He has recently died. Rest in peace, my beloved friend.

CHAPTER III

MONSIGNOR QUIXOTE: THE FILM

THE TRANSITION OF *Monsignor Quixote* to film was not easy. It is a novel in which dialogue is everything; cinema is a medium of action in which there is no place for the long paragraph. Shortly after publication, Thames Television in London bought the film rights. For the first time in his life, Graham retained the right to vet the script and specified a time at which the script would be shown to him for his approval. There had been so many disappointing films based on his books and in most of these adaptations Greene's hand was scarcely recognizable.

It was towards the end of May 1983 that, thanks to our friendship, I was able to hear a little more about the filming. Graham telephoned me from Antibes and gave further proof of immense sensitivity and affection. He was coming to stay with me, but this time for rather special reasons.

'Leopoldo,' he asked me, 'would you mind if someone else came with me to Madrid. He wants to meet you and he wants you to be an adviser on the film of *Monsignor Quixote*. He is Peter Duffield, the director of the film. He already made a film of another of my books.'

What on earth could I say to a proposal like this?

'We'll go with him to El Toboso and to see Unamuno's tomb at Salamanca', Graham continued. 'Then he'll go the monastery at Osera where the film will end.'

'Of course, I'd be delighted.'

'They'll pay your fees . . .'

We then discussed the dates of the next journey, which we had already planned, and made a few changes. We would see each other on 4 June in the afternoon at Madrid. Then we would go to Salamanca and El Toboso with Peter Duffield. Cyril Cusack, the Irish actor, was originally due to play the part of Monsignor Quixote. Graham could only spend a few days with me, but, God willing, he would come back afterwards and spend most of July and August here.

'Do you think we should have dinner here, at my house?' I asked.
'Of course. And we can drink some wine.'

•

First problem over the filming. It is 31 May. At nine o'clock at night I arrive home from the University. The telephone rings and it is Graham to tell me that Peter Duffield is not now coming, and that I should cancel the room.

Why isn't he coming? There is a slight melancholy tone to Graham's voice. In Spain they were insisting that the film director must be a Spaniard. Apparently a certain Spanish company was backing the film financially, and money mattered. Graham could do nothing about it. He only gave me this cursory outline.

This news was something of a setback. Graham mentioned the Spanish director Carlos Saura. He told me he was one of the top directors in the world. But he was frightened he would not accept and that they would end up with a second-rate director. In any case, even if the director was Carlos Saura, Graham wondered how he would be able to control a British cast.

This time I did not know how to cheer Graham up. I felt rather discouraged myself. I cancelled the hotel.

3 June 1983. Graham arrives at Barajas at 4.30 in the afternoon. He looks happy and is apparently in an excellent mood. He jokes with me: 'How is my whisky priest?'

As soon as we are at the hotel, the conversation turns to the filming of *Monsignor Quixote*. Graham is very sorry that Peter Duffield cannot be the director for they know each other well and are friends. He had been the director of *England Made Me*. He did not want a Spanish director to alter the spirit of the book.

We spent four or five days travelling and meeting some friends in Spain, then Graham returned to Antibes, and I stayed in Madrid.

On 24 August 1983, a few minutes after putting down the phone to Graham, his brother Hugh rings up from the Bodley Head. He informs me that the people who are making the film will get in touch with me, either in London or in Spain. I am to be their 'adviser'. Hugh had just been speaking to Graham and they both want me to be involved in the film.

We discuss the subject of Spanish Television [Televisión Española] who might put capital into the production. We agree that it would be most unfortunate if these people appoint a director. 'Is there no way of avoiding Spanish Television interfering?' I ask, and I quote Ortega's remark to Hugh: 'I don't know whether it is possible, but I know it's necessary.'

Hugh is delighted by the quotation. We both agree to meet in London.

•

7 September 1983 was a crucial day for the filming of *Monsignor Quixote*. A meeting took place at Thames Television which Graham had insisted I also attend in order 'to retain the spirit of the book and to explain its true meaning'.

I knew that things were going badly with the film. After several months' work, Peter Luke had submitted his script, and Graham had rejected it saying that it had nothing to do with his novel.

I told the meeting about the origin of *Monsignor Quixote*, about the author's spiritual approach to the book, and how there had been three different settings in the novel whose atmosphere had been vital in Graham Greene's mind since they had provided the stimulus he needed to write the book. They were: the district where the 'Mexicans' lived; the area near Señor Antonio de las Regadas' estate, particularly the patio of his house beneath the shade of that biblical fig tree; and the Trappist monastery at Osera. These places were essential to the film.

Since I knew exactly what Graham's views about it were, I told them that in my view and in Graham Greene's too, a Spanish director or co-director would be a disaster for the film: 'Yesterday Graham Greene and I agreed that it would be better not to make a film at all than to make a bad film. Graham is absolutely fed up with seeing films that destroy the contents of his books.'

After several false starts, Thames Television came up with the ideal solution. The job was entrusted to Christopher Neame, who would be both scriptwriter and producer.

On 4 May Graham rang from London. Christopher Neame had been to see him. He had liked the man and his ideas on the film. He told me that Neame would be arriving in Madrid in two days' time and would be getting in touch with me.

And this was what happened. Four hours of conversation ensued. Rather than read the script, Christopher Neame almost performed a third of it for me. I knew at once that the film was saved. Hearing him read and watching him act out the various parts with his expressive gestures, I began to relive the book that had grown out of those unforgettable journeys.

Seeing my astonishment, Neame admitted: 'This isn't my doing. It's all Graham Greene. It's all here in the book. I've hardly added a word.

'The danger for the scriptwriter who has a masterpiece in his hands,' he went on thoughtfully, 'is to give way to the temptation of putting his personal trail into it.

'Look, I have had a precious stone given to me,' he concluded. 'I have two choices: either to make a jewel of a film, or not to make it at all.'

I believe he achieved this almost unattainable ideal. When Graham telephoned me on 16 May to discover my impressions, I told him: 'This is the man! We're going to have a great film.'

●

The film really does capture Osera. *Monsignor Quixote* is a totally truthful film. There are no studios used; the scenes are shot in the places in which they are set in the novel: El Toboso, Madrid, the Valle de los Caídos, Salamanca, Valladolid, the cathedral of León, Señor Antonio de las Regadas' house and vineyards, the monastery of Osera . . . Only the shameful procession of the Virgin covered with banknotes was shot somewhere else, for reasons of taste, although it is identical to the place that Graham remembered.

We needed to visit these places slowly, and this is what we did on several occasions, before we began shooting, with Christopher, Rodney Bennett and the principal technicians examining everything in minute detail.

Rodney Bennett, the director, deserves special mention. He is the essence of sensitivity: a spiritual, sensitive and very cultured person. He studied at Cambridge and was the gentlest of men. He always smiled and he never had a harsh word for any of the actors. He was a friend to each and every one of them, even those playing minor characters, and he saw his role as one in which he served others. Rodney Bennett is a devout man and I saw evidence of his faith in the fraternal and simple way in which he worked. He was the ideal director, re-shooting certain passages as often as was needed, with the same mild manner that he displayed the first time around. The actual celluloid was, for him, far less important than the actor who was doing his best.

A crucial part of the novel *Monsignor Quixote* is the two friends' picnics in the countryside. The mood of the book is saturated with cheese and Manchego wine, and so we put these frugal provisions in the car for the sake of verisimilitude. We visited the Valle de los Caídos; we stood in silence in front of Unamuno's tomb; at León cathedral we tried to rehearse the scene in which the humble monsignor prays for the robber and for Sancho, and realizes that he has a hole in his sock.

The monastery of Osera, so imposing in its peace and silence, seemed to envelop us like a caress; and the monks treated us with the affection and simplicity that only they can offer. My companions were delighted, almost overwhelmed, by the ineffable feeling which they experienced at every single moment of the filming here, although I sometimes feared for the future of the film. I was worried that all my companions would become Trappist monks!

•

Characters in search of actors. They need to find suitable actors to play the various parts. Graham Greene sent a personal letter to Sir Alec Guinness, asking whether he would play the principal role and everyone is feeling very optimistic because Sir Alec has accepted.

In the novel, however, the part of Sancho is almost as important as that of the priest. They thought of Leo McKern, who was on the point of retiring to Australia after forty years in England, and he has postponed his trip in order to take on the role. I would never have thought it possible to find a more perfect couple to play the two main characters. The film is now safe, at least for the most part.

In *Monsignor Quixote* there are also a number of characters who, though they may be of less importance, nevertheless have an important bearing on the story. They are symbolic characters such as the Bishop of Motopo (Ian Richardson), the Vatican diplomat; Father Herrera (Valentine Pelka), who represents the shallowness of the episcopal and academic worlds; Señor Diego (Maurice Denham), a rural Galician Seneca, who is all poetry and heartfelt feeling; Father José (Joseph Blatchley), the dedicated priest who is a victim of the miserly behaviour of peasant clergy who never read a single book; Father Leopoldo (Philip Stone), who is something of an Unamuno figure – a devout intellectual in a Trappist monastery; the heroic

'Mexican' emigrant who should perhaps do rather more to open his firmly closed mind . . . and many others.

•

From my notebook:
They've started shooting already. It started on 22 April in El Toboso and it will finish on 8 June in Valladolid.

Graham Greene, the chief consultant, is in regular touch with the producer and he must decide everything. He arrives at Barajas on 23 April and he is here until 2 May. We left for El Toboso on the morning of the 24th. The producer was waiting for us in his office. As we leave, we bump into Leo McKern. Graham Greene had been delighted by his performance in one of the *Shades of Greene* television series, but they had never met before. Greene congratulated him and McKern was clearly pleased to be introduced to the famous writer. He is a short, stocky man – a perfect Sancho. His humour is overwhelming and he is always roaring with laughter. He is a fund of endless jokes; a genius of an actor and a man with a wonderfully warm heart. After a short while, I felt I had become this fine actor's friend. In a sort of journal I kept of the filming, he wrote:

> *For Leopoldo (Padre)*
> *from Leo (Sancho)*
> *with warm good wishes from a Communist,*
> *lapsed-Catholic village Mayor!*
> > *Leo McKern.*

Leo McKern had never met Sir Alec Guinness before. They are now good friends, just as they were in the novel. He laughed as he said to me: 'Could you have a more appropriate pair to play the parts of Monsignor Quixote and his friend Sancho? Alec Guinness really is a convert to Catholicism. I'm an agnostic, although I could not detest communism any more than I do at the moment. It's inhuman, unnatural.'

A priest walks into the dining room. A soutane, immaculate Roman collar, a beret in his hand; I really did take him for the parish priest of El Toboso and stood up to greet him.

'Oh, it's Alec Guinness,' Greene exclaimed.

He got up, rushed over to him and they embraced warmly. Then Graham introduced me to the celebrated actor.

There's something rather timid about Alec Guinness when he meets someone for the first time: his humility and naturalness; his charm and obliging manner; his expressive eyes and soft voice ... In fact he did not seem to act so much as live the part of the character he was playing in a marvellously intimate way. At the time, I felt as if it was not Alec Guinness I knew, but rather the former parish priest of El Toboso who had been raised to the rank of monsignor. He is an extremely cultured man and a fine writer himself, who inspires peace in the way a Trappist monk does, because he is a profoundly spiritual person, and his art flows from his fingertips like the words of a poet.

It has all been unforgettably exciting. They were filming the inside of Monsignor Quixote's house. As we were going there, I thought: I must be careful and try not to laugh while they are shooting. We entered on tiptoes. They were filming the scene of Father Herrera's arrival. To my surprise, when I looked up and saw Alec Guinness, Valentine Pelka and Rosalie Crutchley, who played the part of Teresa, I felt quite overcome and I had to pull out my handkerchief. How is it possible for such a gentle boy as Valentine to transform himself into someone so cruel and cutting?

Nobody who has seen them film the meeting of the parish priest of El Toboso with the Bishop of Motopo could dare suggest that Ian Richardson was not a legate from the Vatican. Tall, thin, and with a smile that is simultaneously affectionate and authoritative, 'Holiness and literary appreciation don't always go together,' he would say wisely.

At the Alcázar de San Juan, we watched the first rushes on video; they seemed perfect.

Graham Greene returned to see the filming from 18 to 23 May. From Madrid we travelled to Santiago, Carballino and Osera, where they shot the culminating scenes in that imposing monastery. Everything conspired to create something transcending and there was no need to impose a rule of 'silence' ... I feel sure that the Mass said by Alec Guinness, wearing only his pyjamas, will have made a lot of people think very seriously.

There is a Father Juan here, a very elderly Trappist monk who has become a symbol of tradition in the monastery, and who still has all his wits about him. When the monastery buildings were renovated and somewhat more human sleeping quarters were installed for the monks, he refused to leave his old cell which was almost in ruins.

Not long ago, however, the ceiling of his cell fell in and he was obliged to join the others. I saw him, standing discreetly apart, at the entrance to the porter's lodge, leaning on his walking stick, chin in both hands, and totally absorbed by these people and the strange things they were doing . . . With seventy years' experience of Trappist rule behind him, Father Juan did not want to go to heaven without seeing how films were made.

On 21 May the sun shone and the film crew set off for Las Regadas. I doubt whether the novel of *Monsignor Quixote* would exist without that patriarchal figure Señor Antonio – or Señor Diego – the sanctuary of his wine cellar, and the meals that Graham Greene, the 'Third Man' and I shared with him, sitting at that large stone table beneath his fig tree. A whole day was spent in the house filming the scene with the 'Mexican' and the lunch offered to the travellers by Señor Diego. Señor Antonio was so moved by the occasion that he said to me: 'This is the greatest day in my life.'

He is now ninety-three years old. When he was twelve or thirteen, he used to help his father. They grew their vines on the rockiest of ground and ever since then he has nurtured and cherished them in the way one cherishes a beloved child. When he saw himself portrayed by Maurice Denham, wearing a pale grey suit, a cap and steel-rimmed spectacles, Señor Antonio may well have wondered whether he had ever been an actor in some previous life.

Graham Greene and I left for Santiago feeling very happy because we had had a very moving foretaste of a greater part of the film. We had an hour and a half to wait at Santiago airport. He is not a man ever likely to miss a plane! Graham ordered a whisky and I had a tonic water. I tried to drink a toast, but he refused: 'I never toast with water.'

•

On the morning of the 23rd I took Graham to Barajas airport. Azucena Corredera, a friend of ours, and of Graham's family, too, accompanied us. She had driven us before on several occasions and she was writing a thesis on Graham's work. I once suggested to Graham that I buy a cheap car and that, after a few lessons, I would drive. He dissuaded me.

'Do what you want,' he teased, 'but if you drive, I'll never get in the car with you.'

After that, we always depended on a 'Third Man' or 'Third Woman'.

For some time now, I have been unable to stop thinking about the world of film and the making of *Monsignor Quixote*. Seeing this world from the inside, as I did for a short while, has been a fascinating experience. There is a beauty about the discipline of it all, for I am a great admirer of military punctuality and all aspiration to perfection, and they sometimes shot the scenes over and over again until they had achieved the perfect combination of acting, camera work, lighting etc . . . They were hoping that the film would become a classic just like the novel. And they achieved it. In Spain it has still not been shown, but that doesn't matter – the rest of the world has seen it.

Graham Greene's happiest moment during the making of the film was that day spent at Las Regadas, shooting in Señor Antonio's house and vineyard. Graham knew only too well that for his old friend, seeing all these people wandering around his home was something he had never dreamed of. When we both set foot on the patio which we knew so well that morning, surrounded by all those people and equipment, Señor Antonio was waiting there with outstretched arms, and when the two men greeted each other and remained in locked embrace, I knew for certain that life was still worth living.

Chapter IV

SOME NOTES ON THE BOOKS

'It's a bit difficult for me to answer your questions as I try to forget my books after they are written,' Graham Greene wrote in the first letter he ever sent me (20 June 1964).

Certainly, he never bothered about the books that were already published, and he never used to read them again unless it were for some particular reason. He did so when he wrote his Introductions to the 'Collected Edition' of his work.

As I have said, I think that the reason he never particularly seemed to care about any of those books, well known though they were throughout the world, was that none of these children of his seemed quite perfect. Some were better than others, but no more than that. And some he considered positively bad. When I was with him in Antibes once, he inscribed, among other books, a copy of the French edition of *The Quiet American*:

> *Pour Leopoldo Durán*
> *avec mon grand amitié.*
> *- Graham Greene*
>   *Antibes, 12 avril '79*

'These others won't interest you,' he said. He had in his hand copies of *The Confidential Agent*, *Stamboul Train* and one or two other books. They were in French, a language I was trying to polish up a bit. I didn't say anything, for what he said struck me as being almost selfish.

'All these books are pretty worthless,' Greene went on, 'but I have already suppressed two of them, and if I go on like that I'll suppress almost all of them. Anyway, I had to start somewhere.'

Graham did allow his first novel, *The Man Within*, to be republished, however, and in the Introduction to the novel in the 'Collected Edition', he gives his reasons for keeping it in print.

Graham was usually reluctant to talk about his books, but in this chapter I want to relate some of the discussions we had that related to his work.

On 18 July 1979, we left the *parador* at Mérida on our way to Evora in Portugal, a place that had always attracted us, ever since the occasion of the famous explanation of the Trinity using the two and a half empty wine bottles. Graham was in an excellent mood.

Because we were on the road to Sintra, Graham was recalling certain anecdotes to do with Portugal. On one occasion, after the war, Graham met a certain Portuguese diplomat at the British Embassy who said to him: 'Ah, you were the person at MI6 responsible for Lourenço Marques.'

Graham replied: 'No, that was my friend Malcolm Muggeridge. I looked after Portugal from London.'

This led us on to talking about certain of his books. Graham told me much more than I had expected.

'I wrote two books that were never published,' he said. 'One was about Spain, the other had as its theme the problem of a marriage between a white couple who, through some accident of retrospective heredity, had a coloured child. Of these two manuscripts, one is in a safe in a bank, and the other is in Texas.'

Was he referring to *The Tenth Man*, which was published later in 1985? Apparently not, since Graham said he had forgotten all about this work until a stranger wrote to him from the United States in 1983, telling him that MGM had offered a story of his entitled *The Tenth Man* to an American publishing house.

One year before (27 June 1978), he had told me about a very old friend of his who was now seriously ill. He was thinking of going to London to visit her. This woman possessed part of a novel which Graham had begun but never completed. It was about a twelve-year-old Catholic girl who had committed a crime. Neither the police nor anyone else suspected that the child could have done such a thing. The only person who knew was a priest who was a friend of the family.

Later (6 July 1983), Graham told me that apart from 'The General and Chuchu', previously entitled 'On the Way Back' and finally published as *Getting to Know the General*, he also had a work in progress called 'Getting to Know the Captain'. He described it as a deeply psychological novel. He told me the plot, but I did not take any notes. It had nothing to do with the biography of Torrijos. Given the similarity of the titles, it is possible that he put the pages he had written to one side and concentrated on the biography of his friend Torrijos. We never discussed the subject again.

Even when he had completed a book, Graham had doubts about whether to publish it, or whether to put it away in a box. Graham had seriously regretted publishing his first book of poems, *Babbling April*, and his first three published novels, *The Man Within*, *The Name of Action* and *Rumour at Nightfall*. He did not want to have any such regrets again. He always found it very difficult to deliver a manuscript to his publisher, which is why he sought perfection in works such as *The Power and the Glory*. He was much more decisive about other writers' unpublished manuscripts than he was with his own. *The Captain and the Enemy* had been lying around in a box for many years before it was published. Even when it was completed, I came to the conclusion that he would never be satisfied that it was publishable.

•

Graham had entrusted the fate of his novel *The Human Factor* to his former friend and publisher A. S. Frere. He had not been happy with what he had written, but Frere's opinion mattered enormously to him. Frere was partially paralysed during his later years, but it seemed that anything to do with Graham was sacred to him. One day Graham received a letter; in it Frere said that he wanted to come and see Graham to give him some advice about the novel.

'I was absolutely certain,' Graham told me, 'that Frere found it too difficult to give me a negative opinion in a letter. That is why he had decided to come and see me in Antibes, despite the difficulties of travelling.'

In fact, Frere wanted to go to Antibes because he wished to give his opinion in person: '*The Human Factor* is one of the best novels you have ever written,' he told him. 'Send it to your publishers as it is, immediately. It will have a huge success.'

Graham obeyed blindly, as he always did with Frère, and it was indeed a huge success. In America the hardback edition sold out immediately and a few months later they printed a million copies of the paperback. And it was a similar pattern everywhere.

The novel was dedicated to his sister, Elisabeth Dennys, 'who cannot deny some responsibility'. The responsibility was of having recruited Graham into the Secret Service. Eventually he came to understand the reason he was invited to those parties where there was never any shortage of drink, even when it was unavailable everywhere else.

At the time that Elisabeth, Graham and I went to Berkhamsted to sample the atmosphere of the place where much of the novel was set, we visited the Common where Davis used to go to play with Buller and little Sam. We discussed Davis's death from *aspergillus flavus*, the toxic substance which can be found in old nuts. According to Graham's brother Raymond, who was a doctor, it could cause almost immediate death in animals, but no one had experimented with it on humans. Doctor Percival did so on Davis. Getting rid of a spy in this way would mean less investigation and less of a diplomatic uproar than if he had been assassinated. And Davis would die more peacefully.

Apparently, the priest in the novel is based upon a real priest who Graham went to for confession in London. The priest sent him to a psychiatrist, and he did the same to Castle. Castle forgave his confessor for having been so tactless: 'He was another victim of loneliness and silence, like himself.'

This provided an opportunity to discuss the relative loneliness of the priesthood. We agreed that what one meant by loneliness depended on each individual, on each priest. 'I have always felt that I was not alone,' I said, and Graham agreed with me. A priest's two most important companions should be his spiritual life and his books – and his friendships, of course.

According to Graham, *The Human Factor* ends with two hells: Castle's Russian hell, and Sarah's hell in her mother-in-law's house. We agreed that the one evil person of the book is Mrs Castle and that the dog Buller and Carson were rather lovable characters.

Graham told me several times that his favourite passage in the book is the last paragraph of the third chapter in Part Three. Castle is unable to sleep, and he is lying awake thinking of Carson and Cornelius Muller, Uncle Remus and Prague. He makes sure that Sarah is sleeping before falling asleep himself. He remembers the hero of books he read in childhood before he is 'off on that long slow underground stream which bore him on towards the interior of the dark continent where he hoped he might find a permanent home, in a city where he could be accepted as a citizen, as a citizen without any pledge of faith, not the City of God or Marx, but the city called Peace of Mind'.

Graham told me about the woman friend of his who kept models of owls everywhere, just like Daintry's wife. One American critic said that once Daintry arrives on the scene, the book became utterly tedious! But Graham thought that Daintry was one of the most successful characters in the novel.

I was surprised to hear Graham say that 'Uncle Remus' really existed, though under another name. 'It was less an invention than a prediction,' he said, and he told me about how important South African mineral wealth was for the West.

We talk about Castle's youth and Graham comments: 'One imagines that Castle attended an Anglican church school. This would fit in with his mother practising her religion, at least while Castle was a student there.'

We return to the subject of Otto Preminger's film. Graham was deeply disappointed by it. The actor who played the part of Castle was good, but the part of Sarah was acted very badly. By changing her clothes all the time she ruined the atmosphere of the book.

'I have had a letter from Christopher Hill which pleased me very much,' Graham told me on the telephone one day. 'He tells me that in this book I accord totally with his ideas and deepest feelings.'

Christopher Hill was an English historian who had been a communist, but who left the Party when Hungary was invaded.

•

We frequently spoke about *A Burnt-Out Case*. It is a book I have always liked very much and it pleased Graham when I referred to it as a metaphysical parable on charity, yet he felt very depressed when he had finished writing the book. Was it a premonition of the quarrel between him and Evelyn Waugh? There are many aspects of Graham Greene's life and work that are inexplicable at first sight. Apparently, he had consulted Doctor Michel Lechat about anything to do with leprosy in the book and he had approved everything. 'Obviously,' Graham said to me, 'Doctor Lechat is not Doctor Colin.' He also checked all medical details in the novel with his brother Raymond. When the book was published, a Danish authority on leprosy wrote Graham a scornful and insulting letter. He told him that he failed to understand how he could have dedicated his book to Doctor Lechat, nor how Doctor Lechat could possibly be grateful for the dedication, since it was full of errors and inaccuracies.

Graham replied: 'It is obvious that you are not familiar with the forms of acknowledgement that writers use before dedicating a book to someone. They ask the person to whom they intend dedicating the book for permission to do so. This is what I did with Doctor Michel Lechat. Furthermore, I had consulted him about anything I wrote to do with leprosy, and he read the manuscript before the book was published. He was quite happy with it.'

Doctor Lechat, incidentally, sometimes visited Graham in Antibes. He attended his funeral, and was one of the pallbearers who carried the coffin to the grave. Unfortunately, I never met him, or I would have greeted him warmly.

Graham told me how he had arrived in the Congo aboard a boat belonging to the missionaries, who had always been very kind to him. He lived at the mission for about three months, taking his meals with the missionaries and with the doctor. The missionaries provided him with a 'boy', who is immortalized in the novel as 'Deo Gratias'. He is the boy who dreams of going to Pendele: to Paradise! Reading St Augustine later, I came across the name Deo Gratias.

Graham had his own hut where he worked. He became quite used to it and soon felt at home there. Every day, he went to Doctor Lechat's surgery and watched how he tried to cure the patients. When a husband contracted leprosy, his wife took care of him. When it was the woman who fell ill, the husband forgot all about her and went off with someone else.

Graham told me that what he wrote about the poor quality of the food prepared by the nuns was quite accurate. They lived some way away from the priests, and when the food arrived after being carried beneath the burning sun, most of it had been ruined by the heat.

We discussed the portrayal of the missionaries in the novel. Father Thomas was a man who failed to adapt, whereas Father Superior was someone who was immensely likeable. There is a gallery of attractive and good-humoured priests.

On one of his visits to Antibes, Doctor Lechat told Graham that at one time the nuns at the leproserie – portrayed so sympathetically in the novel – used to make the lepers work too hard. Their fingers became worn away, although there was no pain. Doctor Lechat informed the Provincial, who told the Father General of the mission, and the nuns were immediately replaced. Doctor Lechat did not mention this to Graham Greene when he was at the leproserie, since Graham was looking for characters for his novel and he felt that this information might have prejudiced him.

We often talked about Querry's dream, which was one that Graham himself had dreamt after spending several days unable to write and with his mind a blank. That fortunate dream solved everything and profoundly influenced Graham. In a letter he wrote as an introduction to a book of mine, he said: 'It may amuse you to know that the dream you refer to on page 394/5 was an actual dream of my own which arrived when I was badly stuck at that point in *A Burnt-Out Case.*'

I asked Graham which was the part of the book he most liked. He replied: 'Perhaps the sermon of the Father Superior.'

•

The Heart of the Matter was another of the books which was mentioned occasionally in our chats. I would raise it, because Graham Greene always had a serious antipathy towards the novel. I believe he judged it more harshly than it deserved. According to him, Scobie was a character who would have been more suitable in a tragicomedy than in a novel. Without disagreeing with this, I maintained that Scobie is a prototype of the many men who are psychologically maladjusted.

Graham's lack of appreciation for this novel was only increased by the success of the book all over the world. '*The Heart of the Matter* was a success in the great vulgar sense of that term,' Graham maintained half in anger, half in sadness. Added to this was the amount of letters he received, especially from priests and women. There was one young Berliner who invited him to lead a youth crusade on the streets of West Berlin 'where we were to shed our blood for the Church'. Less appealing to me, however, was the letter from a Swiss girl asking him to come with her to her own country 'where the snow can be our coverlet'. Graham told me he had felt absolutely worn and driven to despair by these letters; he wished he had never written such a book.

As if all this was not enough, someone in the United States had the unfortunate idea of adapting *The Heart of the Matter* for the stage. Graham received a letter inviting him to attend a rehearsal and could not believe his eyes when he read the letter. It was a disastrous venture and Graham was appalled by what he saw. That night he wrote a note to the person responsible, saying: 'Have I come from London to see this?' Fortunately, the play was a failure.

•

On more than one occasion when we discussed his work, particularly when I first knew him, Graham reckoned that *Brighton Rock* might perhaps be his best book. As time passed, I never heard him repeat this, but he always had a high regard for the novel. I often heard him say that he would have preferred it if most of the first part had not been published. He thought it slowed down the pace of the book unnecessarily. Graham did not know whether the character of Pinkie was based on someone in real life or whether he was simply a product of his fantasy. He rather liked the anonymous priest who appears at the end of the novel, and who listens to Rose and counsels her so wisely.

•

The Comedians came into our conversations because of the political situation in Haiti. Graham told me all about his journeys to this tormented little country and the tragic situation under Doctor Duvalier. The last time he had been there, Graham really did fear for his life. After all, he said to me, it would not have been difficult to arrange a motor accident in order to do away with him. The book contains so much actual history that it sometimes reads like a fictionalized chronicle. Duvalier, or 'Papa Doc', looms over the whole novel. In his prefatory letter to Frere, Greene describes the historical basis for the novel quite clearly. Apart from Doctor Duvalier, certain other characters are modelled on actual people. The Marquesa de Lascott Villiers, for example, is based on a handsome blonde-haired woman who Graham had known in Martinique. She had a black lover, and had had a child by another man. She also owned a hotel of sorts, which this son had allowed to go to rack and ruin.

The scene with the seagull, which happened to Brown and his new girlfriend in the Hôtel de Paris, actually happened to Greene in the same hotel.

When Duvalier's son, Baby Doc, was overthrown, I congratulated Graham on the influence his novel continued to have in Haiti. All too soon, however, the deposed Haitian leader became his neighbour and came to live with his family in sumptuous style near Antibes. The Americans had misled the French, telling them that the former dictator was going to spend only one week there, for no one wanted this cruel dictator. He lived in a big hotel, but the owners considered bringing a legal action to make the French government remove him.

•

I asked Graham why he himself considered *The Honorary Consul* to be perhaps his best novel.

'Firstly,' he replied, 'because the characters grow and develop throughout the book. And secondly, because the relationship between the father and the son is a fundamental part of the novel. Charley Fortnum matures as a father, so much so that he comes to regard the traitor Plarr as another son.'

When he gave me the copy he always kept for me, he confessed that he might have created a new theology for his dissident priest, and he read me the passage which speaks of 'the night-side as well as a day-side' of God. 'God depends on our evolution.' I reassured him that there was nothing new about Father Rivas's theology and that it was all perfectly compatible with Catholic doctrine. It was no more than the doctrine of the Mystical Body of Christ, although expressed in a literary and poetic form. As I have already mentioned, Graham referred to this conversation in *The Other Man*.

•

Everything to do with Vietnam and its people had a special attraction for Graham, something he demonstrated clearly on the occasion mentioned earlier when he came to Madrid on the official visit. *The Quiet American* was therefore one of the books that we discussed most frequently in our conversations. Graham agreed that it was fundamentally a political novel.

An American journalist had once said to someone that he thought the novel was outdated and this person replied: 'Read it yourself, slowly, again, and I assure you that any chapter will throw fresh light on the war in Vietnam.'

Apparently, when Heinemann were moving offices in London, they found a packet which had Graham Greene's name on the cover. They gave it to him and he opened it. It was the manuscript of *The Quiet American*! He had no idea how it had come to be there.

•

Before submitting my doctoral thesis at King's College, I sent it to Graham Greene and asked him if he would be so kind as to glance through it. I would feel that much more confident at the viva. He read it with scrupulous care as is evident from the long letter he wrote which became the introduction to the book when it was published. Point by point, he drew small details to my attention which

I should perhaps consider. Among his comments, he wrote: 'You must forgive me if I think you under-estimate *Travels with my Aunt*. In my mind it is the second best book to *The Power and the Glory* and a serious and sad book which happens to be funny.'

Much later, we discussed *Travels with my Aunt*. It is a work which, in so far as any of his works pleased him, he always liked. One of the reasons for his relative fondness for the book was that it had appeal and avoided any obvious Catholic theme. In his Introduction to the 'Collected Edition', he writes: 'I felt above all that I had broken for good or ill with the past.'

Graham was not at all shocked that there were those who preferred this novel to all others. He did not believe it was his best book. It was a humorous work, but a serious one as well; or rather, a serious work that happened, accidentally, to be funny.

Without any doubt, *The Power and the Glory* was the book which we spoke about most frequently during our conversations. Apart from anything else, I devoted a long chapter to it in my thesis, and later I would publish a book about the novel. Graham kindly wrote me a letter as a preface to this book.

The condemnation of this great novel by Cardinal Pizzardo, the Prefect of the Holy Office and a man already advanced in years and dignity; the Dominican, Father Gervase, to whom the novel is dedicated, and his brother Bishop Matthews, two people who clearly influenced Graham Greene on intellectual matters, these were the themes that enlivened many of our conversations.

I believe that, in his subconscious at least, this was the novel that meant most to Graham among all his books, although after the publication of *The Honorary Consul* he asked for special consideration to be given to Charley Fortnum.

Graham was once convalescing in a London hospital. Suddenly the door opened and the chaplain greeted him with a smile and a raised hand: 'Hey, it's the power and the glory!'

●

One of the novels I read before publication was *Doctor Fischer of Geneva*. Without knowing quite why, it always reminds me of Schubert's *Moment Musicale*. Perhaps one of my functions in Graham's life was to make him laugh with my foolish remarks. I told him that from its first sentence, this was the most lyrical book he had written. Graham smiled. Forsaking his usual modesty, he replied that he also thought it was a 'good book'. The first sentence with which the one-armed Jones opens the novel is both original and unforgettable: 'I think that I used to detest Doctor Fischer more than any other man I had known, just as I loved his daughter more than any other woman.'

His first publisher, A. S. Frere, also thought highly of the work. He assured Graham that it was the most 'self-expressing' book he had ever written. Graham reminded me of how much he respected the opinion of his first publisher.

We discussed the critical reaction to *Doctor Fischer of Geneva*, which had been very good. I also wrote a sort of commentary (later mentioned in the *Financial Times*) on the story in the *Clergy Review* which earned from Greene a rare accolade: 'very good indeed'.

When they were filming the novel, Graham occasionally spent some time with the actors. He was full of admiration for James Mason, who played the role of Doctor Fischer, and who, delicate though his health was, put up with the icy Swiss temperatures in the middle of the night.

Graham had already told me, before the showing of the film, that it did not end as the book does. After the 'Bomb Party', Doctor Fischer says: 'I think it is time to sleep', or something similar. Graham agreed to this ending. He explained to me that everything depended on the music. One guessed that he had committed suicide.

•

In the summer of 1985, Graham had finished the books he brought with him to read and he asked me to lend him my copy of *The Ministry of Fear*. He told me he liked it: 'I think it's a reasonably good novel.' He had probably not re-read it since he had written the Introduction for the 'Collected Edition'. Graham reminded me of a father who, having sent his son out into the world, was now seeing him again as a man.

Something similar happened with *Stamboul Train*. He had told me it had no merit, but many years later he read my copy in Spain and said: '*Stamboul Train* now seems to me better than I thought.'

•

Alluding to his play *The Potting Shed*, Graham said: 'I like the first act; the second, rather less; the third, not at all.'

The 'housekeeper' is taken from an actual person whom he met in Belfast when he was on his way to Africa. (Out of this trip would come *Journey Without Maps*.) He had gone to a presbytery in order to go to confession. The housekeeper came to the door and told him in an ill-tempered manner that the priest was eating, and tried to close the door. But Graham put his foot in the way. The priest came and Graham went to confession, though he noted that the priest was rather suspicious when Graham told him he was on his way to the Congo.

The actress who played the role of Charles's mother did not want to have to speak certain remarks in the text that were against her Church. She was a Catholic and she thought them disrespectful. Eventually, Graham insisted to the director that she should say them, for she was playing the part of an atheist. It had nothing to do with the actress's feelings, nor with Graham's.

•

As I have said, we frequently talked about Vatican politics, including the intrigues which emerge from the higher echelons of that divine institution. There is certainly no shortage of people eager to battle for position there. So much for the human element in the Church!

On one occasion, Graham told me – this is more than twenty years ago – a true story that is the basis for the title story of *The Last Word and Other Stories*, which was published in 1990. Someone in a senior position within the Vatican recounted the following. The Pope, Pius XII, was frightened that Hitler might have him arrested, removed from Rome and taken to Germany on the pretext of his personal safety. Rome was occupied by German troops at the time. So Pius XII had had a bell installed in his study – hidden in the desk at which he worked – which, when pressed, rang in the offices of various important officials. The Pope had given them instructions that the moment they heard the bell, all the ambassadors in the world should be summoned to the Holy See immediately and told that the Pope was a prisoner and that he was leaving Rome against his will.

The mysterious story, 'The Last Word', is based on this historic fact. The old Pope, his memory failing on account of drugs and much suffering, is taken to a distant country. There, having been dressed in his robes and formal insignia – which he scarcely remembers – he is shot by a general. The general is convinced that he has killed the last Christian in history. However, 'Between the pressure of the trigger and the bullet exploding a strange and frightening doubt crossed his mind: is it possible that what this man believed may be true?'

Graham actually preferred 'The Moment of Truth' – a story of human superficiality and helplessness – to 'The Last Word', but the title story is an interesting example of the way Graham took his fiction from real life.

PART FOUR

J'ACCUSE

D URING OUR 'PICNIC' of 1978, Graham Greene was beginning to sense a cloud on the horizon and he immediately told me what was happening. He was becoming increasingly worried about Daniel Guy, the husband of Martine, the daughter of his close friends the Cloettas, of whom he had always been very fond. Apparently, Guy's friendships were not quite what they appeared to be.

From the first months of her marriage several years ago, Martine had suffered alone, in silence. She had soon discovered that she had entered a world that she had never imagined existed. Being an intelligent woman, she had quickly realized that certain things were going on that were to do with a criminal mafia that was operating on the Côte d'Azur. Late at night, people would arrive at the house and hide packets there which they would collect at some later, convenient time.

Daniel and Martine had married for love, with all the blind romanticism of idealism, but the wretched sort of life she was leading had nothing to do with love, nor even with human dignity. Their life together was akin to that of sadist and victim, and there were frequent cases of violence against this totally defenceless young woman. Meanwhile, she tried to be heroic, suffering silently, never revealing the tragedy of her life to those who really loved her.

When Graham first told me about the unhappy marriage, he had no inkling of what lay ahead or what he would discover through his own enquiries.

No one can imagine the extent to which Graham Greene concerned himself with friends of his who had serious problems or suffered wrongly. Seeing those he loved grieve in any way made him want to take on that suffering himself, particularly when it concerned someone for whom he would willingly have given his life. I am putting this as plainly and objectively as possible, for that is the way it was.

Graham prepared to intervene wholeheartedly into this matter. He wanted to resolve the problem through legal means, but as time went by he became more and more convinced that Guy and his cronies moved in a corrupt world in which justice could not be trusted. Even Martine's lawyer, it appeared, had been bought by the enemy. He would invite his client to come and see him and then once she had left, he would change his mind totally and recommend absurd solutions that could only favour the other side. The lawyer had become a double agent in the secret service. It was a good thing that Graham knew something about that world.

When you thought you were on firm ground, everything seemed to slip away beneath your feet. You could not look for anyone to defend you, because you would suddenly discover you had been betrayed. Apparently unbiased lawyers representing both parties were actually conniving in favour of one of the parties. At the same time, Graham was quite well aware of the threats of violence that had been made by this mentally unbalanced man against his friends. From 24 April 1979, Graham had begun to tell me about these things in telephone calls from Antibes. He always ended them: 'But you must continue to pray about it all. Especially at Mass.'

•

How many times Graham asked me to say prayers and remember his requests at Mass during those years! On 18 November 1979, he telephoned me at 1.15 p.m. The reason he called was because tomorrow the problem of Martine's marriage would be decided one way or another. He asked me to intensify my prayers. He told me how Martine's little daughter Alexandra had returned home in a very unhappy state after a day spent with her father; how she had gone to sleep in tears on a sofa.

Graham's battle with the mafia 'on what is called the Côte d'Azur' was fought on two fronts: 1) the need to obtain a civil divorce for Martine, and 2) the right of custody of little Alexandra. When he published his bilingual pamphlet, J'Accuse, the courts obliged him to withdraw it from sale in France, though it was published in Britain. Graham Greene defended his right to publish; there was thus a third front on which the battle was to be fought, although this one was of minor importance compared to the other two.

The war on the Côte d'Azur, which lasted from 1979 until October 1984, was a series of starts and setbacks, hopes and disappointments. On 6 October 1979, when Martine was alone in her parents' house, her husband came in and beat her up. But on 19 November the problem of the marriage was settled. Graham telephoned me the next day to tell me: 'Martine has obtained her divorce. It was confirmed yesterday by the judge.' The solution was a fortunate one. It had been no life for her. Of course, this was only a first step. There would be appeals to higher authorities, but this first judgement meant a lot. It would be necessary to change lawyers for quite serious reasons, and there was to be a new judge. There was good reason therefore for further optimism.

On 19 April 1980, Graham telephoned. 'I did not feel I had the energy to reply to your letter,' he began. And then he recounted the last act of the tragedy. This madman had assaulted Martine's father. The girl's bravery had been extraordinary, and she had defended her father with a tear-gas bomb.

Graham Greene then wrote a letter to *The Times* of London describing what had happened to Martine earlier, how she had used a tear-gas bomb to protect her father and other disgraceful episodes. The letter had an enormous impact and ensured that all the authorities were aware of the case of Martine and Daniel Guy. Graham told me all about it on the telephone. He knew that I had been carrying out certain spiritual exercises over several days. When I congratulated him on his brilliant letter, it was he who put forward this surprising interpretation: 'The brilliant letter may have been the result of your visit to Osera.'

I smiled. This was just like Graham. 'You must thank God for the gift of your pen,' I replied.

'I'll do that, of course,' he said. 'But I would give all my books just to be able to stop the suffering of those I love most.'

•

On 19 May 1980, I received a slightly gloomy letter from Graham, and so the following morning I telephoned him. He was feeling a little under the weather. His doctor said he would be better in two or three days' time. We spoke at length on the eternal subject of this endless battle. Graham says he can see no other resolutions apart from resorting to blackmail. He was referring to his threat to write an article which would be published simultaneously in Britain, America and Germany. He did not like to do this, but he could see no other way. I told him he was perfectly within his rights to stand up for the truth and that he should do so without any scruples whatsoever.

The Mayor of Antibes is playing a useful role. He is a decent man and a good friend of Graham's, but perhaps the writer's threat to publicize this business throughout the world has stimulated him. Later, Graham would be somewhat disappointed by his friend the Mayor. He had agreed to be a witness in the case of Daniel Guy, but when the moment came he did not dare appear. Graham was very upset, although in our last discussion on the subject he half forgave him: 'A politician's career is like that. They are frightened to compromise on matters such as this in case it harms their political career and promotion to Paris.'

'Why?' I asked.

'Because they may have to say something in court which could damage the prestige of their district.'

•

On 15 December 1980, Graham asked me for special prayers at Mass. Apparently, someone had said that he would kill X under the semblance of a driving accident. This person really had gone too far.

Graham was quite prepared to fight. Even General Torrijos had offered to intervene. 'I never leave my friends alone when they are in danger,' he had said.

22 December 1980. I was in Antibes. I arrived at the flat at 10.30 a.m. Graham rang Elisabeth and dictated a brief statement issued in advance of the two letters he would send, one to the French Ministry of Justice, the other to the Grand Master of the Légion d'Honneur. Elisabeth would send copies of the letters, as would certain foreign journalists – a German, a Dutchman and a Swede – who had been to see him in Antibes. When Graham gave the word, Elisabeth would get in touch with these people.

Graham returned his Order of the Légion d'Honneur, which had been awarded him by President Pompidou. In his statement he gave his reason for this decision: the corruption of justice on the Côte d'Azur.

His two letters were registered and posted to Paris on the morning of the 23rd. If in about a week there had been no reaction on the part of the authorities in Paris, Graham would send copies of his letters, and his introductory statement, to the world's press. In Britain they would be sent to *The Times*, *Daily Telegraph* and *Guardian*.

The response from Paris came immediately, and, as far as such things can ever be, suddenly. Two members of Daniel Guy's group were sentenced, one to eleven years in prison and the other to an equally long sentence. The Ministry of Justice secretly sent two men to the Nice area in order to discover what was happening and take action. The authorities were convinced that a closed wall had been built by the mafia in these parts that was outside the reach of the Law. One high official assured Graham: 'One day, however, we will find a hold and then the wall will tumble.'

The problem seemed to last forever. By 15 November 1981, Graham was so exhausted – he had been battling for three years! – that he was prepared to go on television and tell the whole world about the appalling corruption that existed in this part of France.

Every day brought its ups and downs in the struggle and I forget how many times he was obliged to change lawyers.

In the worst eventuality, Graham had prepared *J'Accuse*, which in the end he was obliged to have published. It was a great blow to the mafia and their world of falsehood, but it also created a further problem, adding yet another lawsuit to the suits for divorce and the custody of the two daughters.

French justice was on the side of the truth, but how difficult it was to fight against corruption when it extended to a good number of the 'representatives of law and order'.

Graham Greene made countless journeys to Paris and had meetings with the Minister of Justice, Alain Peyrefitte, who was a great admirer of his novels. The Minister did all that was in his power and provided Graham with security, but he could not do everything. The Socialists then came to power and Graham had a private meeting with President Mitterand at the Elysée. Mitterand is a literary man and he had invited Graham to his investiture, though Graham had been unable to go.

•

The final verdict was announced in Nîmes on 7 June 1984. On 2 July at ten o'clock in the morning, the telephone rang.

'Who is it?' I asked.

'Leopoldo, we won.'

It was Graham, happier than I had known him in many years. I whooped down the telephone.

'I don't think you've ever given me better news. I have just finished saying Mass.'

'I waited until you had finished to call you.'

We spoke at length about those six interminable years of head-
aches: the judges, the lawyers, all the constant travelling. He asked
me not to forget the battle with the mafia at Mass. After such a long
time, it had become a habit by now for him to ask me this.

When they went to collect Alexandra after the Nîmes verdict, they
stopped the case at Daniel Guy's intervention. They were deciding
whether or not he should be sent to prison.

A few days later, the lawyer, a legal officer and the police went to
collect the girl from school and they delivered her to Martine.

There was still one further trick to be played: they tried to insist
that Martine be given a psychiatric examination in Switzerland before
they hand over her daughter. Fortunately, the judge had the sense
to dismiss this appeal.

The anxiety for those involved in this business, and I count myself
among them, had been indescribable.

Looking back, I think that two 'miracles' occurred. How was it
possible for Graham to continue writing while he was suffering such
hell? And then why, given the criminal nature of this mafia, did they
not kill Graham? His only protection was a tear-gas bomb which he
never used. That iron will of his held firm for another seven years.
But ordeals of this kind have their effects on human life.

•

On 25 January 1982, *The Times* of London published a letter from
Graham Greene denouncing the mafia in the region of Nice. It
accused police officers, certain magistrates and some lawyers of criminal corruption. And although the writer Max Gallo had already written a novel about the putrid state of affairs there, Greene in his letter
promised a short book about his own experiences. He even announced
the title of the pamphlet, which he would borrow from Zola: *J'Accuse*.

Graham Greene's letter was soon read all over the world. Two or
three days after it appeared in *The Times*, Graham had to travel to
Germany and, to his amazement, even his taxi-driver in Berlin had
read it. On 31 January *The Sunday Times* devoted a full page and
more to 'Graham Greene's private war' in the South of France.
Journalists and representatives of every medium queued up to speak
to this famous but very private writer. I spent Holy Week with him
that year, and it was still impossible to avoid the press asking for
interviews. These three months had been physically very demanding
for him.

After four or five years in which he had tried every other possible means – the police, the law courts, even returning his Chevalier de la Légion d'Honneur (which they refused to accept) – Greene had no alternative but to turn to his most powerful weapon: his pen. A 'Holy War' had been declared. Not even he, with all his modesty, could have imagined the commotion this letter would cause throughout the world. His sister Elisabeth, who acted as his secretary and arranged the interviews that Graham gave, felt completely overwhelmed. For several weeks she sent out about thirty letters a day – and these were just those that demanded urgent replies – dictated by Greene from Antibes. She wrote to me at the time: 'I am glad that his instructions to me are to tell all the journalists that he is not giving any more interviews. I do wish they would let him rest for a bit, but that seems doubtful. I have a feeling that they can think and talk of nothing else, which is not good.' (4 May 1982)

J'Accuse: The Dark Side of Nice was duly published. It was a short book, a bilingual edition in English and French, that ran to sixty-nine pages. I read it in manuscript in Antibes one evening before going to bed. One cannot stop reading it; it's like a thriller, or a rather disturbing play – a tragedy in five acts with documentary appendices. The opening paragraph of the first act is a powerful and grief-stricken appeal:

> Let me issue a warning to anyone who is tempted to settle
> for a peaceful life on what is called the Côte d'Azur. Avoid
> the region of Nice which is the preserve of some of the
> most criminal organisations in the south of France: they
> deal in drugs; they have attempted, with the connivance
> of high authorities, to take over the casinos in the famous
> 'war' which left one victim, Agnes Le Roux, the daughter
> of the main owner of the Palais de la Méditerranée, 'miss-
> ing believed murdered'; they are involved in the building
> industry which helps to launder their illicit gains; they
> have close connections with the Italian Mafia.

These people had access to the most respectable places and there was no secret about the relationship of certain officials with these gangs. By allowing various documents to disappear, or by calling off prosecutions, the police assured the immunity of many of these criminals. In return, they would help the police lay hands on comparatively unimportant delinquents so that the statistics of the fight against crime which they were obliged to produce annually looked perfectly satisfactory. The corruptive role that money plays in this infrastructure is unimaginable! Graham Greene appeared to know the shady places in which these people operate fairly well. He knew about people like Jean-Dominique Fratoni, the general of the casino war, and Spaggiari, the man responsible for 'the robbery of the century'.

In this first act of *J'Accuse* – Greene himself calls the story a drama – he tells us of the background to his close friendship with the Cloetta family, about Martine's artistic qualities and her marriage to Daniel Guy, whose principal characteristics were his cunning and his jealousy. Martine's secret unhappiness in her marriage was reaching a climax. She once said to me: 'I would prefer to die than go back and live with him.' The law is taking a hand, but it is the corrupt justice of Nice. Her own lawyer deceives her, the magistrate allows a divorce under appalling terms, and her ex-husband assaults her brutally on several occasions, promising to destroy her. The young woman's martyrdom has begun.

Graham Greene's powerful pen provides a note of mounting suspense as the accounts turns into tragedy. In the second act he reveals the shady life of Daniel Guy, who has been imprisoned four times in France and Italy for violence, robbery and fraud. His civil rights had been forfeited. Daniel Guy is a sick man. In an interview with Graham, he admits that Martine has been slandered unjustly – Guy had paid a man for his testimony. This man, March, a television technician in Monte Carlo, was a friend of Martine's; and for Daniel Guy this friendship was sufficient: '. . . so far as I am concerned, friendship is the same as adultery,' he said. Graham Greene's portrait of Doctor Fischer in his novel *Doctor Fischer of Geneva* is, incidentally, based upon certain aspects of Daniel Guy.

Daniel's behaviour towards his wife worsens from day to day. He assaults Martine's father. The family complains to the police, but Daniel could not care less, for he knows that complaints will go unheeded, the police are also infiltrated by the *milieu*. Martine goes to her lawyer for help, but he betrays her too. He even presses her to go with him to a *partouze* (a debauched party). Naturally, Martine refused. If she had accepted, she would have been lost. After her years as a television announcer in Monte Carlo, her face would have been recognized immediately. Daniel would then have had an irrefutable argument in his possession. Is this what her own lawyer was attempting to achieve? He had once confessed that Daniel Guy had tried to bribe him.

Not even the most implausible novel could be stranger than these experiences. Throughout the time that Graham was writing his book, the Mayor of Nice himself, Jacques Médecin, was in regular communication with the man who owned most of the casinos on the Côte d'Azur, Jean-Dominique Fratoni, a friend since boyhood. Birds of a feather fly together, as the English proverb has it, and Médecin would eventually have his comeuppance.

Guy's attacks on his wife increased. The law showed further signs of corruption, and one judge rewarded Daniel Guy's 'coup de force' by granting him custody of the child he had already snatched. This same gentleman, during an argument with his current mistress, Mademoiselle Escrivant, broke her nose. The doctor confirmed the fractures and she went to the police. Two days later, he told her that her charges were worthless; they would simply be put in a bottomless drawer. 'It's merely a bore having to go and call at the Commissariat of Police.' A short time after this, a member of the gang broke into Mademoiselle Escrivant's office, cut the telephone wires, and said: 'So busting your nose wasn't enough, eh? Now I've come to shoot you.'

Fortunately, a lorry drove up at that moment and the thug escaped, though not before hitting her on the head with the butt of his revolver. The girl was frequently threatened with death. Guy was discharged.

The pain and anguish seemed endless; no sooner did one door open than another closed, and the situation seemed to worsen. Greene decided to make his accusation. He did not accuse a petty criminal, someone perhaps worthy of compassion, but he accused certain police officers, magistrates and lawyers in Nice. He accused them of protecting criminals and of encouraging them in their crimes by guaranteeing them immunity. They had all helped deliver a young woman and her two daughters into the hands of an unbalanced criminal. And he also accused the 'obscure forces' whose recent manoeuvres were attempting to prevent justice from being done in the Supreme Court. His indictments were based on three years of careful observation, and on a series of converging clues, which neither the police nor the magistrates in Nice wished to pursue.

Emil Zola did not have final legal proof when he published his famous letter *J'Accuse* in defence of Dreyfus. The proofs emerged later, just as Greene hoped they would in this case. And so they did.

My friendship with the writer had kept me in daily contact with every phase of these sad events. My friendship with the Cloetta family, too, goes back some while. How well I remember a long conversation with Martine, walking beneath the trees, not far from the coast, overlooking one of the best views of Nice. There I discovered something about her own views on life and the extent of her silent suffering. I also discovered that her marriage was not recognized under canon law. It was like discovering a star in a dark night.

Shortly afterwards, Sandrine was born and I went to Antibes to baptize her. At the same ceremony, the local parish priest baptized Alexandra, and I accepted the honour and obligation of being her godfather.

I can testify to the absolute truth of what Graham Greene has written in *J'Accuse*. The tension in which we lived – I must write in the first person – is difficult to describe. Anyone who was not caught up in that tangled web, which was as invisible as the air we breathe, cannot really appreciate the feelings of impotence and frustration we experienced. The mafia has a diabolical way of asphyxiating personal freedom, and one wonders how it was possible in those circumstances for Graham Greene to complete *The Human Factor* and also write *Doctor Fischer of Geneva*, *Ways of Escape*, *Monsignor Quixote* and *Getting to Know the General*.

There was no limit to the mafia's tentacles. The moment it was attacked, it arranged for a reporter from the *Figaro Magazine* to be sent to Antibes. He cunningly enticed a member of the Cloetta family to give him some private family photographs, and on 13 February a fully illustrated article appeared which was sordidly defamatory of Graham Greene and the Cloetta family. In one of the many photographs appeared 'the cuckolded, complacent husband, smiling at the author'. This husband of Yvonne and father of Martine was ... a Spanish priest. It was a picture of me! Fortune often so arranges things that the devil has some rope with which to hang himself. Faced with the threat of a libel action for defamation, and alarmed at the level of compensation I might demand (for being represented in the *Figaro Magazine* as a man with a double life, and the consequent scandal among those of my students who read French) through our lawyers in Madrid and Paris, the magazine published a photograph of Graham and myself in colour, printed to the size we demanded, and accompanied by an apology which was dictated to them. In the legal documents of retraction, the *Figaro Magazine* was represented by Jean Allard, a well-known right-wing extremist, and the Mayor of Nice, Jacques Médecin. My telegram to Graham's lawyers in Paris stated: 'Have instructed my lawyer to accept terms of *Figaro* apology.'

Our lawyers demanded that *Le Figaro* provide me with fifty copies of the magazine in which the retraction was published, to distribute among my students at Complutense University. It was essential that I prove my innocence. Today, I am only sorry that I did not insist on the half-million francs our lawyers suggested, which I could have given to charity. My 'sullied' name was certainly worth those few francs.

No one should think that this book does not belong with the corpus of Graham Greene's work. All his novels, from *Brighton Rock* on, are novels of pursuit. Pinkie is pursued by the police, by Ida Arnold and by the memory of his lost innocence, among other things. The 'whisky' priest is pursued by the lieutenant, by his conscience, by the Christians who ask him to leave town. Scobie pursues and is pursued by Eternal Love. Monsignor Quixote is pursued by his bishop, by Father Herrera, by his conscience. Even Doctor Fischer is pursued by his feeling of humiliation, which is transformed into hatred and contempt for everybody.

I don't know whether *J'Accuse* is a clue to our understanding of the theme of pursuit in the novels of Graham Greene (and also his better plays), or whether his entire opus is a clue to understanding this powerful indictment of the mafia in the south of France. We also have here the figure of the eternal defender of the oppressed, and the 'martyr of hope'.

Perhaps Graham's strongest motive in writing the book was the fate of the two children involved: Alexandra and Sandrine. One recalls that the corruption of children in our society is a sin that had always obsessed Graham Greene. Think of Brigitta and Coral, for example, in *The Power and the Glory*.

It took a lot of courage to publish *J'Accuse*. But Greene had always lived dangerously. His life had frequently resembled a game of Russian roulette: in Zigi (Liberia), for example, in 1935, when fever had brought him close to the grave; twenty years later, during the war in Indo-China, when there had not been enough water in the canal to wash away the corpses, and, confronted with the imminence of death, Greene went into the cathedral to make his last confession; in Haiti in 1965, Duvalier and his secret police were well aware of the danger

that his pen might do if he was allowed to leave the country alive –
it was almost a miracle that he did get away; a short time before his
death, he was in Northern Ireland. Even there, the danger was not
insignificant: just because he was a Catholic, because he was English
and because he was Graham Greene. And it was like this everywhere
he went.

Consider the final words of the book:

> I have deliberately given this pamphlet the sub-title 'The
> Dark Side of Nice'. For of course Nice has its sunny side
> also, but I can leave it to the Mayor of Nice, Monsieur
> Jacques Médecin, to talk about that side of the city.

The Mayor of Nice accused Greene of declaring this 'Holy War' so
as to publicize his books; he accused him of being a political tool of
the Soviet government. He even called Graham Greene 'an old
poodle'! When corrupt politicians feel themselves under threat, they
turn to the gutter to defend the indefensible. Not even Monsieur
Médecin really believed any of this. What people did begin to wonder,
both inside and outside France, was by what shady means had the
Médecin family managed to hold onto the mayoralty of Nice for fifty
years . . .

J'Accuse is not, after all, a sad book. If the deeds it recounts are
shameful, it should give us hope that there are still men among us
prepared to denounce them before the whole world.

I am reminded of Graham Greene's final words in his introduction
to *The Comedians*:

> I am proud to have had Haitian friends who fought cour-
> ageously in the mountains against Doctor Duvalier, but a
> writer is not so powerless as he usually feels, and a pen,
> as well as a silver bullet, can draw blood.

When Graham Greene went to Paris to see the French Minister of
Justice, Alain Peyrefitte, and to explain the case of Daniel Guy, the
Minister exclaimed: 'But here's a subject fit for a novel!'

' I've written it already,' replied Graham.

He was referring to the criminal world of *Brighton Rock* and to his
character Pinkie.

The book Graham was writing now was not a novel, but tragic

history. The pamphlet was finished, and a well-known lawyer was very skilfully correcting certain points in the manuscript.

There were four appeals made by Daniel Guy against *J'Accuse*, Graham lost the first three, but won the fourth.

'Not a very good score,' he remarked.

Graham's lawyers did not attach much importance to this. Their view was that the judges were trying to avoid a great scandal. This may have been the reason why the sentence was so mild: a symbolic fine for interfering in a person's life. 'Naturally, we shall appeal,' said Graham. There was a fifth appeal against the book, but I failed to take any notes about this. The case against us had been well planned; they would die rather than allow the truth to be revealed. The book was banned in France, but the first edition had already appeared in its bilingual English/French edition and had been distributed throughout the world.

There were verdicts on three issues: divorce, the custody of the children, and whether *J'Accuse* was defamatory. On 23 February 1983, Graham telephoned me from Paris. He was delighted by the fact that my name had been cited by a witness in court. The girl spoke in a low voice and all that Graham could hear was 'a Spanish priest, Leopoldo Durán...' When he heard this, Daniel Guy jumped up from his seat and shouted: 'I've never met this priest...'

The judge reprimanded him severely.

'What do you think you are doing, interrupting the court like this? Sit down immediately.'

Daniel's lawyers had just assured the court that the defendant was a good and peaceable man, and here he was spoiling everything by flying off the handle at the mention of this name.

•

In the heat of the endless struggle against the mafia, these brief, brighter moments provided Graham Greene with a little cheer. There can be no doubt that this battle 'on what is called the Côte d'Azur' was the toughest ordeal in his life. Were it not for the fact that he would hear about it up there in heaven, we should perhaps give the pamphlet an alternative sub-title to the one he provided: *J'Accuse*, or the incalculable power of one man's pen.

PART FIVE

TWO DINNERS IN LONDON

G RAHAM AND I frequently discussed our respective families. The names of his brothers, Hugh and Raymond, often cropped up in our conversations, but it was a long time before I ever met either the former Director-General of the BBC or the Harley Street doctor.

On 9 July 1980, we were both in London. At 7.30 in the evening, I went to meet Graham at the Ritz. He seemed happy and in good form, although I noticed that he still seemed a little regretful about that brief, but rather brusque, disagreement we had had at the Valencia restaurant in Salamanca. I began to laugh, and I believe my laughter helped erase that triviality from his mind.

When we went out into the street, Graham announced: 'My brother Hugh is coming to dine with us, so you will meet another member of my family.'

We continued walking until we reached Stone's, the excellent restaurant not far from Piccadilly Circus that features in *The Human Factor*. Along the way, Graham pointed out the building in which he worked when he was employed by MI6.

Sir Hugh Greene was waiting for us in the restaurant. He was a giant of a man, beside whom Graham appeared quite short and thin. At Hugh's request, we were soon on Christian name terms, and I was astonished by the culture and depths of this man who had been the Director-General of the BBC for almost ten years. He was not at all happy with the way the Corporation was being run at that time.

'Perhaps mine are the whims of an old man who laments the past,' he remarked.

'They're not the whims of an old man,' interposed Graham. 'They're the truth.'

Our discussion that evening was about books and films, about Hugh's conversations with the Kennedys, the articles he was writing. We moved on to the subjects of Spanish wine, the Pope, the political situation in Poland and marriage between people of different races,

among many others. A conversation between these two brothers is a
glorious thing. They spoke about visiting second-hand bookshops –
something they both loved doing – about foreign capital cities they
both knew, and so on.

This took place not long after the publication of the de luxe edition
of the first chapter of *Monsignor Quixote*. Hugh loved it, and he regretted that Graham did not plan to continue the book.

'Of course he will,' I said without a trace of doubt.

Graham did not say anything. We spoke about the various biographies of Cervantes. Graham had lost the notes he had been
assembling these past three years in connection with *Monsignor Quixote*. 'What a shame!' we both said, but Graham did not seem to mind.

●

Our second meeting also took place over dinner in London, on 25
August 1982. When I arrived at the Ritz, I asked for Graham and
was told that he was waiting for me in room number 423. In the lift,
I bumped into Hugh. We greeted each other warmly and went to
Graham's room.

Graham and I hugged each other, as we always do, but this time
the embrace was prolonged, for we had both been concerned about
my brother Avelino, who was close to death.

Graham had already poured the whisky. The conversation was, as
ever, of great interest. The first subject on the agenda: the Pope's
document on Opus Dei. We discussed the matter at length. I tried
to give an honest appraisal of what I considered to be the pros and
cons of the movement. I mentioned some of my personal experiences.
I described the problems created by some of my students in Madrid
who joined the organization without their parents' knowledge. I told
them of my great friend Alberto Sols, a distinguished biology
researcher, who had been a former member of Opus Dei and an
unquestionably spiritual man. The difficulties he experienced when
he tried to leave the movement – which he loved dearly and continued
to do so – were indescribable. I told them that something similar had
happened to me when I left the congregation of the Vincentian
Fathers. In my opinion, I added, it was the same for anyone who,
having lived a life of prayer, then wanted to leave a religious community, even if he or she intended to continue leading a devout life
afterwards. One's 'superiors' usually went to unacceptable lengths to
oppose the decision when the person in question was someone they

valued. I also assured them that many of the enemies of Opus Dei were, in reality, enemies of the Church.

We set off to dine at Bentley's. The dinner was not exactly a Good Friday fast. There was all sorts of seafood, accompanied by a rather special wine.

The conversation of these two men was what mattered. In the hotel, Graham had given me my personal copy of the Bodley Head edition of *Monsignor Quixote*. We compared it with the American and Canadian editions. We liked them all, but preferred the British edition. The purple of the jacket of the book was the same colour as the pechera and socks which the Monsignor so hated wearing. Hugh found the last chapter of the novel very moving.

Graham said he was eagerly awaiting Maria Couto's study of the political aspects of his work, which would be published under the title *Graham Greene: On the Frontier*.

The war with the mafia was then at its fiercest, but the three of us were nevertheless in excellent mood. Graham did not yet know what the lawyers would decide about the appeal to the Supreme Court to ban *J'Accuse* in France, but the splendid Monsieur Azoulay was optimistic about the issue of Martine and the custody of the child and that was what mattered to him.

Graham loved anecdotes and so did Hugh. Graham told us that one local Chief of Police had told X that they knew that Alexandra was Graham's natural daughter, and that he was intimately involved with both Yvonne and Martine. When Graham first heard this he had burst out laughing. Now he just smiled and looked amused, whereas Hugh and I could not contain ourselves. Not long ago, two men from the French secret service had been to see him; they had discussed a number of things and had arranged for his telephone number to be changed.

Hugh told his stories too. As a student at Oxford, he had once bought a car for £7, even though he had no idea how to drive. All he knew was that cars needed petrol to move. No one had ever told him that cars also needed oil, and so it was continually breaking down. Once he crashed into a church; he could see the church coming towards him. Graham interrupted: 'That is the fate of all the Greenes.'

After the accident, Hugh sold his car. They gave him £3 for it.

●

We discussed dreams. Hugh described a recent dream in which he had been walking through Oxford looking for friends from his student days. They had all died.

We moved on to politics. Both brothers agreed that Antonio Tovar ought to write a short account of the celebrated conversation between Franco and Hitler that took place in Hendaye. I told them that an interpreter was strictly bound by secrecy.

Graham joked: 'What about a dictator?'

Hugh recalled Hitler's comment: 'I would prefer to have all my teeth taken out than have another conversation with Franco.'

Neither Hugh nor Graham cared for Franco. We disagreed about this. But Hugh pointed out that 'Britain owed it to Franco that Hitler never invaded Gibraltar'.

•

Norman Sherry had just spent some time with Graham in Crowborough. Graham told us: 'He will take another six years to finish his biography. The later the better. In that way I won't see it.'

On 13 April 1982, speaking about his biographer, Graham had also said: 'I am pleased that he is working so slowly. I can hope to be dead before he finishes it.' Nevertheless, he admired the superhuman effort Sherry was putting into his research.

•

Hugh hailed a taxi, and Graham and I walked back to the Ritz. I told him that I had felt very drawn to Hugh ever since our first meeting at Stone's, and that he was delightful company. And Graham must have said as much to Hugh.

Graham was happy to see the brother he had always loved in such good spirits and he painted an impressive, if slightly depressing, picture of Hugh for me. On his last visit, he and Elisabeth had gone to visit Hugh at his home in Suffolk. They found him stretched out on a hammock in the garden, reading, while a crow flew around him in circles and a rabbit nibbled on the lawn beside him. Hugh had lost his wife not long ago, and he lived alone. Now, however, Sarah had given him new life and he was happy again.

Hugh Greene married Sarah Grahame on 19 December 1984. I was sorry not to have been able to be present at the wedding. In an affectionate and very trusting letter, in which he mentioned his sudden plans to get married, Hugh wrote: 'I expect you will give us your blessing in an unofficial sort of way.'

A few days later (23 November 1984), in a note accompanying the wedding invitation, he wrote the following: 'All the same, [Sarah] very much likes the idea of your saying the Mass for us, as I do.' My friendship with Hugh had achieved its fullness in a very short time.

The letters Hugh wrote to me after his marriage to Sarah were always full of good humour, and I spent some very happy hours with him and Sarah at his flat in Palace Gate, and at the comfortable restaurant next door to their home.

Graham and I had a gentle discussion about Hugh's marriage on 31 December 1985, when I was in Antibes. Graham thought it might be difficult for the marriage to be successful, largely because of the great difference in the couple's ages. He hoped that marriage would bring them closer, and, as time went by, Graham was very happy at the success of the union and the marvellous role which Sarah, despite her age, was playing in Hugh's life.

I told Graham that I had received two charming letters from Hugh before he got married, informing me of what he was about to do. As he told me, when he had received my letter of 6 October, he had no idea of what he would shortly be announcing in his letter of 10 November. This is what he wrote: 'Meanwhile something has happened of which I never dreamt at the time I received [my letter]. I am going to be married!' And he ended: 'This is something I should never have expected for a moment. With much love, Hugh.'

I went on with what I had been saying to Graham: 'At first I was very surprised by these letters. I should have liked to speak to you about them, but they were about such a private matter! And a priest must be a man of unswerving secrecy.'

Graham understood perfectly. 'The extraordinary thing,' he replied, 'is that Hugh, who is not a Catholic, should have told you all these things. This must mean he has great trust in you, and great affection for you.'

When I told Graham that Hugh had asked me for my 'blessing in an unofficial sort of way', Graham was very happy, but also 'puzzled'. I told him that I had waited a few days before replying to the letter and that when I did, I had told him that my only wish had been his happiness and that perhaps the fact that he was lonely was reason enough for the step he was taking. My university classes prevented me from going to the wedding, but I had asked Hugh to tell me the exact date, because I wanted to say Mass for them that day. Hugh had replied that he was very pleased to have Mass said and, enclosed with his letter, he sent me a photograph of Sarah taken when she was making a film in Israel.

This was just one among thousands of private conversations that I had with Graham. It was a very happy one for both of us.

•

Hugh's new-found happiness did not last long. On 20 February 1987, at nine o'clock in the evening, Graham telephoned.

'Leopoldo, Hugh is dead.'

He was in London. He told me some of the circumstances, which I already knew, for Elisabeth had rung me a few days beforehand. Graham had been in Moscow and they had been trying to reach him via the British Embassy. Hugh had said that he wanted to see him and Elisabeth. Graham flew back on the first available plane.

'I arrived at the hospital one hour before he died,' Graham continued. 'He did not recognize me, but at least I was able to see him before he went. He looked horrible. But still . . .'

Hugh had not been well when Graham left for Moscow. He had tried to shorten the visit as much as possible, for this was what he had promised Hugh he would do.

Graham spoke to me in a very authoritative way. I believe he was trying to cheer me up. He knew me very well, and he knew how much Hugh and I meant to each other. He said to me later: 'Sarah was wonderful with him. I had suggested that they give Hugh a stronger injection in order to see whether he would recognize me. But she said: "I don't know whether it's worth it. It would cause him even more suffering just in order to extend his life a few moments more." Sarah was right.'

He went on: 'Sarah remarked that at least Hugh had not had the distress of seeing me die before him.'

I assured him that Sarah was quite correct, for it was true that Hugh adored him. And I told him how, in his last letter to me, Hugh had mentioned how much he regretted seeing so little of Graham in recent months. Whenever Graham came to England, it was always when he was away. Most recently, Hugh had been in Germany making a film.

'One thing that Sarah said impressed me very much,' Graham

recalled. 'She said, "Now that he is in heaven he will be rejoicing because he can see his wife again." '

'It's a lovely thought,' I said. 'For a woman jealousy has power even in a situation like that.'

'Exactly,' Graham agreed.

'I do understand, dear Graham, what a hard blow this is for you,' I then said. 'But life is like that. All we can do is pray for him, as he will pray for us. God's scales are very different from those of men.'

'Of course I have prayed for him,' Graham replied.

At the beginning of our conversation, he had told me that he already knew that I was praying for Hugh at Mass, for Elisabeth had told him she had spoken to me. I said that I prayed for him as if he were my brother.

I want to emphasize how authoritatively and calmly Graham spoke. From the time of his conversion, his faith had sustained him at difficult moments in his life, and he always prayed, even though he did not go to confession or take communion in those years.

I told Graham that when I first spoke to Elisabeth, I had not known what to do. I thought of dashing off to London, but that would have meant letting Hugh know that his condition was grave.

'There was no reason for you to go to London,' said Graham. 'He knew how ill he was. But there was no question of calling for a priest.'

'I understand,' I replied. 'But I would have gone purely as a friend.'

'That's another matter,' agreed Graham.

This telephone conversation lasted about an hour. I reminded Graham how very helpful Hugh had been to me over the filming of *Monsignor Quixote* and my honorarium.

'He was always my favourite brother,' Graham said. 'I loved Raymond, but in a different way.'

I thought to myself: in some ways, the person to blame for so much may not have been Raymond, but someone else who was very close to him.

Hugh and Graham were quite different from one another. They both spoke very slowly, with great precision and clarity. They were both unusually clear-minded in fact. Both were extremely cultured men and tireless travellers. But perhaps Hugh had more self-control and was more balanced in the true sense of that word. And Hugh was the only one of the siblings who would sometimes burst out with noisy peals of laughter. I would say he was quite 'Latin' in this respect. Elisabeth and Graham would smile, although when Graham was enthusiastic about something, and especially when he was told something ridiculous, he would laugh quite freely, uttering a high-pitched 'Oh', followed by words that were muffled by genuine laughter.

Hugh's death was one of three heavy blows that Graham suffered during the time I knew him. Another was his sister Elisabeth's illness, and the third, the wretched battle with the mafia.

•

Graham used to tell me about his family from the moment we first met, just as I would talk to him about my own. I would also tell him about my little home town, Penedo de Avión in the province of Orense.

Graham had often spoken about Elisabeth. He told me that she had been recruited by MI6 and had worked for the Secret Service before Graham did. But it was only when Elisabeth was discharged of all her duties that he felt able to discuss them. I began to realize just what Elisabeth had always meant to him.

My correspondence, and later my friendship, with Graham had existed for some years before Elisabeth began to look after Graham's affairs, yet I soon came to know her personally. She had very kindly invited me to her home at Crowborough, Sussex, on several occasions, and I went there for the first time on 23 August 1977. She met me at Crowborough station and drove me to her house, which is a real sanctuary of peace and silence. Were I able to choose anywhere I would wish to live, it would be her beautiful house and garden.

I believe I knew who Elisabeth was the moment I first saw her. She is a person of perfect sweetness, shining intelligence and consummate tact in everything she does. After that first occasion, I visited her home many times. At each meeting, I thought more and more highly of this admirable woman. I do not exaggerate when I say she is one of those human beings upon whom God appears to have showered boundless gifts.

My first visit lasted from about midday until seven o'clock in the evening. We discussed everything imaginable and it felt as if we had always known one another. I took enormous pleasure in seeing her collection of Graham's books and of books about him, and the folders full of press-cuttings. Later, every time I went there, I inspected everything over again and I always found some new treasure. On my next visit, she showed me the telephone box in Crowborough from which Sarah called Castle's office in *The Human Factor*, and we drove through that region of East Sussex where Mrs Castle was supposed to live and where she was visited by her family once a month. It was here that the Greene family had lived after their father had retired as headmaster of Berkhamsted School.

Everything impressed me; but if I had to pick upon one thing that delighted me more than anything else, it was the two letters written by Graham as an Oxford undergraduate to his sister when she was nine or ten years old. In those two letters I saw both a symbol of the enormous affection and mutual appreciation which had always existed between the two, and an unconscious intuition on the part of the little girl of what her brother Graham would one day become.

Life took them along different paths. Graham, the eternal wanderer, was constantly travelling all over the world, and so this brother and sister who were so close met only rarely. However, one day Graham's secretary decided to retire and Graham thought of his sister as a possible successor. It was Rodney Dennys, Elisabeth's husband, who advised Elisabeth that she should accept the job, in spite of all the other work she had. If she didn't do it, she would always regret it, for she loved her brother and had such a high regard for his work. She accepted Rodney's advice and never regretted doing so.

•

How very fortunate Graham Greene was in his sister! I began to have some inkling of this in 1964, and later it became quite obvious to me. When Elisabeth was there, Graham was a different man. She was not just a 'supersecretary', the perfect adviser, or the sister with whom he discussed everything on the telephone from Antibes several times a week, dictating letters and making all his arrangements. Elisabeth also provided extraordinary moral support and a complete harmony existed between them: a certainty that whatever she decided would be for the best. Here are Graham's exact words, spoken in Antibes on 2 April 1985 while I was staying there.

It was providential that Elisabeth took charge of all my
affairs. She went through all my correspondence,
picking out only the letters which she thought I should
see, and she would send them to me in a weekly packet.
She dealt with the others. And she was always right.

From 1976 onwards, he frequently said much the same thing in different ways! I was often with him in Antibes, or here in Spain, when he would mention his sister and we would comment on her virtues. I am absolutely certain that, in so far as every one of his problems was concerned – whether personal or to do with business – the opinion that mattered most to him was that of Elisabeth. Graham was always a free, independent spirit. 'I don't like to be protected,' he would say. Yet whatever Elisabeth, with her sweetness and perfect tact, suggested always achieved its effect in one way or another . She would choose exactly the right moment to raise a tricky or delicate matter. What is more, she would keep her own problems to herself so that Graham would not have to worry about her.

I often thought that it was a great shame Elisabeth had not been in charge of Graham's affairs many years earlier. How many trials might have been avoided! With Elisabeth beside him, he was at peace (in so far as Graham could be at peace in this world). He often said to me: 'Perhaps you, or perhaps we, should ask Elisabeth's advice.' For Graham, Elisabeth was a visible sign of God's providence.

As I have already mentioned, it was on 25 February 1989 that Graham told me that Elisabeth had had a stroke.

He recounted what had happened very slowly, with all the self-control he had at times like that. Nevertheless, he said something which I had never heard him say before, nor ever heard again: 'I don't know what to do.'

It was one of the most difficult moments of his entire life. We spoke for a long time. We resigned ourselves to the sorrow – trusting to God's mercy – of Elisabeth's prolonged illness. But, in human terms, we were both overwhelmed. One of the problems that arose immediately was to do with who would take over the work Elisabeth did for her brother. The name of his beloved niece Amanda suddenly came to my mind and she took up the reins from her home in the Midlands and coped perfectly with everything.

•

Elisabeth was also enormously helpful to me personally from the moment she became what I call a 'supersecretary' or 'super-adviser'. Through her I was able to find out everything I needed to know about Graham and his work. She was always wonderfully good-humoured and one had the feeling that she was even happier when one gave her yet another problem to solve. Over the course of the years, there were many such occasions when I was not sure whether I should raise a particular matter with Graham or not, and I would consult Elisabeth in the knowledge that she would always advise me which course I should take.

Whenever I went to London, I could never leave without calling on Elisabeth and her husband Rodney at least once, and in our conversations we took stock of everything that had taken place over the year.

I once commended a Spanish friend of mine to her and she looked after her as if she were her own daughter. She always treated anybody connected with me with the utmost care. She was one of a number of people in London who did things for me that they would only have done for the very closest of their families: Mrs Dunn, my 'adopted mother' as Graham called her; Elisabeth and her family; Dymphna McGregor; Betty Sharrock and countless others.

To return to Elisabeth, the eighty-one letters I have, not counting notes written after her stroke, are a testament to a wonderful friendship and to her enormous warmth of heart. I am convinced that Elisabeth has always been the mother figure for the entire Greene family and someone who represented peace and tranquillity for all of them. In her company, one always felt safe and happy. She sustained us all.

Those who have met Elisabeth know that my words are no mere homage to her character, but rather a faint echo of all that could truthfully be said of her. I do not doubt that it was in no small way due to her that my friendship with Graham developed as it did.

CHAPTER II

EXHAUSTION

GRAHAM GREENE WAS a tireless man. His singular mental clarity and agility remained with him until the very end of his life, and his physical energy virtually kept pace. In 1989 he was with me in Vigo for a few days and we travelled around Spain as we usually did. In July that year, I went to Antibes and we took the same long walks that we always had. Graham walked quickly, and because his legs were so long it was sometimes difficult to keep up with him. (The only time we ever went to the cinema together was in London and we were a little late leaving; I had to ask him to please walk a little more slowly.) I never knew where Graham's physical strength came from, for he ate far less than an average person. He was well over six foot, and I believe it was his nervous energy and his constantly active mind which instilled such agility into his tall body.

I began to hear Graham use the word 'tired' frequently during 1989, but I noticed that he only said it when he was worried. I do not deny that he was physically tired, but in my view the exhaustion was as much psychological as physical and it was the former that was largely responsible for the latter.

The period from 1979 onwards had been perhaps the most exhausting period of his life. This was when his battle with the mafia in the south of France began, and the problem continued to worsen until the end of 1985. After this there was a period of relative calm and Graham Greene reverted to being, for the most part, the man I had always known. On the telephone, when asked, 'How are you?', the reply was frequently, 'Well, but a little tired.'

Although he was no longer preoccupied by the struggle with the mafia, it had left its mark and thereafter he was nearly always 'a little tired'.

On 6 July 1989, we planned our holidays. God willing, he would be at Barajas airport on 9 August for the start of our annual 'picnic'. But before that, he would spend a few days in Capri 'to work and

relax'. In his quiet little house on Anacapri, work was the best relax-
ation, because he could write without anyone disturbing him. He was
happy psychologically when he could see that his work was pro-
gressing. For Graham, tired though he was, his work, in the strictest
sense of the word, was his life.

Nature, however, has its own laws. As that sceptical philosopher
rightly said: '*Quam difficile est exuere natura*' – How difficult it is to
cast nature aside.

Without realizing it, Graham Greene had refused to confront the
evidence. When I asked him how he was on 5 April 1987, he
answered: 'I am well. Sometimes I feel a little tired, but I am well';
a month later (15 May 1987), he said: 'I am well. But these endless
festivities in Antibes leave me feeling totally exhausted. The telephone never stops ringing. Everybody wants to come and see me.
It's as if everyone is trying to follow my every footstep.'

He felt worn out by events: journeys to Latin America and Switzerland, mountains of letters waiting to be answered. And, as if that
were not bad enough, his dictaphone had broken down. He took
refuge in Anacapri where he could work on *The Captain and the
Enemy*.

In my notebook I wrote: 'I have never seen him looking quite so
tired, dejected and overwhelmed as on this occasion. He is travelling
too much, Antibes is too noisy, and there are too many selfish people
asking to see him . . . He cannot go on like this!'

I heard the dreaded word again two months later (22 July 1987).
Slightly later than usual, we had a telephone conversation. Graham
was happy, but he replied to my usual question: 'And how are you?'
with an emphatic 'Exhausted.'

'I arrived in Capri, but I am feeling very tired,' he went on. 'The
flights were all delayed and no one leaves me in peace.'

In my notebook at the time, I wrote: 'I felt upset and worried when
I heard him. Graham becomes involved in so many problems that he
then feels "exhausted" – that is the word he used – and has no
energy for anything else. Then, when he recovers a little, he becomes
involved yet again and compromises himself here and there. And so
it goes on.'

Our conversation continued. And I wrote: 'And now for the bad
news.'

'I cannot see how we can go on our picnic until October,' Graham
said. 'Sunday Dimitri is arriving [a Russian correspondent friend of

both of ours]. Then someone else is coming from Russia who tells me he is my Russian Chuchu . . .'

He went on listing things. I interrupted him.

'If that's the way things are . . . how terrible to be so famous!'

'You are quite right,' he replied.

For Graham Greene this had always been the case ever since 1940, when the publication of *Brighton Rock*, and, especially, *The Power and the Glory*, made him a celebrity.

As I have said, the summer of 1988 was an awful time for Graham Greene. His friend Max Reinhardt was setting up his new publishing firm and they wanted to launch it with a new book from Graham.

On 30 November we had a very long telephone conversation.

'Why this unusually late call, dear Graham?'

His voice was full of warmth, but it sounded terribly tired. 'The summer and the following months are going to be exhausting. I am very tired. The flood of correspondence weighs one down. At this moment I have more than fifty letters on my table. What's more, I also have the first volume of Norman Sherry's book [the first part of his biography of Graham]; it runs to 750 long pages which I have to read very carefully.'

And then he told me about his recent visit to Russia: to Kiev and Moscow, where he was awarded an honours degree by the University.

'It's all rather a lot.'

'I don't know what I can say that I haven't already said a hundred times,' I replied. 'I don't know how you survive with such a vast amount of work, all the appointments you keep arranging . . . on top of everything else.'

'The trouble is that I organize things badly. I do find it hard to keep afloat.'

And he added, with a certain dismay: 'We're going to have to wait until January for you to come to Antibes.'

Plucking up my courage, I tried to sound enthusiastic. 'Don't worry. I'll come in January, February or whenever.'

I sat down at my table and this is what I wrote: 'I have never heard Graham sound so tired on the telephone. It is all too much, far too much.'

I did not go to Antibes. Between March and April 1989 Graham came to spend a week with me in Vigo. As ever, we enjoyed ourselves, in spite of the serious problems that confronted us, but I did observe that he had little strength.

We spent some time planning our summer picnic rather like two children on the day before a fiesta. Graham always felt restored by these informal excursions through the countryside. But two months after he had left Vigo, he rang me to say that he would prefer it if we could alter our plans; he felt tired and he asked me if I would come to Antibes for a few days. After consulting our calendars, we agreed that the best time for Graham would be around 1 July, and it was on the afternoon of that day that I arrived at Nice airport. This was the occasion when he told me about how he had travelled to London, without realizing that he had broken two or three ribs, in order to help Daniel Ortega on his visit to Britain.

I did not know whether to laugh, be furious, or cry. I preferred to try to make him laugh: 'You have published a book entitled *An Impossible Woman*. You are an impossible man!'

And Graham did laugh.

•

With his birthday coming up, and the publication of two books – *Why the Epigraph?* and *Yours Etc.* – there were countless letters to be written and telephone calls to be made. In September, he cancelled his trip to Russia, as well as another to London where he was due to sign copies of the limited edition of *Why the Epigraph?*

He had, however, agreed to go to Ireland to award a literary prize. He returned to Antibes on 1 December 1989. There was a letter from me waiting for him. He read it and telephoned me at once. He had been treated with 'too much fuss, a special plane etc.' All these honours bestowed on him meant a tremendous sacrifice. By nature, he was averse to publicity, and he needed only two things: to have time and be alone. He returned from Ireland worn out both physically and mentally. When his illness became irreversible, he told me more than once: 'Ireland killed me.'

Graham Greene's physical and psychological resistance were unimaginable, but the human body has its limitations. He had arrived at the frontier. And 'you can't cross the frontier'.

•

Correspondence was a form of martyrdom for Graham Greene throughout his life. He himself wrote very few letters. He wrote to his children perhaps once a year, but he had an allergy to writing outside the hours he spent creating his books.

Official correspondence was another matter. He needed to keep in touch with his various publishers, film-makers and people of this sort, but he could dictate these letters to his secretary. When Elisabeth took over his affairs, she would send out the vast majority of these letters herself, though in Graham's name. Using her own judgement, she would only send Graham a small batch of the letters which she considered he should reply to personally.

The letters I am referring to were those sent to Graham at his home address in Antibes, the letters that would await him on his return from our holiday. Sometimes he was able to forget about the thought of all this correspondence, but the moment he did so, something would remind him of it and he would moan: 'There may be a hundred or more letters waiting for me in Antibes.' The mere thought of confronting all that post would cloud his happiness.

He certainly had good reason for his anxiety. On 29 October 1984, he told me: 'I am correcting the proofs of the French edition of *Getting to Know the General*. I don't have time for anything. In this month alone, I have received 266 letters.'

On 25 September 1985, on his return from Capri, he found a further 63 of these wretched letters.

The problem of his correspondence seemed to go from bad to worse. On 17 September 1988, I rang him in Antibes. I was about to leave for Osera and I wanted to give the monks his greeting. We spoke for a long time. When I enquired about the state of his health, he replied: 'I am well, but tired.'

He went on: 'The main problem is the post. If I go away for even a week, it means that I may find a hundred or more letters awaiting my return. When I return shortly from Russia it's possible there may be several hundred. Of course, I don't have to reply to every one of them, but at least I have to open them.'

Some of these letters went straight into Graham's huge waste-paper basket, which was capacious and almost as tall as his writing table. Dark pink in colour, it was a waste-paper basket that had witnessed a great deal and really deserved a poem to be written about it. Most of what was thrown into it had to do with Graham Greene himself: there might be magazines with articles about him, plastered with photographs, or editions of his books whose appearance he disliked. Each day's post brought an enormous amount of material destined for that waste-paper basket.

Whenever I went to Antibes, I could not resist sifting through this waster-paper basket. There always seemed to be something worth-while there and I began to resemble one of those beggars one sees in the evenings, sifting through the rubbish people have discarded – although I believe I was luckier than most of them.

On my trips to Antibes I would sometimes try to find out who some of these people were who wrote letters to Graham which he threw away. On 19 December 1979, for example, the post brought the following: two letters from Moscow – one from the woman who had looked after him when he was last there, the other from his former literary agent, telling him that *The Human Factor* had been praised by the entire Soviet press. There were letters from South Africa, from Argentina, from all over the world; there was also the most recent batch of British press cuttings. Graham threw everything except the Russian letters into the waste-paper basket. There might be letters from some slightly unbalanced young woman, or from priests or nuns who were even more unhinged, and who would write extraordinarily audacious letters to him. It is quite impossible to cope daily with this amount of post.

Some people would even register their mail. The postman would arrive, Graham was not in, and so he left a note telling him that there is something to collect at the post office. Poor Graham would go along there and, after waiting in a queue for half an hour, he would collect a registered letter from some crank. There are some people who spend their time writing to famous people in order to collect replies.

One morning I leave early to accompany Graham to Cannes where he had a dental appointment. When we return home, the post is waiting. A professor in the Canary Islands has sent Graham a copy of a recent photograph of him published in *El País*, and asks Graham to sign it. A fifteen-year-old English boy writes to ask if Graham would explain the meaning of one of his short stories. There is a letter of congratulation from a Chinese publisher or translator. Another young woman takes the opportunity to send him Christmas greetings out of the blue and at the same time to ask his advice about how to settle and work in France. She would be most grateful and promises to visit him.

Then there were those tragic, pathetic letters that I have already mentioned, occasioned by the publication of *The Heart of the Matter*: a stream of letters from women and from priests asking if he would be their spiritual director. For a time, the terrible sense of impotence he felt in being unable to help would drive him mad. But that was short-lived; he was soon able to laugh about the letters and his scruples. Nevertheless, the shadow cast by the thought of the correspondence that always awaited him, and the terrible reality of coping with it, was a constant torture for Graham.

Postal strikes had often caused him great inconvenience, but when he was already ill, on 15 February 1990, he said to me: 'I am pleased about the postal strikes in various parts of the world. It means fewer letters.'

'Let us pray for the post office strike!' I muttered.

Graham rather approved of the prayer. For the time being, at least, that large waste-paper basket was no longer needed.

PART SIX

GREENE ON GREENE

O N 22 JANUARY 1977, I wrote a most fortunate letter to Graham. Fortunate, because the letter produced a very happy outcome, one which was far from being what I expected and something I had never imagined possible. As I have said, I asked Graham whether he would mind writing the occasional brief sentence or few lines, from time to time, in an album which I would send him. The album could remain with him at home indefinitely. 'I shall call this album my Picasso,' I told him.

Graham was in Switzerland when my letter reached Antibes. On his return, he wrote to me on 7 February. Among other things, he said: 'Of course, send me your "Picasso".' In fact, he had already started to work on it two days before he wrote to me. I expected it to be no more than a simple autobiographical keepsake, written simply as a souvenir. However, on my next visit to Antibes, I saw the album lying on top of a small table at the entrance to his study. I noticed that he had written a few pages. He told me that he kept the album there so that he would not forget his promise. He even asked me to remind him about my 'Picasso' from time to time in case pressure of work should make him forget about it. I said I would do so, although he did not mention it again until two or three years later.

'Whenever we speak on the phone or you write to me, remind me of your "Picasso",' he said.

'But isn't it a bit much?'

'No, always remind me about it.'

Naturally, I never forgot to remind him, although I did not always mention it in our telephone chats. I felt rather awkward. I did cast a glance at it whenever I went to Antibes and we would sometimes discuss what he had written. And when Graham came to Spain, the blessed 'Picasso' did not go unnoticed. Slowly but surely, it grew longer. Sometimes, without being asked, he would say to me on the telephone: 'I've written a few more pages of your "Picasso".'

In December 1983 I received a letter from my friend Joseph E. Jeffs, the librarian at Georgetown, the well-known Jesuit university. He and his wife had been to see Graham in Antibes. He wrote in his letter: 'He even showed us the "commonplace book" that he is assembling for you. What a wonderful memento of your friendship!'

Graham presented me with the 'Picasso' on 9 August 1984 at the *parador* in Oropesa. He offered it to me in the same way that he might have handed me a glass of water. I knew only too well what he was giving me. He had been writing it, bit by bit, for over seven years.

Occasionally, Graham had filled entire pages; at other times, just half a page. The book contains his comments and reflections, as well as many of his own poems. What he wanted to do was to produce a rather special sort of anthology – a commonplace book – in which he would jot down passages from books he had been reading over the years that he felt worth recording. The quotations thus came to be his in some way or other; the album became a mirror of his tastes, his thoughts, and of the authors he read with most enjoyment.

There are quotations from 138 well-known writers. Some are quoted just once, others more frequently. Unamuno, for example, is quoted six times; G. K. Chesterton, William James and St Augustine each four times; Rilke and Nietzsche, three times. Graham used those ideas which were tied in most closely with the way in which he lived and thought, whether they were concerned with aesthetics, theology or literature. In the passages written by him, the subject of religious faith is crucial to an understanding of the man, as are those in which he refers to the effects on him of the six-year struggle with the mafia.

•

It is not my intention to provide even a short resumé of this book. I only wish to quote certain passages which are relevant autobiographically.

Graham loved solitude. This is where the false idea arose that he was a man of mystery, when all he was trying to do was find the silence he needed to write creatively. At the beginning of my album, my 'Picasso', we see how determined he is to avoid any disturbance on our 'picnics', and how he looks for the sort of quiet atmosphere a Trappist monk enjoys. He then provides an appropriate quotation:

A motto for all the journeys we hope to take, from
Unamuno:

Avoiding the Casino, avoiding the town, avoiding a
human society which invents jails, I've taken to the woods,
as far as possible from the highway. I shun the highway
because of those trees used for signs, which are like
prisoners too or like foundlings, which is almost the
same, and then all those billboards. They all have
something to proclaim, all kinds of products, some of
them agricultural machinery, most of them liquor,
others tyres for automobiles that rush about everywhere.

Greene's embattled faith was rather like Miguel de Unamuno's. It
was a faith that troubled him, for he was a man obsessed by faith,
but he never stopped praying and begging God for hope.

Was Thomas Becket a Saint?
He had faith, he was a martyr, but . . .

'If I have all faith, so as to remove mountains, but have
not love, I am nothing. If I give away all I have, and if
I deliver my body to be burned, but have not love, I gain
nothing.'

Did Becket love?
Unfortunately St Paul gives a definition of love which
includes hope. And many of us today find hope even more
difficult than love. There is an English hymn which I
have always liked, 'Abide with me', and I always
misquote one line. The hymn reads, 'Help of the helpless,
O abide with me', but I always find myself saying, 'Hope
of the hopeless'. Feb 5

Like any mortal, Graham had his low points, his periods of discouragement or despondency. Then, suddenly, he would feel himself reju-
venated and he would come alive again and be able to write, thanks
to this inner light. These lines of George Herbert, which he chose,
describe the phenomena taking place within him:

Do all things like a man, not sneakingly:
Think the king sees thee still, for his King does.
George Herbert

And the sad man is cock of all his jests.
Ib.

Although there were some forty heavens, or more,
    Sometimes I peer above them all;
    Sometimes I hardly reach a score,
    Sometimes to hell I fall.
Ib.

And now in age I bud again,
After so many deaths I live and write;
I once more smell the dew and rain,
And relish versing: O my only light,
    It cannot be
    That I am he
On whom thy tempests fell all night.
Ib.

In a few magnificent lines that are full of simplicity, Graham Greene describes those spiritual ups and downs with which he struggled constantly and silently all his life:

> After the right number of drinks with a snack meal and
> alone – perhaps two bottles of Carlsberg and three
> Swedish *akvavit* and a tin of sardines – I believe that I
> can carry on, an idea may come, perhaps the last book
> has not been written ... but tomorrow morning ... the
> euphoria will have left me.

This is one of the most revealing passages Graham Greene ever wrote.

•

Ever since his adolescence Graham Greene had to struggle against boredom. It was one of the crosses he bore. Here, Steinberg provides the words with which to reflect on one of life's most secret and painful realities:

> The life of the creative man is led, directed and controlled
> by boredom. Avoiding boredom is one of our most
> important purposes. It is also one of the most difficult,
> because the amusement always has to be newer and on
> a higher level ... Not everything that amused me in the
> past amuses me so much any more.
> *Samuel Steinberg*

Like Unamuno, Graham Greene spent a lifetime struggling with himself. For both of them, the reality of life appeared to be a conflict, an 'agony' in the etymological sense of the word. One has only to think of Unamuno's book *La Agonía del Cristianismo*. The great Russian writer thought as they did:

> As for tranquillity – it's spiritual business. That's why
> the bad side of our soul desires tranquillity, not being
> aware that its attainment entails the loss of everything in
> us that is beautiful – not of this world, but of the world
> beyond.
> *Tolstoy*

Was this not what St Teresa of Avila taught in her poetry:

> *Ya no durmais, ya no durmais,*
> *Pues que no hay paz en la tierra.*

Graham Greene had one goal as far as his style was concerned: simplicity. There are two masterly passages on the simplicity of style for which he yearned:

> It had been the dream of his life to write with an
> originality so covert, so discreet, as to be outwardly
> unrecognisable in its disguise of current customary form
> of speech. All his life he had struggled after a language so
> reserved, so unpretentious as to enable the reader or the
> hearer to master the content without noticing the means
> by which it reached him. All his life he had striven to

achieve an unobtainable style, and had been appalled to
find how far he still remained from his ideal.
Boris Pasternak

The other passage which Greene adopted is a prayer:

Of all the prayers that writers have addressed to the deity,
I know of none more touching than the one Tolstoy
wrote in his diary as a young man: 'O God, grant me
simplicity of style.'
Henri de Montherlant

Quite clearly, the Lord did listen to Tolstoy's prayer asking for simplicity, as he did to Graham's.

•

I will conclude these extracts from my 'Picasso' with two memorable
pages. The first begins with a note he sent to me after I had spent a
week with him in Antibes, just before the battle with the mafia had
begun. That week had seemed a little more hopeful, but trouble had
broken out and it was going to be a cruel ordeal.

The second page contains one of the most illuminating passages
Graham Greene ever wrote about his faith and his belief.

Leopoldo, this is April 14, 1979. The day after you left a
shadow of hope arrived – a meeting between Martine's
lawyer and Daniel, the husband, in the Alps tomorrow and
a possible agreement. Today we still have to pray and at
lunch I was reading this quotation from Newman – he is
referring of course to the Church and not to human
relations, but it seems very apposite.

What is commonly a great surprise when it is witnessed
is the particular mode by which Providence rescues and
saves ... Sometimes our enemy is turned into a friend;
sometimes he is despoiled of that special virulence of evil
which was so threatening; sometimes he falls to pieces of
himself; sometimes he does just so much as is beneficial
and then is removed.

4 May 1980
The problem still unresolved – perhaps the last but one

solution the most possible. We have now been warned by the Mayor of Antibes, who is helping us, that Daniel and his group of the milieu are highly dangerous. The lawyer has already been changed – he had tried to persuade Martine to go to a group-sex party at Cannes where her ex-husband was trying to get the guardianship of the children, there has been violence and threats, and the Nice police seem to be his protectors. The next week is likely to be critical and dangerous.

30 April 1984
Then finally I had to write *J'Accuse* – 1984 will perhaps see things settled.

I am to a certain extent an agnostic Catholic. I am quite unable to believe in Hell which contradicts my faith that if there is a God he must be a loving God or else why bother to invent the Devil? As a separate Person? Nor do I accept Rome's teaching on contraception which in this poor overcrowded world goes against all reason – a teaching which in Catholic countries or rather among Catholics is one of the principle reasons of abortion.

One must distinguish between faith and belief. I have faith, but less and less belief, in the existence of God. I have a continuing faith that I am wrong not to believe and that my lack of belief stems from my own faults and failure in love.

Now paradoxically in the affair of Father Hans Küng and Father Schillebeeckx I find myself grateful to those two priests for reawakening my belief – my belief in the empty tomb and the resurrection, the magic side of the Christian religion if you like. Perhaps that is the unconscious mission of Father S. when he writes of the resurrection as being a kind of symbolic statement of the spiritual impression which the apostles experienced after the crucifixion. I remember again in St John's Gospel the run between Peter and John towards the tomb. Peter leading until he lost breath, and then the younger man arriving first and seeing the linen cloths but afraid to go in, and then Peter overtaking him . . . it's like *reportage*. I can be

interested in the *reportage* of a mystery: I am completely
uninterested - even bored - by a spiritual symbol equally
'unhistoric' in Küng's sense as the *reportage*. The attempt
to get rid of the fairy tale makes me for the first time in
years begin to believe in it again. I am against the condemnation of Father S. for he has communicated belief to at
least one Catholic.

G. G.

In Chapter Ten of the first part of this book, I tried to elucidate a
little what Graham Greene meant by 'faith' - unadorned faith that
does not take into account any of the rational arguments that may
help us to believe; and 'belief' - something that is based on our
reasoning processes and which tries to demonstrate what is rational
in our faith. When we make our act of supernatural faith, these
reasons are rejected, since they are natural, whereas our faith is something divine and supernatural.

Here is one illustration. Before saying 'I believe in the Trinity',
reason tells me three things: that God exists; that he cannot be wrong,
nor can he deceive me; and that he has told me through the Gospels
that in God there are three persons in one being. Nevertheless, one's
reason goes on asking: how is it possible that one being can have three
persons? But then grace intervenes, and through the illumination of
the mind and the will with divine grace, man is able to say on both
a rational and divine level: 'I believe in the Holy Trinity.'

By praying this way, reason accepts what it cannot see and pays
great homage to God.

OUR CORRESPONDENCE

Strolling with Elisabeth Dennys in the garden of her home near Crowborough, she told me that Graham Greene's correspondence had to be divided into two sections: the letters addressed to me, and those sent to everyone else.

I have already mentioned the genesis of our friendship. I had been preparing a dissertation on Graham Greene at the Complutense University in Madrid. I was planning to go to London University to prepare a doctoral thesis on the role of the priest in Graham Greene's work. It occurred to me to write him a short letter – a note more than a letter – asking him two or three questions to do with the work I had in mind. Rather apprehensively, and in order that his reply should be as little trouble to him as possible, I had enclosed a list of his books so that he need only put a cross alongside the relevant titles. I was greatly surprised when, a few days later, I received a letter from Graham Greene which was much fuller than mine, replying to each one of my questions. Today, that letter actually strikes me as being rather affectionate:

C.6 Albany,
London. W. 1.

30 June 1964

Dear Father Durán,

I wonder if you are any relation of an old friend of mine, Gustavo Durán, who now lives in America? It's a little bit difficult for me to answer your questions as I try to forget my books after they are written and I don't myself see some of the problems which other people see in them. However, as you have suggested, I have put a cross against certain books in answer to your question one. I suppose the answer to your question two would be *The Power and The Glory* and *The End of The Affair* and *The Heart of The Matter* – in fact the same ones as I have marked for question one.

Two short stories I think you should read: 'A Visit to Morin' in *A Sense of Reality* and 'The Hint of an Explanation' in *Twenty One Stories*.

Thank you very much for your memento in your mass.

Yours very sincerely,
Graham Greene

To begin with, I think I was careful not to bother him with my letters; later, our correspondence became more regular. After a few years, I sent him a fairly basic outline of the thesis I proposed to write, which he was kind enough to study, and he subsequently sent me a long letter giving me his opinion about what I planned to do, offering detailed and subtle criticism. I did not write to him again until I sent him a copy of my thesis, having defended it at King's College at the University of London.

From that time on, our correspondence increased, until our first meeting. Then, his letters were quite lengthy, but later we both preferred to communicate by telephone. This made it easier for him, and it was very rare for us not to be in touch with each other at least every month.

My considerable correspondence with Graham Greene gives a very compete picture of the man's inner life. Written over a period of twenty-seven years, these letters reflect his absolute sincerity, his tenderness, his almost childlike dreams, the things that made him happy, his anxieties, great and small. Everything is there.

Broadly speaking, I would divide the letters into the following groups: letters of friendship, although they are all friendly; letters to do with politics and his travels; humorous letters; letters planning our 'picnics'; letters about those picnics and the photographs that we took; letters (many of them) concerning the battle with the mafia in the south of France; letters to do with my retirement from the University and my pension; final letters (of which there are only three, for Graham was unable to write much, and we communicated by telephone).

Many of Graham's letters touch on political matters. Up until the death of Omar Torrijos, and even several years afterwards, Greene travelled a great deal in Latin America; mostly in Central America: Panama, Nicaragua, Haiti, Cuba. Before that he had been in Mexico and Argentina. But above all, it was Panama and Nicaragua. The political problems of Central America were of great concern to Graham Greene. He had often met the guerrilla leaders of some of those countries, men who later rose to power. By word and through his writing, as well as a small amount of financial aid and, above all, through the fame of his name, he always supported them in their fight. The intervention of the United States in these parts of the world was something he tried to counter with whatever limited means he could, particularly during Reagan's presidency. With his unfailing humour, Graham wrote to me: 'I go off on December 3 to Panama to fight the Americans!' The assassination of Archbishop Romero and the war in El Salvador were continually on his mind whenever the subject of America arose, particularly after the murder of the Jesuit priests from the University of Salvador, whose work on behalf of the people was so admired by Graham.

Talking about El Salvador on one occasion, he recounted the tragic death of Caetano, a Salvadoran *guerrillero*. He had been to Libya to meet Gadafi. While he was there, his girlfriend was stabbed to death. When Caetano returned to Managua he committed suicide with a gun which Chuchu had given him. It was a mysterious death and the whole affair was surrounded in mystery too. Graham had known Caetano in Managua and Caetano had inscribed a book to him very affectionately, referring to himself as 'your brother'.

One of Graham's happiest moments was the signing of the Canal Treaty by President Carter and Omar Torrijos. He had been present, and on 24 September he wrote to me:

> My dear Leopoldo, I have only just got back from Panama via Washington with the Panamanian delegation to see the signing of the treaty! It was quite fun. I keep a Panamanian passport as a souvenir.

And on 4 October he wrote as follows about the same Treaty:

La Résidence des Fleurs,
Avenue Pasteur,
06600 Antibes

4 October 1977

My dear Leopoldo,

Thank you a thousand times for the beautiful album of photographs which arrived today. These are a better lot than last year's, I think, and just as much drinking. Sad that we haven't got Maria among them.

I can't remember whether I have written to you since Panama. I had an equally bizarre time and almost as amusing as the first. This time I spent a good deal of time with one of the leading Nicaraguan guerrillas whose brother, since killed, organised the spectacular kidnapping of several Ambassadors and several Ministers in one swoop and gained the release of prisoners in Nicaragua. Then the General wanted me to go with the Panama delegation to the signing of the treaty in Washington and off I went with a Panamanian passport to be lodged in a magnificent suite! It was quite amusing seeing all these villains like Pinochet and Stroessner in the flesh and also all the American types – Kissinger, Ford, Ladybird, Carter, Rockefeller, etc. at the signing. They all seemed peculiarly insignificant. The General spoke much better than Carter, who was deplorably bad. It seems more and more doubtful whether the Senate will confirm the treaty and if they don't I imagine it means guerrilla war in Panama next year. The General won't be sorry. At the end of the negotiations he had a dream that he was in the forest, the guerrilla war had started, and he found he had no boots so that he was doomed to the humiliation of capture at the very start of the campaign. I hope that doesn't happen.

With much affection
Graham

P.S. Capri, alas is off this October as the nice woman who looks after me there has broken her arm, so I am having one or two small holidays instead. The book is going very

well before publication. It is the choice of the American
Literary Guild and in England they are able to do a first
printing of 75,000. Of course you will get as early a copy
as possible.

From 1979 to 1984, the war against the mafia cast a shadow over
our correspondence, but the promise and expectations of our annual
'picnics' were always eagerly anticipated.
   On 11 January 1978, he wrote:

   I begin to look forward to our summer holiday. What
   about Barcelona to be included this time? An English
   writer whom I like very much, V. S. Pritchett, who knows
   Spain pretty well, says that there is a wonderful hellish
   landscape behind Elche. The trouble about Barcelona is
   that it is far away from the places we love – Salamanca
   and Orense – and we ought really to look in on Maria
   Newall. Perhaps we ought to do Cordova and Seville and
   come into the far south of Portugal? Anyway, we have got
   plenty of time to think about it. Much love, Graham

Or there is this marvellous letter in which he anticipates the imminent
'picnic' with childlike zest:

   La Résidence des Fleurs,
   Avenue Pasteur,
   06600 Antibes

              18th June 1979

   Dear Leopoldo,
      I have been looking up maps and things and I begin to
   wonder whether our best plan is not to go say after lunch
   of July 16 to Oropesa which is only 148 kilometres from
   Madrid and spend the night only of the 16th there at the
   parador – the telephone number is 172 – and then go on
   and spend the night of July 17 at Mérida, which we briefly
   visited last year at the parador again, which is an old convent and the telephone number is 301540, and then on
   into Portugal spending the night at Evora, which we only

briefly saw at the Pousada dos Loios – another ancient convent – Tel 240 51 – that makes it the night of July 18 and we are only 142 kilometres from Lisbon, so that we could arrive at Sintra on July 19. These would be fairly easy days. If you agree, I suggest that at any rate we book our rooms in Oropesa and Mérida and perhaps from Mérida we can book our rooms in Evora. We would therefore have several quiet and not long days on the road before we came to Sintra and after that we could be more energetic!

Lots of love from myself, Yvonne and Martine

Graham

P.S. The highlight of our trip again will be in the north with your vine grower!

P.P.S. If the Professor was only available in the evening of July 16 then we just do the same route but arrive at Sintra on the 20th instead of the 19th which is after all what we planned and we spend the night of July 16 in Madrid. In other words, it would be July 17 Oropesa, July 18 Mérida, July 19 Evora and July 20 Maria.

There was no subject of importance that was not alluded to in our letters to each other. Sometimes he would mention the progress of the books he was working on. Here is one example. He had already spoken to me about an earlier novel to which he had returned after many years. Later, he wrote to me:

7 February 1977
... Enough for now as there are other things to write which I find more difficult, and that wretched novel.

9 March 1977
... Your letter arrived today (March 9) when I had just written the last words of a not very good novel which I began ten years ago. Even if I don't publish it, it's a relief to have it off my back because I couldn't get settled down to write anything else as long as I was carrying the pack.

11 June
... and proofs of my novel – now called *The Human Factor*
– which I must correct promptly.

In another note he had told me: 'I marked this passage of Dickens as a possible epigraph for *The Human Factor* (which I was then calling 'The Cold Fault'):

They say he has sold himself to the enemy; but you and
I know better – he don't buy.

In his letter of 4 October dealing with political matters and reproduced earlier in this chapter, Graham also told me about the great success of this book before it was even published; a success that was totally unexpected by the author.

I have already alluded to the dream I had in which I saw Graham Greene in the sacristy at Osera, taking off his vestments after celebrating Mass. I had mentioned it to him in a letter I wrote in the first free moment I had the next morning. This was his response:

2 March 1976
... I was amused by your dream. I remember that the day
I became a Catholic I was quite frightened at the length
to which the commitments might take me! Luckily they
did not take me as far as your dream.

The notorious Chuchu was always an unending source of humour for us. Greene considered him an 'intelligent bohemian', and on his return from this first visit to Panama, Greene described him and General Torrijos, in a long letter, as 'most sympathetic characters'. The General had arranged that he should look after Graham. On the face of it, the omens were ill-fated! Graham wrote:

28 December 1976
... Just before I arrived [Chuchu's] car had been
destroyed by a bomb, so we had one of the general's cars
instead. He claimed to be 60% Mayan, 30% Spanish, 5%
Negro and a mixture for the rest. He was a charming
companion. Altogether it was a real holiday and a bizarre

experience. I really will have to begin to learn Spanish
again.

In the following letter, dated 19 January, he told me that Chuchu
'took a degree at the Sorbonne and was a Professor of Philosophy
and Mathematics with nine children by four women'.

   This Chuchu (José Martínez), who is mentioned at various times
in the letters, was also 'a very funny man. He used to recite Rilke as
we drove around, or helicoptered around, to which I would reply
with Thomas Hardy.'

   Graham never tired of talking about Chuchu. In appearance, the
two men looked like Don Quixote and Sancho, but Chuchu had a
perfect command of English, French and German, in addition to his
native Spanish, and could recite 'Spanish poetry and Rilke in German', so he hardly resembled Cervantes' Sancho in other respects.

CHAPTER III

REFLECTIONS ON OUR 'PICNICS'

A T THE END of one of our journeys through the countryside, I asked Graham if he might jot down a few lines that would provide a summary of our travels, and this is just what he did on each occasion from then on. Occasionally, he would spot some apparently insignificant detail which, on a journey of a fortnight, would go unnoticed by most people. They are not so much short, literary paragraphs, as mathematical formulae that reflect the events of two weeks.

I shall give six examples only, each preceded by a rather longer passage in which I give the background to what he wrote.

1. Graham Greene was, as I have said, an enemy of all dictatorships, whether of the left or the right, but he carefully weighed up the circumstances in each case. On 28 December 1976, he wrote to me as follows:

> I found General Torrijos a most sympathetic character and in spite of what you might call a military dictatorship there was a great deal of grass roots democracy and the system excellent, I thought, for a small country, though probably impossible for one even as large as England.

He was less enthusiastic, however, about General Franco's period in power. I had been seventeen years old when the Spanish Civil War began and I lived throughout his rule. Subsequently, I have lived through ten or eleven years of Socialist government. I have frequently tried to compare these two periods and I have reached the conclusion that there is nothing more dangerous, deceitful or cruel than a dictatorship that speaks for a democracy that is false. There is a vast gulf between true freedom and freedom that is no more than hot air! In the name of the latter, corruption of the most atrocious kind has been thrust upon us, and it flourishes today.

Yet there was no way of convincing Graham that Franco had any ethical qualities. He was a dictator, he told me, and his political system had, from the very beginning, denied the basic liberties.

Where Unamuno was concerned, on the other hand, we agreed about everything. On this occasion, we had visited the Valley of the Fallen. The church there and all the grandeur that surrounded it, from the esplanade as far as the cross, reminded Greene, ever a bitter enemy of pomp, of a pharaoh's tomb.

Two or three hours later, as I have already recounted, we were standing in silence in front of the 'box – one cannot call it a tomb –' that contains the remains of Spain's great thinker . . .

> After visiting the Valley of the Dead – that monument of bourgeois bad taste with marble halls resembling the Palace Hotel – it was a pleasure to be directed in the cemetery of Salamanca to Unamuno's latest home – "Unamuno – he is Box 340". General Franco too had fashioned himself a suitable resting place.
>
> Graham Greene
> 26 July 1976
> Madrid

2. Engraved on Graham Greene's mind was the memory of the Roman collar and the black suit I wore when I went to visit him for the first time at the Ritz Hotel. Graham did not care for that form of dress. It seemed far too formal, and he thought such clothes risked alienating me from my students and might restrict their trust in me. I was not easily convinced about this but, after all, he was my 'spiritual adviser'.

Our friendly 'discussions' about General Franco had continued as before, and at the end of this particular journey he alludes to our political disagreements. Humorously, he wrote:

> After our third voyage as your spiritual adviser I have succeeded in persuading you to leave off the bourgeois vestments of a Roman collar and a black suit, but I have failed to open your eyes to the wickedness of a certain Generalissimo. Perhaps next time . . .
>
> Graham Greene
> 26 July 1978

3. Graham was captivated by Salamanca from the first moment. He fell in love with the city. However, the soutanes that many priests wore struck him as being rather archaic and outmoded.

To begin with, he would have liked it if I had tried to live in Salamanca. Now, he is not so sure ... He jokes, telling me that I should perhaps return to wearing my old clerical clothes – the black suit and the Roman collar. He alludes to someone who, according to him, I had rescued from I know not which galleys.

> The fifth occasion and the fourth pilgrimage to Salamanca. The Roman collar buried deep and only a scrap left in the intestine – but this time I have my doubts of Salamanca –might the scrap begin to grow in those surroundings until it left the intestine and enclosed again the neck? Don Quixote rescued the galley slaves and you have rescued somebody whom I have only known in photographs.
>
> Graham Greene
> August 1979

4. Graham Greene believed that a glass of good wine or a decent whisky were social pleasures. It made him happy to see me sharing a bottle with him during our unforgettable suppers in Antibes and we would discuss wine as if it were something sacred. This was the only word used to describe it. Sometimes, however, I found it difficult to sleep, and then I preferred not to drink wine. A little melancholically, Graham counselled me:

> The fifth pilgrimage to Salamanca and I am even more convinced that Salamanca would be wrong for you. The costume-revolution is still there in the intestines – your consumption of wine has fallen strongly – the clerical collar becomes more of a threat as the level of wine falls. "The priest close to ETA" has become the priest close to ... ? Be careful, Leopoldo!
>
> Graham Greene
> 24 July 1980

5. From Madrid we had travelled to Roncesvalles, passing through Santo Domingo de Silos and some historical sites in Navarre. On our return journey we had stopped at paradors and seen some places of great artistic beauty . . .

Graham forget all about them when he came to write down this brief summary of our pilgrimage. All he remembered was one quiet corner of the cathedral at Santo Domingo de la Calzada:

> Three days with Octavio in a new region, Navarra. Perhaps the high point of the journey was the cage in a cathedral containing a live cock and hen and an engaging history.
>
> Graham Greene
> August, 1985

6. It had been an unusual afternoon and the two of us had been alone at my home in Madrid. After lunch and a short siesta, we had planned to keep the afternoon free so that I could ask him questions about his work. How patient and clear-headed Graham was! The session lasted until supper. Graham had certainly deserved the Spanish omelette.

This is how he described what had been an exhausting afternoon for him:

> 17 August 1986
> After the traditional journey thanks to Octavio – picnics by the road – the Trappists – *Paradores* of varying quality – and now in Madrid and interrogation by Torquemada stretching back over half a century about books whose character I can't always remember. However Torquemada ends by giving me a Spanish omelette not the steak – I mean stake.

CHAPTER IV

DEDICATIONS TO HIS OWN BOOKS AND OTHERS

T HERE WERE COUNTLESS occasions when I pestered Graham to write an inscription in my copies of his books. I have many inscribed books in fact, everything he wrote, except for the four last ones which reached me during his final illness. There were also books by other writers, most of them given to me by Graham.

I may have mentioned some of these already, but I list a few of them now in order to give a precise picture of the skill with which Graham dedicated books. I never saw him stop for a moment to consider beforehand what he was going to write in a book. They just seemed to flow like clear water from a fountain.

At the end of one of our journeys, it occurred to me to ask him to inscribe the 'Collected Edition' of his novels so as to reflect in some way what had happened on our 'picnic'.

Some of the dedications are slightly cryptic and need a word of explanation. Others refer to some detail or other from our travels and also need clarifying. Each one included my name and was usually signed 'affectionately, Graham'.

I have already mentioned the ghastly noise made by the visitors, pilgrims, the children and the clergy 'praying' the psalms aloud in the cathedral of Santiago. The din was such that we both had to leave. Later, Graham wrote in my copy of *Brighton Rock*: 'For Leopoldo, who shared my feelings at Santiago . . .'

We would often arrive at the 'San Miguel' restaurant in Orense feeling very hungry and thirsty. Graham reflects this sorry state of the travellers in my copy of *It's a Battlefield*: '. . . in memory of three hungry people at Orense and a great wine.'

Then, when we arrived at the college of the Vincentians in Marín, where those dogs wanted to eat us, Graham recalled the scene in

England Made Me: ... in memory of the four barking dogs of Marín ...'

How we laughed as we travelled along God's highways on our 'picnics'! Graham dedicated his comedy, *Our Man in Havana*: '... in memory of a laughing journey ...'

The intimate stillness of the Carthusian monastery at Miraflores, in Burgos, impressed Graham deeply, so in *The Power and the Glory* he wrote: '... in memory of the Carthusian Silence ...'

Graham never cared for *The Heart of the Matter*. He makes this clear in his dedication to my copy of the novel: '... this tired product of war ...' and, in the case of *The Confidential Agent*, a novel about the Spanish Civil War, he inscribed the book as: '... this superficial story of your Civil War ...'

Many other dedications refer to specific incidents on our travels together. Thus: '... Don't you think it's time to stop the car and have a little wine?' (*A Gun for Sale*);'... Is there any ice left in the thermos?' (*The Ministry of Fear*); '... in memory of the Valencia at Salamanca ...' (*The Quiet American*); '... No more camera shops, please!' (*Stamboul Train*); '... after, so many wayside wines and whiskies ...' (*A Burnt-Out Case*).

In *The Lawless Roads*, my friend describes our preparations for the road: '... ready to start on the lawless roads of Spain, with the Third Man, 2 bottles of "Tonic", three bottles of whisky and 15 bottles of Galician wine.'

In his dedication to *The Human Factor* he refers to the novel's epigraph – the tie of friendship which brought about Castle's ruin: 'For Leopoldo – the tie we have formed I hope will not lead to his corruption.'

There are some inscriptions in other editions of his works, too: 'For Leopoldo who has written so understandingly of Father Rivas and who introduced me to a living Father Rivas in Salamanca ...' (*The Honorary Consul*); '... my "flop" ...' (his play, *Carving a Statue*).

One of the four famous children's books Graham wrote is entitled *The Little Train*. In my copy he wrote: 'For little Leopoldo, with love from grandfather Graham ...', and in another, *The Little Steamroller*: 'For Leopoldo, this exciting crime novel.'

Heinemann/Octopus once published seven of Graham's novels in one massive volume. The print is worse than microscopic. The inscription says it all: 'For Leopoldo, this horrible edition for people who don't like books enough to read in bed.'

The Tenth Man is inscribed as '. . . this forgotten bastard child . . .', whereas the American edition has '. . . with the Author's corrections, after a good wine and Señor Antonio's Tonic.'

I have copies of both the novels that Graham Greene suppressed. In *The Name of Action* he wrote '. . . this bad book of which the title alone is good – and that was suggested to me by an equally second-rate novelist, Clemence Dane . . .'; and in *Rumour at Nightfall*, '. . . perhaps even a worse book than *The Name of Action* because more pretentious and under the malign influence of *The Arrow of Gold*, Conrad's worst novel.'

A Sense of Reality is inscribed: '. . . these secrets from outside the confessional . . .'; *The Power and the Glory*: 'FOR GERVASE [to whom Graham dedicated the book] – who alas! is dead and for Leopoldo who is so much alive . . .' and *Babbling April*, his early poems: 'These adolescent verses written between the age of 18-19 are for no eye but yours, my dear Leopoldo. Pages 4 and 5 have been suppressed by the photographer!' 'Now 4 and 5 are back – none the better for that. July 16, 1979.'

●

These are some examples of books by other authors, which Graham inscribed for me.

In *Bygone Berkhamsted (pictures selected and introduced by Percy Birtchnell)*, Graham recalls: '. . . a visit to Berkhamsted in the summer of 1979 "in search of a character" . . .' [the character we were looking for was Castle (*The Human Factor*)].

Faith and Fiction, Creative Process in Greene and Mauriac by Philip Stratford is dedicated:

'. . . This book, with your own, is the best on my work', whereas in *The Power and the Glory, Text, Background and Criticism*, edited by R. W. B. Lewis and Peter J. Conn, he wrote: '. . . Save me from these American academicians . . .'

Graham was an admirer of the Japanese novelist Shusako Endo. In my copy of *Silence*, he wrote: '. . . My pen-friend Endo would love to know that he was read by my travel companion in Spain . . .' and *The Samurai* was: '. . . This book by one of my favourite friends and novelists . . .'

Finally, in my own book, *La Crisis del Sacerdote en Graham Greene*, Graham Greene wrote in the Spanish edition:

Dear Leopoldo, I am very honoured by Bishop Butler's introduction, not to speak of the book itself. I wish it could appear in English, for in England I am regarded as a bit of a heretic. Affectionately, Graham.

PART SEVEN

CHAPTER I

GRAHAM GREENE: MASTER OF THE ANECDOTE

I N THE DEDICATION to another of his books, *The Other Man*, his conversations with Marie-Françoise Allain, Graham described me as 'the master conversationalist'; but I know only too well that I am far from deserving of this tribute. It really belonged to him.

Graham Greene's conversation had a quality of suspense about it, for it was always spiced with a story or anecdote concerning something that had happened to him, or with a joke, for his humour was inexhaustible. His stories were the distilled essence of almost seventy years spent travelling all over the globe. He would relate experiences of every kind imaginable, more or less confidential conversations that he had had with ecclesiastical or political dignitaries; a flow of endless experiences to do with whatever subject might arise.

I don't know if it is possible to try to describe a man by recounting three anecdotes. Conversation, for this man, was one of the most important things in life and his own contained a fair dose of humour. The extraordinary thing about him was that however diverse the subjects we were discussing might be, he always had a relevant anecdote relating to some experience of his own.

At the 'Michel' restaurant in Lisbon, for example, something we said in passing gave rise to the subject of night life in the big cities. Greene told us how he had once come to Lisbon with Carol Reed. They decided to go to a 'smart brothel' where they asked for a bottle of brandy. The girls were very obliging too . . . Later, when the time came to leave, they were only charged shop prices for the drink and were told they could take away anything that was left in the bottle. Naturally, they did not do this.

I looked askance at Graham, and asked him whether he had confessed what he had done that night, whereupon Graham proceeded to tell us three stories about going to confession.

One day he had gone to Westminster Cathedral to see a priest. Apparently – and unfortunately, too, for he clearly lacked the basic principles of moral theology – the priest in the confessional began to ask him questions about his past life which had nothing to do with the matter at hand. Finally, this penitent sinner lost his patience and said to the priest: 'Father, I think I am making you waste your time, and your are wasting mine. Good-bye.'

Graham left and went to call on a Jesuit priest at Farm Street, and two minutes later the confession was over.

When he was in Vietnam, he felt himself to be in constant danger and so he decided to go to a priest for confession from time to time. Noticing that the river water had still not carried away the corpses, Graham went to the cathedral where he met a young Chinese priest who, it seems, had a perfectly angelic face. Graham felt anxious and upset, not so much about what he was confessing, but because he was worried that he might harm this immaculate priest by putting wicked thoughts into his mind.

On another occasion, he went to confession and mentioned birth control. The priest advised him drily: 'Go and see a doctor.' Graham refers to this priest in *The Human Factor*, when Castle goes into a church and tries to talk to the priest who he sees sitting in the confessional. He tells the priest that he is not a Catholic; that he does not belong to any religion; that he simply wants to talk to him for a moment. The priest, who is not much of a psychologist nor very human, replies: 'Then I think what you need is a doctor.'

The priest immediately drew the little curtain of the confessional and Castle walked away. The confessor had lost his great opportunity.

Graham forgave him. 'He looked about him reluctantly. His eyes were bloodshot . . .' Perhaps the priest, like Castle, was prey to loneliness and silence.

We left the 'Michel' and set off for Sintra. That day, the anecdotes that kept coming to Graham's memory reminded me of bees settling on a tree in blossom. I did not stop laughing until we reached Maria Newall's house. Seeing me doubled up, she laughed herself, and asked me: 'But what's been happening?'

'You must ask Graham,' I told her. 'He is responsible for everything. Ask him to tell you about the angelic Chinese priest in the cathedral in Saigon.' And Graham told her.

CHAPTER II

WAS GRAHAM GREENE HAPPY?

I AM AWARE that this question is somewhat unsubtle. Human happiness is always relative, but it is this relative happiness that I am discussing. As far as happiness or misfortune are concerned, appearances can often be deceptive.

Graham Greene published *The Power and the Glory* in 1940. From that moment on, his international fame became firmly established and his literary reputation grew every year and with each new book. His fame was not the trivial, brittle fame of politicians and bankers that is measured in applause and sacks of gold. It was due to his intellectual gifts and the exquisite power of his pen which, to quote again, 'had invaded and shaped the public imagination more than any other serious writer of this century' (*Time*, 15 April 1991). From a superficial point of view, it would appear that he had every right to be happy.

I used to talk to Graham Greene about absolutely everything and I would ask him about anything that came into my head. Dining at the 'Mesón Casas Colgadas' restaurant in Cuenca, Graham once mentioned his famous game of Russian roulette. We then discussed suicide. What he said was more or less this: 'Anyone contemplating suicide should think of the consequences his death may have on others: those closest to him, his family.'

Returning to the game of Russian roulette in which Graham put his life at risk, I asked him why he had done something so dangerous; whether he considered himself to be happy or unfortunate in life. He replied that there had been only one chance of dying to five of staying alive, except for that time when he fired twice. As far as happiness or misfortune were concerned, he said: 'The years from thirteen to fifteen or sixteen were happy ones. They were followed by troubled years. At about the age of forty, I had some happy moments as well as some wretched ones.' And he went on to list some personal reasons.

Glancing through my books one day, he came across a typescript of my Ph.D. thesis at the Complutense University. He wrote the following in it:

> My goodness, Leopoldo, what a book! Longer than *War and Peace* – but it deals only with the war and occasionally peace in the mind of one friend of yours. How many volumes would be required to deal with all your friends?
>
> Graham (Greene)

In his modesty, Graham considers himself to be just one among so many other friends, and nothing more. Greene affirms that his life was one continuous battle, a mental struggle with himself. Only very occasionally did peace smile on him.

How well I understand the truth of this autobiographical testament! Just as Jacob fought with an angel from dusk to daybreak, and just as Unamuno turned his life into a tragedy, either through struggling at times with his conscience or by doubting his God – see *El Sentimiento Trágico de la Vida* – so something very similar happened to Graham Greene. In this book I have made it clear that Graham had always been obsessed by faith, but I would even go so far as to say that faith was present continually in his conscience. He knew that there were certain 'rules' of the Church which he had broken: 'I broke the rules.' It is necessary to use his own words. Graham never used the word 'sin', except in his books. His sin was 'to break the rules'. He did not distinguish between the two. In this respect, there was not necessarily any moral fault, as far as he was concerned, but there was unfaithfulness to the rules of the Church. He had committed himself to observing these rules, and he felt guilty if he did not fulfil them.

This obsessive faith of Graham's and this feeling that he was sometimes 'breaking the rules of his Church' made him not so much 'a martyr of hope', in Charles Moeller's words, but a martyr of faith, as I described in Chapter X and a martyr of conscience. Moeller does of course say that 'with Graham Greene the true face of evil is revealed: sin is present everywhere; in time, because childhood is besmirched; in space, because the same cruelty and violence which bring corruption to our schools is as present in our great cities and the most distant countries'. I do not deny this; it is true. But if Moeller had known Graham Greene as I did he might possibly not have paid so much attention to high-flown ideas and realities, and he would have concentrated more on the eternal battle which Graham felt stirring within himself, with only 'occasional flashes of peace'.

In the wider sense, Greene was someone who was scrupulous in his beliefs or, rather, in his religious experiences. In this respect, he lived in a state of constant inner struggle, a state of 'war and occasionally peace'.

I saw Graham Greene many times when he was radiant with happiness – when I arrived in Antibes, and when he arrived in Madrid ready to embark on another 'picnic' along the roads of Spain and Portugal. I saw him quite overjoyed when he arrived in Spain to spend a few days following the filming of *Monsignor Quixote* . . . He was entirely happy after the defeat of the mafia on the Côte d'Azur.

For a time after this, although he was not sad, some of the shine of that happiness had turned to serenity and his mood became slightly more subdued. Perhaps his outer euphoria had to give way to the sterner reality he carried within himself. This reality was a continual 'war'. The rest was 'occasionally peace'. Graham Greene was a warrior, and a warrior at war can never be happy.

•

On one occasion, Graham told me about his grandsons Andrew and Jonathan. He loved them both and he dedicated *The Monster of Capri* to them. The book consisted of a series of postcards written to them, and it is probably the most beautifully produced of all his books.

As we ended our conversation about these boys, he said: 'One is very balanced; the other is rather like me.'

Graham Greene recognized that his temperament was not stable; it was not perfectly balanced. Thus his moments of peace were often fragile. And if there is not permanent peace in one's heart, there can be no real happiness.

Graham Greene carried a 'dark angel' that tormented him as it did St Paul; and this malign angel was, in Graham Greene's case, his rather unbalanced temperament which resulted from a character that was afflicted by sudden bad temper and psychological depression, as well as boredom. He was thus never able to enjoy permanent happiness in this world.

Graham Greene's external world appeared to lead him towards happiness, as did his intuitive intellectual gifts. But he was psychologically incapable of complete happiness. We must remember the psychoanalysis he underwent in his adolescence. He would never be cured; some things never are. Some people may choose to call this sort of psychological imbalance an illness, but such conditions are ways of being. And that being does not change.

It was his unstable temperament that gave rise to his anxiety, his need to be constantly travelling, to be always on the move so as to avoid or forget his boredom. Once, when we were in Logroño, we specifically discussed this problem; Graham believed that it had decreased with the years. I am sure that was the case.

•

Graham Greene and Vivien were married on 15 October 1927. Some have said that their marriage was unhappy from the start, but if that had been the case there would have been harsh words in that house, at least occasionally. It was simply not true. Vivien's character was essentially opposed to quarrels and argument – she was just not the type. I have read the letter Graham wrote to Vivien on their tenth wedding anniversary; he was far away, but his letter was full of tenderness. Many years later, Graham told Vivien – and I have no doubt that he meant every word – something to the effect that he was 'the base Indian who threw the pearl away, richer than all his tribe . . .' I know exactly what Graham thought about marriage and about his wife, and I can assure readers that there is no basis for saying that the marriage was unhappy.

The problem with Vivien and Graham's marriage was far more serious than this. They both made a bad mistake: Graham in marrying, and Vivien in marrying Graham.

Graham was not made for marriage. I don't know whether marriage at the age of fifty or sixty might have been more stable, but at the age of twenty-three, which was how old Graham was at the time of his wedding, it was a union that was headed, irretrievably, for disaster. At that time in his life, Graham lacked the necessary temperament to endure the unbreakable bonds of a Catholic marriage. Without the necessary stability of temperament and character, or the ability to commit himself to a more or less ordered family life, it was impossible for such a marriage to succeed.

What is more, it is not simply that Graham was too young nor just that Vivien was not the right woman. It was the fact that Greene's more or less unstable psychological make-up was such that he felt continually restless; he was born to be constantly travelling – he had to be in order to develop into the type of writer he became. Graham needed to be totally free, to live in his own way, scarcely ever knowing one day where he would be the next or what he would be doing the following morning. The trappings of marriage made him feel hemmed in or, as he put it in one of this favourite phrases: 'I don't like to be protected.' This phrase does not express literally all that I am suggesting, but it is a symbol. At the age of twenty-three, when he got married, Graham was a sort of anarchist as far as law and life were concerned.

Very deeply in love – which, in his way, he was – Graham married out of passion, blindly, and unaware, at least relatively so, of what he was doing. We must remember that Graham's 'first love' was Gwen Howell, his sister Elisabeth's governess, who was considerably older than him; it was a pseudo-love affair that might have led to his suicide.

Nevertheless, it was his marriage, bound as it was for disaster, which was the cause of Graham becoming the great writer he was. I mean the writer who decided to make theology the backbone of virtually everything he wrote. Thanks to Vivien, Graham became a convert to Catholicism. Vivien was the channel for grace. And Vivien's faith was, and continues to be, something real, vital and unshakeable. She herself became a convert to Catholicism at the age of fifteen or sixteen, against the wishes of her mother, and her belief today is as strong as it was on the day of her baptism. The faith of this extraordinary woman – a faith purified in a crucible of fire – left an abiding mark on Graham and on all his work. His particular temperament transformed this mark of faith into a veritable obsession. This is the precise truth. To put it in any other way would be pure misunderstanding.

•

Although Graham jumped into marriage rather hastily, he confronted the responsibilities of a married man seriously. For many years the financial burden of bringing up a family weighed heavily upon his shoulders. To try to overcome the situation, he set himself the task of writing ceaselessly, sometimes working on two books at the same time, as I have stated: in the mornings he wrote *The Confidential Agent*, which he finished in six weeks; in the afternoons he worked, a little more calmly, on *The Power and the Glory*. As the work was exhausting, he took Benzedrine as a stimulant, which produced a temporary negative effect on his nervous system. Fortunately, Vivien was an excellent organizer, and with the publication of *The Power and the Glory* the financial strain began to subside.

We sometimes discussed these matters. Graham felt that he had done what he could to solve the family's financial problems; but he felt remorse that he had not given more time to his children in their early years.

It is well known that Graham was unfaithful to his wife, both before and after their separation. Without any doubt whatsoever this was the most serious failure in Graham Greene's life. Yet in spite of everything, he always retained a great affection and admiration for his wife.

He always defended Vivien. When a person very close to both of them once tried to speak ill of her, Graham intervened immediately and told him that he was not in a position to say anything against Vivien.

Graham told me that when he separated from his wife, his mother wrote a letter in which she suggested that Vivien was to blame for the breakdown. 'It's not true,' Graham wrote back to his mother. 'I alone am to blame. She is innocent. The fault is entirely mine. You should not have written to me in this way. Your duty was to side with Vivien.'

Graham quite often spoke to me about Vivien. In 1976 he told me that he went to see her whenever he went to England. On 13 July 1977, he told me: 'I mustn't forget my wife's birthday. If I can't go to see her, at least I can send her a cheque.' He said the same thing in April 1979; he told me that when he got to England the first thing he would do was to go and see her. I believe that later he was not quite so dutiful, but he always provided her with an allowance and this continued after his death.

Life, however, had taken its toll, and it may have been that when Graham did return to the sacraments, it was not the right time to try to restore his relationship with his wife. It may have been that he did not want to do so, or it may not have been prudent or even possible – from a human point of view. For my part, taking everything into consideration, I never tried to involve myself in these matters. All that mattered to me was that he should live in God's grace.

I never knew Vivien during Graham's lifetime. I feel sure that Graham would not have minded anything I might have tried to do; given my closeness to Graham, however, it always seemed to me to be wiser to keep away. I only met Vivien in Switzerland at Graham's funeral. We were both staying at her daughter Caroline's house.

When we were first introduced, she greeted me with these words: 'I want to thank you very much because you made my husband so happy.'

This was Vivien Greene, the woman who, in spite of her own regrets, told Graham with great fondness one day that she was always happy to grant him a legal separation, or a divorce, should that be of help to him in any way. Graham rejected her offer a little angrily. It was a good sign!

I developed a great fondness for Vivien and I admire her enormously. We understood each other very well in a short time. She reminds me of St Monica. Both women had to shed many tears: Monica for her son Augustine, Vivien for her husband Graham. Both women had been responsible for the conversion of the two men. Monica mourned Augustine for thirty-three years; Vivien would grieve over Graham for much longer. I believe that each of these women brought her son and her husband – men of 'so many sorrows' – much closer to God.

Chapter III

A MONASTERY AND
TWO CHARACTERS

T HE MONASTERY AT Osera, as I have said, is a place that is intimately connected with Graham Greene's trips to Spain. A visit here became something essential for him. I would go further: it was an inner inducement to him throughout the year to know that in a certain spot in Spain he would find peace.

The Cistercian Abbey of Osera has been my spiritual refuge ever since 1947. Divine Providence had introduced me to a young lawyer, a clerk at the Ministry of the Interior, by the name of Carlos Martínez Suarez, who had decided to withdraw from the world and enter the Abbey at Osera in order to purify himself. His monastic name was Father Gonzalo. Apparently he was sanctified very quickly, and God decided to call him while he was still very young.

Before Graham ever came to Spain, I had told him on one of our innumerable conversations about this oasis of peace at Osera. I had also told him how I had met Carlos Martínez at Villafranca del Bierzo (León) the month after I was ordained as a priest, and how he had become a Trappist monk. I remember Graham urging me: 'We must visit this monastery as soon as possible.'

After this conversation, Graham Greene did not delay long in coming to Spain. And he asked to be taken to Osera because he wanted to know, as he put it, 'this abode of peace which you have told me about so many times'.

Neither of us could have imagined the impression the monastery of Osera would make, even on this first visit, on the soul of the writer. Graham was always enthralled by it, and the memory of Osera remained alive in his heart until his death.

Our very first visit lasted only two or three hours. From Orense we had been on our way to Marín, but Graham was anxious to see the famous monastery. The effect of this first visit on him was extraordinary. The sudden view that the visitor has of the mass of the building, having driven along a road bound by a eucalyptus wood on both sides, would remain etched in his memory. The other great surprise was the plateresque style of the simple sober, symmetrical façade that the visitor sees the moment he enters the garden at the entrance to the monastery. When we arrived, there were just four or five stonemasons up there on the scaffolding, beginning their work on what seemed a labour of eternity: repairing the ravages of seven centuries.

Guide and companion among these stonemasons was Father Juan, a self-taught architect, 'the distinguished master of the scaffolding' as Graham Greene called him, somewhat dismayed to see the labyrinth of wood needed to hold up the Gothic refectory. I am writing this two months after Father Juan died, his lungs worn out by so much dust from chiselling stones.

Yet what most affected Graham in his innermost being was entering that enormous building and not hearing a word spoken. The only noise might be the silent tread of a monk crossing one of the cloisters. We spent a little time, deep in thought, wandering very slowly about those immense stone cloisters. We whispered to each other, then we entered the choir of the Cistercian church in which, true to the tradition and style of the order founded by St Bernard, elegance and asceticism always go together.

Father Damián and Father Honorio were expecting us and they showed us around the most important parts of the abbey. Both these monks, who were old friends of mine, had a permanent place in Graham Greene's heart. From that day forth, Father Honorio was christened 'Saintly Face', and Father Damián, the librarian, became one of the men who Greene genuinely admired.

Before we left, Graham wrote a few words in the visitors' book at the request of the fathers: 'Many thanks for these moments of peace and silence. Pray for me. Graham Greene.'

Next year we returned to Osera. We ate and slept in the monastery and spent an entire day in this house of God. The silence, the way the monks went about their lives, and that sense of peace which the world cannot give, were creating something eternal in the innermost being of this great man. The expressions on the faces of those monks were something so different from those one sees in the outside world. These faces radiated peace; they radiated God. It was the first time that Graham had spent any time in a monastery. And perhaps it was Providence that it should have been a Trappist monastery and one such as Osera, where the monks lived according to the Rule of St Bernard, and where, true to their calling, they received visitors in the way they would receive Christ himself. The simplicity and absence of all luxury and finery, in short the poverty of the monastery, spoke to Graham with more eloquence than anything he had seen anywhere else in the world.

We joined in the singing of the 'Salve Regina'. Before retiring for the night, the Cistercian takes his leave of Mary, his mother, in whose honour everything he has achieved that day is done. The singing of the Cistercians' 'Salve' has to be heard. I believe the exact phrase is this: 'This "salve" pierces the soul of the visitor who hears it for the first time; and whenever he hears it.' As we were walking in the direction of our rooms, Graham whispered in my ear the little prayer of François Mauriac: 'Oh Jesus of the evening'.

At the beginning of the 'Salve' the image of the Virgin Mary, which stands high above the centre of the main altar, is illuminated and when this last prayer of the day is over, a monk walks down from the choir into the church and, very slowly, with a pause between each three chimes, he rings the Angelus bell. The Angelus bell is a reminder to the people to remember God and his mother. By now, it was night and everything was completely silent. Graham whispered, in a voice I could hardly hear, words that were roughly these: 'The bell is silent, let silence speak to us.'

●

Graham never once came to Spain without us paying a visit to his beloved monastery at Osera. At least once every year, up to and including 1989, we would call upon those Trappist monks who, in their life of prayer, work and silence, showed us how we could improve ourselves. It was not that the visits became a ritual, so much as that Graham Greene needed to listen to that silence once more and to see those marvellous men who seemed to express the same grace in their bearing that was hidden in their hearts.

We would always spend twenty-four hours at Osera. We used to arrive in the mid-afternoon, and we would leave at the same time the next day. Occasionally, we would stay two nights at the monastery, but we would then spend the day in Orense, at Las Regadas, or with friends or family somewhere nearby. When they were filming *Monsignor Quixote*, we spent about a week at the monastery, though we slept at Carballino.

If Graham yearned for this monastery so much, why did we not spend three of four days there resting and meditating? Because Graham was born to be constantly on the move. He only stayed in his flat in Antibes to work. He might spend a fortnight in Anacapri, where he always worked very fruitfully. He might be in Vigo two or three times in one week, but every day would be spent travelling in Galicia or Portugal. The same would happen in Sintra. An 'angel of Satan' prevented him from staying in one place for any time. He, too, might have written: 'Indeed, I am nothing more than a traveller, a pilgrim in this world.' Are any of us anything else?

Nevertheless, although our visits to Osera were brief, I am convinced that those encounters with the monks were a decisive influence on Graham Greene's inner life. In its poverty, simplicity and joy, the monastery at Osera gave Graham the only wealth that mattered to him; the only wealth he needed.

When Greene said goodbye to his monastery, he took away with him a rich treasure given by the monks, And he, in return – apart from some much needed financial support – bequeathed them the final chapter of *Monsignor Quixote*, a poem to the monastery, later filmed with Alec Guinness and Leo McKern; and he left them something much more important, something highly regarded by the monks: the example of his own extraordinary simplicity.

•

It is just a few kilometres from the monastery at Osera to the small town of Las Regadas. It used to take us half an hour to get there. This was where my great friend of many years, mentioned frequently in this book, Señor Antonio Nogueiras Romero, lived. Graham often heard of Señor Antonio before he met him, because I frequently mentioned him. He knew that over sixty years ago, Señor Antonio, his father and a few labourers had hewn a vineyard from the rocks; that he had often been awarded the first prize for his Ribeiro wine; that he was a great lover of music, well known in the region as a *gaitero* and a versifier. He could improvise rhyming couplets indefinitely. He was a philosopher of the countryside, rather like Seneca, and Graham also knew that he had knelt on the ground to thank God, contemplating the beauty of twenty different varieties of geraniums.

We actually called to see Señor Antonio on Graham's very first visit to Spain. In the penultimate chapter of *Monsignor Quixote* he gives a masterly fictional portrait of the man he met at that time.

Señor Antonio, like Señor Diego in the novel, is first and foremost a poet, a man whose heart overflows with humanity and poetry.

Señor Antonio and Graham were drawn to each other from the first moment they met. Physically and mentally, they were very alike. They were both tall and thin, like Don Quixote, and they were also very natural, unaffected men, who were highly intelligent and had the souls of artists. Within his own small world, the *gaitero* of Las Regadas was as well known as Graham was in the world outside.

As a specialist in making excellent wines, I don't think Graham could have found a better friend anywhere in the world with whom to drink a glass or two of wine than Antonio Nogueiras. The difference was that he would drink twice the amount Graham drank: he still drinks three-quarters of a bottle at lunch and the same again at dinner. He drinks his own wine, grown on his own vineyard and lovingly matured in his own cellars. Exactly half one of these bottles was sufficient for Graham and for me.

Needless to say, Señor Antonio was a supreme connoisseur of wine. And Graham was reasonably knowledgeable too. 'A vine is alive like a flower or a bird,' Señor Antonio would say. 'It is not something made by man – man can only help it to live or to die,' he would add with such deep melancholy that his face lost all expression. In *Monsignor Quixote*, Graham Greene gave literary form to Señor Antonio's natural expressions.

One afternoon Señor Antonio took us to see his vineyard. It was as if he were visiting one of his family whom he had not seen for a long time. There were a few stones that had fallen from the wall and a few roots in the central pathway of the vineyard that were poorly secured. As we walked back towards the house, he whispered in my ear, so that neither Graham nor the 'Third Man' should hear: 'The vine spoke to me and said, "You and I must go." '

Later, I recounted this to Graham, but presumably I did not explain it clearly, for the phrase Graham uses in the book does not have the force of Señor Antonio's remark: '. . . and I thought: "It is time for me and the vineyard to go." '

Graham Greene captured, as only he knew how, Señor Antonio's dignity and his good-heartedness. Señor Antonio is still alive today. He is over ninety-seven years old and has had his fair share of suffering. Many years ago he lost both his sons. When his wife was ill and dying, their only daughter came over from Brazil to see her mother and to look after her father for as long as he lived. Her own husband

and daughter returned to Brazil. A few months later, however, God took this daughter who looked after him and understood him so well, leaving Señor Antonio alone in this world. I was astonished when I saw him again after the death of this daughter. I had expected to find him in complete despair. But no; although he was shattered by grief, he just said simply and nobly: 'God works in mysterious ways. Pray for her at Mass.'

I was in London when she died. When I told Graham what had happened, he could scarcely believe it. He knew that his friend had already lost his two sons, and he just murmured: 'Incredible, incredible . . .'

One needs to know this in order to appreciate Graham's portrait of his friend in *Monsignor Quixote*:

> An old man with great dignity came out on to the terrace.
> He had the sad and weary face of a man who has seen too
> much of life for far too long. He hesitated a moment
> between the Mayor and Father Quixote . . .

Señor Diego, on this occasion, entertained Father Quixote and Sancho with his best wine. Graham, the 'Third Man' and I had even better luck. For on hot summer days, beneath the shade of that cool fig tree by the side of his patio and seated at the large concrete table used for drying grapes, we ate and drank his best wine on dozens of occasions. Whenever we were at Osera we would come and eat on our friend's patio. As I have mentioned in passing several times, the dialogue between Graham and Señor Antonio was quite wonderful. It did not matter that Señor Antonio spoke no English, or that in recent years he was almost totally deaf. They understood each other perfectly. When two people really care for each other, words are unnecessary. The eyes and Señor Antonio's expressions, each as clear as any code, were enough!

Graham and Señor Antonio's friendship went very deep. Graham knew life's masquerade all too well, and in Señor Antonio he found the true gold of a generous and affectionate heart. This friendship would be one of the impulses that continued to draw Graham to Spain. 'How is Señor Antonio?' he would ask me whenever I went to Antibes, or on the telephone sometimes.

From the moment they first met, Graham and Señor Antonio always embraced, and there were tears in their eyes when they parted.

In 1989 Señor Antonio said to Graham: 'Don't leave it too long before returning, for you might not find me here.'

The reverse happened. Graham was the first to set off on that final journey. Today, whenever Señor Antonio and I meet, he always speaks about *el inglés* whom he loved so much. He never called him Graham. It was a name that was a bit too unusual for him.

•

On 11 June 1977, as we were making plans for the next summer, Graham said to me: 'Do you feel inclined for a little trip across the frontier to stay a few days with my old friend (old in both senses) Maria Newall in Sintra? If so, bring your passport. She can lodge the two of us and get a room for our friend in a nearby pub. She's a wonderful 85 and I got to know her during the Mau Mau rebellion.'

He planned to arrive at Barajas airport on 17 July. In telephone conversations between his letter and his arrival, he often mentioned his friend. She was a devout Catholic, and Graham felt sure that it would make her very happy to have Mass said in her house.

I first met Maria Newall on 19 July. Graham had already described her to me perfectly. He had told me that during the Mau Mau uprising and the years that followed, she guarded her own lands and crops. In the night, bandits would roam around pillaging, robbing and destroying what they left behind. Maria Newall knew just what to do. After dusk had fallen, she would order her chauffeur to drive out into the country. Seated next to him in the front of the car, she carried a large revolver on her lap and would bravely tour round her fields until she was sure that everything was safe.

Maria and Graham greeted one another very affectionately; they were very fond of each other and it had been a long time since they had met. Maria Newall had lived in Kenya for many years and when Graham was sent there as a reporter she had been very helpful to him. She had been a leading nurse in the Red Cross, I believe, and was highly respected.

Maria Newall was very thin, almost as tall as Graham and, at eighty-five years of age, unusually beautiful. Elisabeth told me that when she was young she had been 'devastating'. She was dressed elegantly in a blouse with a white belt, and her complexion was as fresh as it must have been on the day of her wedding. Everything about her suggested naturalness. She used two sticks to support her, and she issued orders to her maids in a voice that was both imperious and kind. Her words sounded like a military command, but the kind look that followed was all sweetness. She would smile at us after she had given her instructions as if she were making fun of herself. 'Yes, my lady, yes, my lady,' the maids would answer with great respect, but with great affection too, for though they worked for her, Maria Newall was like a mother to them both.

Her house was set in the middle of an enormous garden, full of fruit, vegetables and fruit trees. The spacious drawing-room was tastefully decorated and there were flowers everywhere. There were many books, and beside her armchair, which lay next to the English chimneypiece, there were half a dozen devotional books which she read by day and by night, for Maria Newall hardly ever slept. This period of her life was totally given over to spiritual matters. A priest called on her every week with communion. The Masses which her visitors celebrated in her house were the crowning moments of a visit in which she had looked forward so much to seeing Graham after so many years. I would say my Mass every day in that drawing-room, and in future years, if she were unable to get up in the morning, we would say it in her bedroom. Communion was her one desire. She lived more in the next world than the present one.

During the last few years she was occasionally ill, and she moved around in a wheel-chair, assisted by her maids. It made Graham happy, whenever we were there, to see that she still managed to keep fit.

Graham had not only great affection for this woman, but veneration and enormous respect too. His behaviour towards her was tinged with an admiration that bordered on wonder, and a cheerful obedience. Occasionally, she would reprimand him with a few sharp words and a smile, and Graham would accept her opinion. She was the only person I knew who could order Graham around in this way. He saw very special qualities in her. I must admit that, as far as I was concerned, I had never met anyone like her. She was the superwoman who recalled Nietzsche's superman, and who does not exist.

After dinner, Graham would spend some time with Maria, playing a game that resembled draughts. He was sometimes quite inhibited in her presence and would walk about on tiptoes, obeying her every instruction and behaving with the utmost kindness and respect towards her. And Maria also had extraordinary affection and admiration for Graham, whom she treated rather like a brilliant son.

Our conversations at Maria Newall's home might touch on any

subject, for she was a cultured and highly intelligent person, and she had enough knowledge of theology to participate in any heated discussion that Graham and I might embark upon.

Making allowance for their very different personal qualities, Graham Greene's attitude towards her was very similar to the way he behaved with Señor Antonio de las Regadas.

From 1977 on, we used to spend a week in Sintra almost every year, but in the summer of 1984, on arriving at Oropesa, we telephoned Maria Newall who, in recent letters, had asked us to come quickly, to tell her that we were on our way to her home. 'The señora died a month ago,' the maids told us. 'But you would be welcome to come and spend a week here as usual . . .'

The news stunned us. Without giving our decision much thought, we decided not to travel to Portugal, but to return instead to Galicia. Later, we rather regretted this. We should have gone to visit her grave and to pray for her. Farewell, Quinta de Piedade!

CHAPTER IV

ILLNESS AND AN EXEMPLARY DEATH

I N T H E M I D D L E of July 1989, I was spending a week with Graham in Antibes. It was the second part of the celebration of the silver jubilee of our friendship.

I left Antibes on the 24th en route to Madrid. Graham knew that I was only going there to collect a few things before travelling on to Mexico. I reckoned on spending about a month or six weeks there, which was what I told Graham, but my stay was prolonged for almost three months, and Graham grew tired of ringing Vigo and not getting any reply.

When I arrived back in Spain at the end of October, I wrote to Graham, and he telephoned me a few days later. All sorts of things had been happening. We chatted on the phone quite calmly and as affectionately as ever. He had had so many letters and telephone calls on his birthday that he was still feeling tired; there was also the work to be done for two new books of his. He had decided not to go to London to sign 950 copies of the limited, numbered edition of *Why the Epigraph?* 'It's too many copies,' he told me. However, he was going to have to travel to Ireland, because he had been asked to judge a literary prize for fiction. He would have given a lot to have been able to cancel the arrangement.

We agreed that I would write to him as soon as possible, and I did so at the end of the month. Graham arrived back in Antibes on 30 November and he rang me the following morning. He would be able to rest a little now. On about 22 December, he would leave for Switzerland to spend Christmas with his daughter Caroline.

•

The month of January 1990 seemed to me to last forever. I had not had any news of Graham since our telephone conversation on 1

December, something most unusual for us, especially around this time of year. What a wretched month it was! Was it a harbinger of bad tidings?

It was not until February that I received a letter from Graham, dated the 5th. In it, he revealed what had been happening:

> My dear Leopoldo,
> I have only just got your letter of December 19 because I went to Switzerland for Christmas and was rather ill – in hospital twice – and I have only just returned to all my mail, so forgive a short note. I think your letter a good one and I wonder what the result will be. Don't telephone for the moment because I am rather weak on my legs and have to take a rest.

I hardly need to describe the effect this news had on me. I replied to his letter immediately, trying not to reveal how anxious I was, although it was not easy to disguise my concern. The last thing I expected when the telephone rang on 15 February at 11.15 a.m. was that it should be a call from Graham. My heart leapt to hear his voice. He began by saying, 'I have just received your letter. Things have not been going too well, Leopoldo . . .' and he told me all about his illness and his present condition. It was a long conversation, much longer than it ought to have been. To begin with, he spoke continuously, with the occasional brief interruption from me.

Graham's voice was tired, with the odd sign of weakness, but it was relatively normal. Mentally, he was as lucid as ever. Apparently, what had happened was that he had fainted one day and fallen to the floor – something to do with a lowering of his blood pressure. They needed to call on two policemen to help put him to bed. He was staying at his daughter Caroline's house.

He had had two spells in the Hôspital de la Providence in Vevey. Now, he found he had no appetite, and he had not drunk any alcohol at all during this time. He would start to take a little vodka, for this made him feel better. He was taking masses of pills, because his blood pressure was very low.

He spoke very affectionately, or rather, tenderly. He told me he didn't want to speak to anybody. I told him that I left it to him to let me know when I could come to see him.

'I will.' He pronounced these short words very decisively. We just had to hope that he would recover a little.

I told him how I said special prayers for his health in my daily Mass. And I prayed for Gorbachev. Graham always asked me, whenever we spoke, not to forget the providential man in my Mass. We spoke about him, as we so often did, with great admiration.

He asked me whether I had received my copy of *Yours Etc.*, an anthology of his letters to the press. I told him I had.

'It was very well published,' he added.

'Yes, marvellously,' I agreed. 'And so was *Why the Epigraph?*'

Graham was glad that there had been a number of postal strikes. 'Let us pray for the post office strike!' I added.

The conversation continued for a long time and eventually I said: 'This call has been rather a long one. Perhaps we should stop, my dear Graham.'

'Yes, we ought to stop,' he agreed.

We took leave of each other with the same deep and mutual affection that we always displayed.

From my diary: 'My conversation today with dearest Graham has quite affected me. I have never heard his voice sound as weak as it did. God knows what he must have gone through mentally these past months, imprisoned in Switzerland through illness.

I am reminded of the true reality of human life, and still more that of such brilliant individuals as Graham. I feel a sort of emptiness that fills my whole being. This most wonderful of friends is getting on for eighty-six years of age. And, my God, what a strain his life has been! How can he put up with so much?

I have a sort of premonition that tells us that everything comes to an end. Would that he live for a few more years yet!

... He has been very sensitive as far as I am concerned. But to have telephoned me today when he received my letter, feeling as he does, touched me to the bottom of my heart.'

A synthesis from my diary:

Second telephone call Vigo, 27 March 1990. Graham rang me from Antibes this morning at ten o'clock sharp. The call was a disaster. I could hardly hear anything clearly because the line was so bad and his voice kept coming and going. When the line was clear, his voice was calm and natural, but that was not often. We had to curtail the conversation because I could hardly hear a thing. We bid each other a fond farewell. What I did hear during the conversation, however, was the pleasure in his voice when I told him that I would visit Elisabeth when I went to England at Easter. 'Very good,' he said.

I also talked about some of the things we might do when he was better.

'If I get well,' he said.

This remark, and the whole conversation, left me feeling sad and worried. Nothing had been clear on the telephone. I immediately called Graham's niece Amanda in England. She explained everything very concisely. Everybody was very worried about Graham. Amanda could scarcely control her tears. She tried not to show it, but I was aware how upset she was. Graham was a bit better, but even yesterday they had had to give him a blood transfusion. This alarmed me very much, both because of his age, and because he had hardly eaten anything for some time. It was almost impossible to continue like this.

I rang Antibes and Graham answered. I felt so moved that I did little more than greet him. I told him that I would write that day, telling where I would be, and at what times, between now and Easter.

May God preserve us, and may He keep Graham in whose work God is everything!

These are difficult days. I long to go and see him. But that may not be convenient for him. We shall have to see what we decide. I feel I need to go there, even if it's just for one day, and even if we do not speak very much.

Note Neither Elisabeth nor Rodney know about Graham's condition: Elisabeth has been told nothing; Rodney very little.

Third telephone call Vigo, 3 May 1990. Great happiness today! At ten o'clock sharp in the morning – our usual time – Graham called. I jumped for joy, for JOY! to hear his voice. On 27 March I could hardly hear a word. Today, on the contrary, the line was sharp and clear. I heard every syllable he spoke, just as if he had been here beside me. How badly I needed this conversation! I am only sorry to say that I felt so delighted to hear Graham talking in his normal voice that I forgot about time and how weak Graham was. We chatted for twenty long minutes. At the end, Graham felt tired. This must not happen again.

1. Today I noticed that Graham's memory was very clear.
2. I asked him how he felt. He told me that he felt all right; however,

I noticed that his voice, which was clear and firm, gave the impression that he was having difficulty breathing. 'I feel better after the blood transfusions,' he told me. 'They gave me the last one three days ago. They do one every three weeks. I shall ask the doctor whether it is possible for them to do so every two weeks.'

3. Goodbye to the house in Anacapri. It's been sold, for Graham doesn't think he'll use it any more. He thought it would be better to buy a house in Switzerland and to spend a little time there each summer. Graham always loathed the summers in Antibes. The noise prevented him from writing. The house in Switzerland is a great idea. What's more, his daughter Caroline and her two sons live there; so do Martine and her daughters, whom Graham loves so much.

The address of the Anacapri house was Villa Rosario, 5 Via Cerelle. It was the quietest and most peaceful place in which to work. He hated the telephone and had only had one installed recently in case some emergency should arise. He always longed for this oasis of peace where he could work and make his characters come alive.

I asked him about his appetite.

'Not very big,' he said.

'Are you able to drink a little wine with your meals?'

'I cheat a little.' He was referring to the doctor. He continued: 'I drink a little vodka before lunch, a drop of wine with lunch and a little beer at supper.'

Graham always went out for lunch at midday. I asked him if he was still doing so.

'Yes, Yvonne takes me there and brings me back again. On Sundays she takes me to Félix – or wherever – and then the son of the owner drives me home again.'

Graham tells me all this in the most unaffected way. There is no reason to make a tragedy out of such things. He is still a great man. I mention these details as evidence of Graham Greene's exemplary behaviour during his long illness and in the shadow of death.

When Graham tells me that drinking wine at meals is what he misses most, I tell him: 'Look, some time ago I started to drink wine with my meals. I've stopped doing so now until you are well again.'

He interrupted me: 'Nonsense. You must drink your wine just as you did before. It's nonsense.'

He said this affectionately and with absolute sincerity. I promised him I would go on drinking a little. He was much happier.

'You even used to drink a little whisky with me,' he went on.

'That's true. Occasionally.'

I was a fool to mention this minute sacrifice. I don't know why I said it; perhaps it was to give him courage. If only I had kept my mouth shut and could continue to do so!

We spoke for a long time about Elisabeth.

'Do you spend your time reading?' I asked him.

'Yes, I read,' he replied. 'I am not really doing any writing.'

He was referring to his creative work. I am almost sure he is writing something. Not long ago he said he was working on a book about his dreams.

I asked whether I should still refrain from calling him. 'I worry sometimes, when I don't have regular news of you,' I told him, 'and yet I am frightened of telephoning you in case I ring at an inopportune moment.'

However, he reassured me: 'Ring me at ten o'clock whenever you want. That's our usual time.'

Yes, that is our time. It has been for all these years. What a relief! Let us hope that the line is clear whenever we do speak.

. . . He spoke to me about his daily injections and any amount of pills. One can see only too clearly that my great friend is partly being kept alive by all these medicaments.

We then said goodbye. This conversation did me a lot of good. It was calm, relaxed and heart to heart, and we could hear every word. But it was too long, and by the end of it, Graham was exhausted.

When I had finished making these notes, I wrote a prayer to the Virgin. This is how it ended: 'Look upon Graham and at how much good his work has done! His small faults are a drop in the ocean of what he has written concerning God and the life hereafter.'

Fourth telephone call Vigo, 5 June 1990. Graham began: 'Leopoldo, I haven't replied to your letter.' He laughed as he said this.

'That is unimportant. What matters is your health and that you are looking after yourself. Your voice sounds pretty good to me.'

'I am not at all well,' he said. 'I continue taking the same medicines and everything else.'

I tried not to interrupt too much so as not to prolong the conversation. Graham then turned to the principal purpose of this call: my proposed visit to Antibes. He explained: 'As you know, I have sold the house on Anacapri and bought another in Switzerland where I will spend July and August. I want to get away from the ghastly noise in Antibes at that time of year. What I wonder, Leopoldo, is this: if it is not too far for you, I would prefer it if you came to Switzerland and spent a few days with me there.'

'I'd be delighted, Graham.'

'Good,' he went on. 'Because here, with all these blood transfusions, injections, pills, I seem to get worse. Whereas there, at least, I may improve a little.'

'I agree with you, Graham. Of course I'll come to Switzerland. You will get better.'

We spoke of various other matters which I have omitted here. Then I interrupted the conversation: 'I don't want to tire you with a long conversation as I did the other day. Perhaps we should stop.'

'Yes, I do feel tired . . .'

'Give my love to Yvonne. Oh, and if you have the address and phone number of the Swiss house, please can you ask Amanda to send me a note with the details?'

'Yes, I have them, and Amanda will send them.'

'Thanks very much for everything. All my love.'

'Goodbye.'

Fifth telephone call Vigo, 5 August 1990. Today I rang Graham at his new house in Switzerland. It was another long conversation. Yvonne replied. She is so wonderful that she decided to go and look after Graham while he is there. I was therefore able to talk to her at length and find out a few more details about the problem. She said to me several times: 'Wait until Graham comes.' But I didn't want to tire Graham and I went on talking to her until I understood exactly what was wrong. A team of specialist doctors is attending to Graham, among them the doctor who looked after him at Christmas when he collapsed. Although he still needs these blood transfusions and the injections, the doctors are optimistic: they are almost certain that the medicine will make the bone marrow start working again, which will produce the amount of blood he needs. I was overjoyed to hear this. May God help the doctors!

Graham came to the phone. His voice sounded completely normal. He sounded not depressed, but rather jolly.

'Leopoldo, I can't speak for very long, because I'm sitting in a very uncomfortable chair.'

I interrupted him: 'Look, Graham, Yvonne has told me absolutely everything. All you need to do is to rest, rest and rest. Don't say a word. I send you an enormous hug. Goodbye.'

He laughed, for I was not usually so emphatic, and he said simply: 'Goodbye.'

I had been a little hard in order to be kind, but I wanted it to be like that, and it made me feel better.

God willing, they would return to Antibes at the end of August when I would go and see them at a mutually convenient date.

What I had said must have worried Graham a bit, for after we had said goodbye, he dictated a letter to me. Among other things, he said:

> I too am pretty tired and I think it would be much better to delay a visit until we are back in Antibes for some weeks in September. I still have to go every two weeks for blood transfusions and every three days have injections of vitamins. Sometimes I am too tired to talk to anyone. However, patience, and I hope all will be well in the end.
>
> Lots of love from us both,
> Graham.

One month later I received the last letter he ever wrote to me:

> La Résidence des Fleurs,
> Avenue Pasteur,
> 06600 Antibes.
>
> September 7, 1990
>
> Dearest Leopoldo,
> Thank you for your letter and Yvonne sends her thanks for your letter to her. I am returning to Antibes for a few weeks on September 11, but I hope to get back here as soon as possible where it's quiet. I think you should postpone any visit until I feel a bit stronger. I depend very much on these blood transfusions and sometimes they go a bit wrong.
> You will be getting another book from me very soon called *Reflections* – a collection of essays going back to

1923! All good luck to your doctor book, though I can't imagine how you can make it interesting!

We shall welcome the time when we see you again and hope it won't be too long before I am fit to receive visitors.

Much love,
Graham

Sixth telephone call Vigo, 13 October 1990. About a month ago I wrote a letter to Graham in reply to one of his, and I told him about the death of my brother Manuel, which had been a terrible blow. I was slightly surprised that he did not write back to me about this, but his health was poor and I understood perfectly.

Last week I sent another letter wishing him many happy returns on his birthday on 2 October, and I mentioned various other matters, including the death of my brother again, since it came to the point.

Graham received this letter today and has only just learned the news of my beloved Manuel. There had been a ten-day postal strike in Antibes, and they had still not distributed the mail.

When he rang up, he said: 'Leopoldo, I am very sorry to hear about your brother and I send you my most sincere condolences.' He always uses restrained and truthful words. Then he told me about the postal strike and how he had just received my news.

Graham seemed determined to talk about my brother's death at length. He sounded so normal and so strong that one would not have thought his health was affected. He wanted me to tell him about Manuel. I told him that my brother had never been ill; how he had been on his way to Vigo airport and that the last thing he had said was: 'My leg hurts a bit . . . this is getting serious'; how his wife had told him to drive on the other side of the road, but that he had veered over to the left and then the right where there was a steep drop. She said he had been unable to brake and the car eventually came to a stop by itself. At the end, his wife was calling him by his name – 'Manuel' – but he was unable to utter a word. He made some unintelligible sound, gave his wife a kiss, and collapsed on her shoulder.

While I related all this in detail to Graham, he said 'Extraordinary' a number of times. He was very moved, for he knew both my brothers well.

Meanwhile, I was getting anxious because the phone call was going on a long time, but Graham continued to ask me questions.

Changing the subject, I asked him to tell me frankly how he felt.

He said that all was much as before: the blood transfusions every fortnight, and the usual injections. As far as he could gather, this would continue for good, and it seemed to me that he believed there was no remedy for him. However, he said this completely naturally, as if it was of no importance whatsoever.

Then he went on speaking in a slow, detailed way about his new house in Switzerland. He is delighted with this house, which has views such as he has never had from any of his other homes. Above all, there is complete silence there. Total quiet. He told me that during the week he went to live with his daughter, Yvonne had transformed the place, putting flowers everywhere. When he arrived, it was like a new house. In a word, delight.

He told me that as from next Saturday he would return to his house in Switzerland and remain there for Christmas. There were two reasons: firstly, Antibes was becoming noisier by the day; and second, Yvonne would go with him and would be able to look after him without her having to go from one house to the other. When he told me this, I had no doubt about the wisdom of the plan. Fate's mysterious ways have meant that Yvonne has become the visible sign of Providence for Graham. Without her care, Graham would not be here now.

Next, he described the flat to me. One large bedroom, another smaller one which Yvonne used for the time being, a small study, kitchen, bathroom, and a sitting room. He used the word 'tranquillity' several times. Graham cannot endure the slightest noise. His sensitivity to it is so acute that he is badly affected by any sound when he is concentrating on his work.

I asked him whether his book *Reflections* had been published yet; in his letter of 7 September, he had told me that a copy would reach me shortly. He was shocked to hear it had not arrived. He hopes it will arrive in the next few days, and if it doesn't he would get in touch with Amanda.

Discussing this book, he says, with the true modesty of genius: 'I think it's readable.'

I laugh and say that I am sure it is.

In my previous letter, I told him that I had not telephoned him because I was worried I might ring at an inopportune moment: after a blood transfusion, or something of the kind. But today we agreed that I should ring him from time to time, however briefly.

Several times today I tried to bring the conversations to a conclusion, but I formed the impression that Graham was in no hurry to stop. Graham is so courteous that he wanted to console me today in whatever way he could, and even though the call lasted for some twenty minutes, he sounded completely normal and natural while we were speaking. It was I who said: 'We must stop.' And we said goodbye in our usual affectionate way.

Seventh telephone call Vigo, 27 November 1990. Graham began by saying that he felt guilty not having called me more frequently; every day he had it in mind to ring me at our usual time of ten o'clock, but then later he would forget.

I interrupted him, telling him that no blame should be apportioned: that it was a question of health, and nothing else.

'And how are you?' he asked me.

I told him that I was fine and asked him the same question.

He answered: 'All right. I'm still having the blood transfusions and everything else. The transfusions are not exactly straightforward. One spends six hours lying on the bed while the blood is added drop by drop. There are two containers – one with blood, the other with something to prevent any ill effects from the transfusion, or of the blood getting into the organism.'

'Do you feel a little better after all this?'

'Oh yes; much better with the new blood. But only for a few days following the transfusion. It is not a permanent cure.'

We agreed that there did not seem to be any possibility of knowing when we might see each other with any certainty. I asked him where he would spend Christmas. He replied: 'Yvonne will go to Antibes to spend a few days with her daughter. In the meantime, I'll spend two weeks with my daughter Caroline who lives nearby.'

'When, approximately, do you think you will be back in Antibes? Perhaps we could see each other then.'

'I'll go for a fortnight in the winter. I'll telephone you to let you know when I'm going.'

I asked after Yvonne.

'I'll put you on to her.'

We said goodbye. I told him how grateful I was that he had called. And I assured him: 'I remember you in my daily Mass and you are present all the time in my prayers.'

I know how much of a consolation this was to him. And I have rarely said anything truer. When he spoke I noticed a weariness in his voice.

Yvonne came to the telephone. She said, very affectionately: 'I feel very guilty, Leopoldo. I haven't written to you; but I am so busy all day.'

'Don't bother about writing. Your role is very clear: to look after Graham. How is he?'

'Well . . .'

'As before?'

'Yes . . .'

She told me of the improvement on the days following the transfusions. But, later, the effect of the transfusions wears off. She said: 'He is very weak on his legs.'

She means, his legs especially . . .

The telephone line went dead. As we had been speaking for some time, I decided not to call back, but to ring again next week, God willing. I told her I felt worried about Graham. She understood perfectly. Her last words were: 'Graham is not seeing anyone, practically. He gets tired the moment he starts speaking.'

Today I have lost all hope of Graham recovering. We need a miracle. Human means are not enough. Graham is leaving us. Only God can help now.

Eighth telephone call Vigo, 9 December 1990. I called Graham in Switzerland at the usual time. There was some delay in his replying. He told me that he was going through his daily post.

Once we began talking, his voice sounded animated, quite normal and even happy. I asked him how he was feeling, and he replied, 'The same as usual.' But at least he sounded in relatively good spirits. We chatted about this and that.

I then told him how much I had liked *Reflections*. Talking about this book, he sounded quite lively and happy, and he said: 'I'm going to tell you something that will please you.'

He proceeded to tell me about a letter he had received from the Cardinal of Sao Paolo, enthusing about *Monsignor Quixote*. The letter had greatly cheered Graham and I was delighted at how happy he sounded. I joked with him about how our trips together and our 'picnics' were famous even in Brazil.

I asked him this: 'When you do go to Antibes – you told me that you planned to spend a couple of weeks there in the winter – do tell me beforehand, as you promised you would. It's not a question of whether we talk or not. It's simply that I want to see you. As you told me I would. I'm quite serious about that.'

'I'll let you know when I'm going. Don't worry.'

He never was able to spend those days in Antibes. Because of the continual blood transfusions, a few days after he had them and especially two or three days before the next one was due, he felt he had no energy whatsoever and did not want to talk. He had no more strength than a corpse at the time; only his will-power kept him going. This is the problem, and it is an insuperable one.

On several occasions we agreed that I should come to Switzerland; but his strength was failing and so I did not go. Now I feel as if I have little hope of seeing him, until his last moments. And I beg God that I am given enough time to talk to him slowly, as he has asked me so often to do.

Before saying goodbye, I assured him: 'I want you to know that you are continually on my mind, especially in my prayers. I am going to say my Mass now. My very special intention is for you. I am referring to the blessed fruits of the Mass, Graham, which are bestowed on the celebrant himself. I pass them to you.'

And he replied with enormous affection, gratitude and faith, as he uttered, very slowly and with emphasis, the words: 'Thank – you – very – much.'

Note It is such a pity Graham has not the strength to speak. He feels so tired as the effects of the new blood wear off. Otherwise, I would have gone to see him before now, in Antibes or in Switzerland. Without warning. But I shouldn't do that. It would be too painful for both of us. I don't mind pain for myself, but I would mind it where Graham is concerned.

Ninth and last telephone call Vigo, 12 February 1991. At 9.30a.m. Graham rang me from Switzerland. How I had been longing for this call! It had been about two months since I had had any news of him. This was because he was very ill and extremely weak.

It was Yvonne who made the call and spoke first, calmly and slowly: 1. She and Graham had telephoned on a number of occasions and I had not been there. They thought that perhaps something had happened. Later, Graham had joked, saying that perhaps I had decided to change my life and go off on a spree. Graham may well have used the word 'gallivanting', as he does in *Monsignor Quixote*.

Thank God for humour, however brief, at moments of ill health!
2. Yvonne explained to me that Graham was even weaker than before;
that there was nothing he wanted to do; that he was not writing
letters etc. etc. We spoke very calmly although, naturally, I was on
tenterhooks. We went on discussing Graham's condition which was
certainly not good. I believe he is only able to keep going because
of the colossal strength of his will-power. These are very troubling
moments!
3. Graham will not go to Antibes during the next fortnight, as we
had all thought he would. Obviously, it's impossible for him to travel
in his present weak condition. We had agreed that I would go to see
him in Antibes and that he would advise me when he would come.
But that is not to be.
4. I told Yvonne about my proposed visit. But Graham's situation is
so bad that he has scarcely any will or energy for anything. Yvonne
said: 'We must wait and see whether he improves a little and then
you could come. We shall see.' Graham would want to feel rather
better if the two of us were to speak alone. I soon realized it would
not be helpful, or very opportune, for me to arrive in the present
circumstances. Graham knows only too well that I am very keen to
jump on a plane, but one has to be aware of the situation and to
know Graham as I know him. He can't cope with anything else. The
man has no strength for anything, he can't write letters or even dictate
them. I know what it must be like.

Graham came to the phone. He spoke very clearly: 'We have rung
you several times . . . The fact that you haven't had a letter does not
indicate any lessening of affection *at all*, Leopoldo.'

These words of Graham's moved me to the bottom of my heart.
As if I hadn't known of his great affection throughout all these years!
I told him that I understood everything; that he wasn't to write; that
all I wanted was what was best for him . . .

Graham then told me: 'All I do is go from one room to another . . .'

And I, who know him so well, see a psychological state of pain
which, in my Christian faith, I would term 'tragic'.

'I feel very tired,' Graham continued. 'I don't write any letters . . .
nothing . . .'

And he added, with particular emphasis: 'Thank – you – very –
much – for your – prayers.'

And then the perfect remark: 'We must see if your prayers bring
about a miracle.'

A moment later, he said to me: 'We must stop now, for I'm feeling very tired.'

We bid each other goodbye in the way we always did. Graham spoke so tenderly, but he was exhausted. He who was always so tireless; a man who had been able to walk heroic distances all his life! Liberia, Tabasco, Vietnam, virtually everywhere in the world . . .

That afternoon I wrote a short letter that I wished had been written by some miraculous angel.

I have never felt so impotent, either naturally or in a supernatural sense. I feel so sad.

There is only FAITH. I knelt down to pray. I don't know whether I was crying.

Note This was the last conversation I was to have with Graham in this world. For in Switzerland I arranged everything so that he did not have to speak. I did not want to invite superhuman efforts from him. It did not seem to me to be necessary.

●

Death

On my return from Switzerland, I waited several months before writing these notes describing Graham Greene's farewell to this world. The idea of writing about his death did not appeal to me, but I felt I had to do so.

Graham had often told me that he wanted me to be beside him when he quit this life. And this is what happened. I had been without news of him for about six weeks. I did not want to ring up, because the last time I had spoken to him he was already more dead than alive. All his energy had deserted him.

But the problem resolved itself at Mass on the Monday before Holy Week. Only St Joseph and I know how. In *The Other Man* Graham wrote of me, 'He is not a conventionally pious man.' Still less am I devout.

Apparently they had been trying to get in touch with me from Switzerland throughout that week. I had been taking part in the Holy Week ceremonies with the Carmelite fathers; at other times of the day I was at home. Graham had told them that they must keep me informed. Perhaps they should have persisted a little more with their calls. I know very well that Graham would have done so if he could. I would have given the world to have been able to spend the last week of his life in his company. For me it is something that will always be a sword in my heart.

At last, on Easter Sunday, at 9.30 in the evening, the telephone rang. It was Yvonne: 'Graham has reached the end. He wants you to come. But there's no need for you to hurry...'

Early on the morning of Easter Monday, I rushed to Vigo airport. There was no problem in getting a flight to Madrid that same afternoon, nor in obtaining one to Switzerland on the Wednesday. But an inner voice told me that I should fly to Switzerland on the very first available plane. Thanks to Chelo Sacarrera, an air hostess with Iberia, I was able to fly to Madrid that afternoon with a reservation on the 8.00 a.m. flight to Switzerland next morning. Without the diligent efforts of Chelo Sacarrera, who has now become a great friend, Graham would have died without seeing me at his side.

At about midday on Tuesday I was with Graham at the Hôpital de la Providence in Vevey. He recognized me immediately, the moment he opened his eyes. The people who had been with him left and went out into the corridor. I administered all the sacraments, including the last rites, and anointed him with the oil of *chrism* and the Apostolic Blessing.

I spent the whole day with him. In the afternoon he seemed to be more rested, and then he became fully conscious. Amanda mentioned something to him to do with the Secret Service which had been worrying him in recent days. Although he had difficulty articulating the words, he was completely conscious when he replied.

I spent that night at the home of Graham's daughter, Caroline. Having said Mass in the house that morning, I was having breakfast when the telephone rang. Caroline told me that we had to leave at once because Graham was dying.

We left in a hurry. Graham was sinking fast when we arrived. I said a few words to Graham and gave him absolution again. The family left the room to make telephone calls. No one anticipated that the end would come quickly. I remained alone with Graham, gazing at him steadily, taking his pulse, praying and thinking.

After a while, I noticed that his breathing was softer. It gradually grew slower and more distant. I took his pulse and it was still beating.

But then I had the impression that Graham was going. I said to him: 'Dear Graham, I believe God is expecting you now. When you arrive in his presence, please say a word for me. I will give you absolution once more.'

Five minutes after I had done so, I became aware that his breathing was gradually fading away ... Then it seemed as if there was no longer any breath at all. I took his pulse again. There was none. I took his hand in mine. It was cold. I was certain that he had made his way towards God.

I was in no hurry to leave and I stayed by his side, watching him, my face almost touching his. I kissed his forehead many times. It did not occur to me at the time to kiss the hand that had written such wonderful books. For me he was not dead. I did not in the least have the sense that I was sitting with a corpse. I was with Graham, just as I had been before. It is impossible even to begin to describe that experience. I was happy being there alone with him. I did not want to leave, neither did I want to call anyone. I tried to pray, but I neither wanted to, nor could. I just thought to myself as I gazed at him fixedly.

I would have been quite happy to have stayed where I was, alone with him, a while longer, but after about a quarter of an hour, I went to look for the family. I could not find anyone. I returned to Graham's room, but only for a few moments. It was the first time in my life that I had been alone with a dead person; the first time I had ever helped someone to die on my own.

I went out to look for the nursing sister. I told her that I thought Graham had passed away. She replied that that was impossible, but she came with me and took his pulse and looked into his face. It was obvious to her that he was dead. She went out to call two other nurses. A little later, the family arrived. A feeling of desperate sadness slowly overwhelmed me; I no longer had Graham. I had to grip hold of my faith with all my strength to dispel the terrible sense of loneliness that threatened to envelop me ...

At the Hôpital de la Providence in Vevey they will never forget Graham. There could be no easier or more perfect patient. He was admired and loved by everyone, and he did everything he could not to be a nuisance to the nursing staff. When they realized that even with the help of the most modern medicaments his days were numbered, Doctor Morandi, with the sensitivity and discretion that are characteristic of him, informed Graham of the gravity of the situation. Graham had understood immediately – I am certain that he had understood for some time – that his terrestrial life was over and it did not affect his serenity in the slightest. We are born for this. A few days before my arrival at Vevey, Graham had said these words to his family: 'I understand why you should lament my death, but there is no need for you to be sad. There is reason for sorrow, but not for sadness.'

I was not in the least surprised at Graham's utter serenity in the face of death. We had often spoken about this; for him death was just one of the stages in life. From the beginning to the end of his life, Graham was an absolutely outstanding person. I take it for granted that many of my statements will seem exaggerated. I am well aware of the fact. I would think the same were it someone else writing this book who had not known the man in the intimate way that I have. And yet even so, I think I was constantly surprised by him each time we met, and in every single one of our discussions.

•

Graham died on the Wednesday after Easter, 3 April, at 11.40 in the morning. They prepared his body beautifully – I had never seen him dressed so elegantly; it really did not suit him – and his body was laid in one of the chapels the Hôpital de la Providence uses for such circumstances. Each day we all went to spend a little time with him, praying for his soul and simply contemplating his face. He had an expression of perfect peace and serenity.

They needed a few days to prepare for the funeral. It had to be a formal, official ceremony, for Graham was a member of the British Order of Merit. Buckingham Palace had to be informed of his death before anyone else could be told.

The funeral took place the following Monday at the church in Corseaux, and it was attended by the British Ambassador. Three priests concelebrated the Mass, and I gave a short homily.

From the church we went to the cemetery to bury Graham. The coffin was lowered into an open grave. And there we left him in his last resting-place, covered by countless wreaths of flowers. Here, forever, will lie the remains of this great man who, in the words of Dr Octavio Victoria Gil, a close friend and our companion on many of our travels, 'in spite of his many and varied experiences, retained the pure heart of a child, and the tolerance of a sage of old'.

•   •   •

One evening, two days after the funeral, Doctor Morandi, who had looked after Graham on his sickbed, came to call on us at Graham's house. He explained to us, as far as he could, the nature of the illness that had cut short this great man's life. We asked him how he explained his supremely restrained and graceful acceptance of death.

Doctor Morandi replied: 'I can only find one explanation for such an admirable attitude. It is the first time I have ever seen someone respond to the circumstances with such greatness of heart. I believe this was due to the exceptional clarity of his mind which enlightened him up until the very end.

'But in my view,' he went on, 'there must be more to it than that. Only a faith free of any doubt can explain such complete serenity at the moment of death.'

It is hard to conceive of a more fitting funeral oration.

Index

story. If I hadn't, the concealment would've grown into contempt. That's what happens when you keep a secret from someone you love: you start to hate them for allowing you to prove your own willingness to deceive them.

So I told him, but the feeling of infidelity didn't entirely vanish. Hasn't entirely vanished.

I finish the cigarette and walk back to the pool. The patio smells are benign: chlorine; clean stone; sun-tan lotion; lavender. I can hear basketball commentary from indoors.

I'll see you another time.

Eight months. Twenty thousand years.

I can't pretend a part of me isn't still waiting.

In the house I discover Walker has fallen asleep on my bed in his underwear, with a twin nestled (also asleep) in each armpit. I draw the comforter over them and turn out the light. They won't roll off. He won't squash them. Species certainty. Species gravity.

In the lounge, my dad snores, open-mouthed, in the recliner. I cover him with a blanket, mute the TV and set a glass of water on the side table next to him for when he wakes up, parched. I should be sleepy myself, after so much booze and sun and food, but I'm not. I'm alert, restless, vaguely bereaved. It occurs to me that for the first time in a long time I'm not worried about anything.

I hadn't thought peace would feel like this.

It won't last, of course.